REX WALFORD AND COLIN DOLLEY

the **one-act play** companion

a guide to plays, playwrights and performance

A&C BLACK • LONDON

Published by A & C Black Publishers Ltd
38 Soho Square, London W1D 3HB
www.acblack.com

Copyright © Rex Walford and Colin Dolley

ISBN 0 7136 7428 8

A & C Black uses paper produced with elemental
chlorine-free pulp, harvested from managed
sustainable forests.

Rex Walford and Colin Dolley have asserted their
rights under the Copyright, Designs and Patents
Act, 1988, to be identified as the authors of this
work.

A CIP catalogue record for this book
is available from the British Library

Typeset in 10pt on 12pt Sabon

Printed and bound in Great Britain by
Creative Print and Design (Wales), Ebbw Vale

contents

acknowledgements

We are very grateful to the many people who have helped us in our research for this book. In particular, we wish to thank: Sir Alan Ayckbourn for his Foreword; Nick Warburton for his contributed chapter; the many playwrights we consulted in relation to their own one-act biographies; Amanda Smith and Paul Taylor of Samuel French for help with information about some authors and for clarification of some copyright and licensing issues; Derek Palmer and Jenny Armstrong of the Welwyn Drama Festival; Harold Stull who has meticulously recorded much of Welwyn Drama Festival's history; staff at the Drama Association of Wales and at the Scottish Community Drama Association for their time given answering our enquiries.

Our publisher Jenny Ridout has encouraged and guided us helpfully throughout, with a light but firm touch and helped to bring the book to its present form.

We are also much indebted to our respective wives, Wendy and Judith, themselves both keen students and practitioners of the theatre; they have contributed much to the discussions which have surrounded the eventual form and content of these pages.

Rex Walford and Colin Dolley
Cambridge and Shepperton, February 2006

foreword

by Sir Alan Ayckbourn, CBE
There is a mistaken belief in some quarters – presumably quarters that don't include playwrights – that writing a one act play is somehow *easier*, requiring less skill, less expertise than its full-length counterpart. Would that it were. I would personally have written dozens by now – as opposed to the handful I have done.

Of course, the truth is that like its equivalents in other media, the short story as opposed to the novel, the small scale chamber piece compared to the full blown orchestral symphony, it is neither harder *nor* easier. It is different.

I consider a good one-act play as the personification of what good art is really about. It's the living embodiment of that all-important choice of artistic selection. In other words, what you choose to put in, and equally, what to leave out. A good picture, a fine piece of literature, a superb acting performance or a wonderful jazz solo, all are regarded as this largely because of their (apparent) effortless simplicity, as opposed to moderate, due to their effortful intrusive clutter.

When I started writing at the end of the '50s, one act plays linked together in double or triple bills were not, I was informed by producers, popular with the public at large as an evening's entertainment. One or two cleverer dramatists got away with it – Rattigan with his craftily disguised *Separate Tables* and Noël Coward – simply because he was Noël Coward. For the rest of us there was essentially the choice of either the two or three act form: though during my career I have used the latter only once and these days it is a virtually obsolete format. The theatre managers' love of bar profits having evidently been out-weighed by the public's resistance to sitting in an auditorium till nearly midnight. Instead there is an interesting trend lately with the emergence of the long one act play.

Maybe, stealthily, the spurned one act play is gradually being welcomed back to mainstream theatre having spent the last decades on the professional fringe or flourishing at the centre of amateur drama festivals. It would be nice to think so. Small, as they say, can at times be very beautiful. But be warned. It is also very, very difficult.

Alan Ayckbourn
July 2005

introduction

'The one-act play is one of the neglected jewels of the theatre', said the noted British actress Sheila Hancock a few years back. Her view succinctly captures both the potential value and the general lack of attention from the media to this particular art-form. It was no accident that this view was expressed when Hancock was attending the prize-giving ceremony of an amateur drama festival, since it is within such festivals that the life of the one-act play lives on most vigorously in the 21st century.

Yet, in its various forms, the one-act play has had a long history. Its earliest days were in Greek theatre, and there was frequent use of short pieces of drama in mediaeval church liturgies. As a broadening professional theatre grew in the 19th and 20th centuries, the one-act piece was frequently found as a 'curtain-raiser' in the professional theatre. Then, standing on its own feet as an increasing number of writers became attracted to the form, it became the staple fare of many burgeoning amateur drama groups in the period following World War I.

Today, the one-act play stands apart from its longer counterparts as a distinct art-form, with some writers specialising in this style. Current writers such as David Campton, Nick Warburton and Gillian Plowman have followed in the footsteps of mid 20th century specialists such as Philip Johnson, HF Rubinstein and TB Morris. Yet a large number of major dramatists (e.g. George Bernard Shaw, Tom Stoppard, Harold Pinter, Caryl Churchill, Alan Ayckbourn, Edward Albee, Tennesee Williams, Georges Feydeau, Jean Genet), though best-known for their full-length plays, have provided work of quality in smaller packages.

The origins of the one-act play have become more diverse, since, besides the genesis of specially-crafted scripts for the theatre, plays first aired on radio or television are now frequently re-shaped for the stage. And these days, as professional theatres seem to offer less and less for the money of their patrons, the difference between a long one-act play (many drama festivals allow a maximum playing time of up to 55 minutes) and a short full-length play (some recent plays presented in the West End have lasted little more than an hour and played without an interval) has become increasingly blurred.

the aims of this book

The main aims of this book are twofold: to provide a useful general compendium of information for anyone wanting to play in the one-act form; and to widen the horizons of both performers and audiences who are interested in the one-act form for itself. Play publishers' catalogues provide basic information about cast and plot only for individual plays that are currently in print; we have sought to enhance those catalogues by providing comment and advice about ix

aspects of presentation and performance, a history of the one-act form, and specific biographical material about leading writers of one-act plays.

biographies

We have provided about 250 biographies of one-act playwrights and overviews of their work specifically in this field, so that anyone searching for plays may have some idea of what there is to choose from. These biographies and play-listings do not claim to be comprehensive, and the choice of those who appear is inevitably a subjective one. Nevertheless, we feel confident that almost all the major one-act plays published in the last hundred years written in the English language (or at least, of those which have proved actable on the stage) are included.

We have included the best-known practitioners of the genre – but alongside them you will find equally worthy but lesser-known authors, popular playwrights from previous generations whose work may be worth revival, and playwrights from beyond the UK. So, to take a snapshot, Don Nigro, Joe Orton, the Hon Mary Pakington, John Patrick, Harold Pinter, Luigi Pirandello, Gillian Plowman and James Prideaux rub shoulders in our list of biographies, and there are entries for playwrights who are not usually noted in other theatre guide listings.

The octet of playwrights listed above gives an indication of the range of styles, periods and nationalities included in this book, and one of our hopes is that readers will discover playwrights whose work they may not have previously known.

Through the 20th century, thousands of short plays have been published and performed; there were periods when a play publisher's catalogue often had as many one-act plays as full-length plays within its pages. The quality and style of writing has varied widely over the years, but we have included in our 21st-century listing some playwrights who are little-known or who might now be thought 'out of fashion' (a view aided if their plays have gone out of print). Hidden away in their works you may find nuggets of originality or excellence worth a second look in a later age. We both know from our own experience of having adjudicated thousands of one-act plays in drama festival over the last 35 years that compelling moments of theatre can be manufactured by skilful casts and directors from apparently unpromising and almost forgotten material. We hope that this book will help both armchair readers and active performers discover more of the rich but relatively unknown land of the one-act play.

the characteristics of the one act-play

What are the particular characteristics and challenges of the one-act play which make it distinctive? Clearly the simplest distinction to make is that the one-act play is played without interval and is shorter than a play designed for a full evening: it usually lasts under an hour. One-act plays are often presented in twos or threes. But, as John Ferguson (himself a short-play writer) noted in his introduction to a collection of one-act plays published by Penguin:

> The short-play is not a full-length play in tabloid form, any more than the short-story is a full-length novel in miniature … the two forms are separate and distinct, as distinct and separate as is the art of the portrait-painter from that of the landscapist.
>
> … In the long play, as in the novel, the author can, by piling up word on word and phrase on phrase, make fairly sure of obtaining the precise result at which he aims. In the short play, however, the author has no time in which to develop character and situations. His characters must be flashed on the audience, in the round, so to speak, like figures passing a window: his situation must be apprehended quickly like a picture hung on a wall. And in reading the best type of short play, it is maybe not the least point of interest to perceive how all this is achieved with the extreme of verbal economy …

And a similar point was made by JW Marriott, an editor of several anthologies of one-act plays in the mid 20th century, who stressed that the one-act play is by no means an easy art form to practice successfully. In one of his introductions, Marriott commented that to suppose that a one-act play demands only one-third of the ability needed for a three-act play, 'is too naïve to be seriously controverted …'

Perhaps the hey-day of the one-act play in Britain was between the 1920s and 1950s, when the desire to be involved in amateur theatre was spreading steadily amongst those who had moved to new communities in the fast-growing suburbs and villages, and who had newly-found leisure time from shorter working hours. In this period, published one-act plays not only proliferated in numbers, but also extended their range from the light comedies and early farces of the Edwardian period, to a much wider range of subject-matter.

In America, too, the one-act play has flourished. Two American editors offered the following comment in their introduction to a set of one-acters in 1958:

> … the one-act play has come of age on Broadway. It always was popular and appreciated in arty theatres tucked away in Greenwich Village cellars and converted stables and in amateur circles throughout the country. Unsung, underpaid, and truly dedicated off-Broadway producers understood the appeal and validity of a full evening's worth of three or four varied expertly wrought one-acters. Only big-shot managers on the 'Main Stem' did not …
>
> … Even on Broadway today, however, the one-act play enthusiastically fostered by popular playwrights like Noël Coward, Thornton Wilder, Arthur

Miller, Tennessee Williams and William Inge has come into its own ... Their taut construction and economy of dialogue will hold a special appeal for readers who have been ploughing through some of the padded, endless, thousand-page novels publishers have been foisting on an arm-weary public. These one-acters may raise another thought in your minds too: how many full-length plays of the past four or five years would have been infinitely more rewarding – and successful – if they too had been compressed into a single act.

Despite this enthusiastic prognosis, the professional theatre has only rarely staged bills of one-act plays, either before these words or since. Ivor Brown, a noted British drama critic, puzzled over this.

Why is it that people who are paying for their seats at a professional show resent the idea of getting three separate one-acters instead of three acts of one play? Is it that readjusting yourself to three new starts is a strain and that playgoers are so lazy that they will not face even so small an effort? After all, if you reckon up your chances of entertainment, the three one-acters are really the safer investment.

In the case of a three-acter, you may realise before the first scene is over that the show is 'not your cup of tea' and has no likelihood of becoming so. In that case your evening and your money are wasted. In the case of three one-acters, dislike of the first effort need not utterly dash your expectations for the evening. You may heartily enjoy the other two. In a variety bill, however feeble the start, there is always hope of something turning up and it usually does. The evening of one-acters applies the variety principle to the legitimate stage ...

On the other hand, some would argue that the full-length play usually provides more depth of character, more development of plot and sub-plot, more time to become fully involved in on-stage lives and situations. For many 'an evening at the theatre' usually means there has to be a single focus to it. But there is no intrinsic reason why a programme of one-acters should not provide as much satisfaction and entertainment as Ivor Brown suggests. One suspects that it is tradition and a reluctance on the part of audiences to experiment, which has confined the one-act form largely to amateur ranks.

There are other virtues to the one-act form. For drama groups and performers who are dipping their toe into the world of theatre for the first-time, the one-act play is a suitably-sized project, which can be rehearsed in a relatively short period of time, and presented in a variety of situations. One-act plays can be presented as adjuncts to other situations, say a social evening or a church service, without monopolising the whole time. Put on in that way, such plays may well attract much more of a 'passing' audience than a full-length piece of theatre might do.

Writers seeking practical performance of their work to establish themselves as playwrights stand very much more chance of persuading a group to perform one of their shorter plays, if they have not so far been published. In a similar way, drama societies and repertory companies are more likely to risk tackling new or experimental material in the one-act form than in a longer version. So, the one-act play serves any number of practical functions. The curious thing is that, apart from play catalogues which briefly describe the synopses of published one-act plays, hardly anything has been written about the genre. The last general book in the English language about the one-act play which we could trace in our researches (*The One-Act Play Today*, edited by William Kozlenko) was published in 1939.

Yet, as the 21st century gets underway, the one-act play is showing signs of vigour, growth and renewal. The advent of new technologies is encouraging more multi-media experiments and the profusion of TV and radio channels now provides more material with potential for adaptation. At the same time, there has developed a profusion of small studio and fringe theatre venues, both amateur and professional, in many cities, and a greater willingness of writers to tackle controversial themes and experimental styles. So, it seemed timely to try to bring together some thoughts about one-act plays and some background history, allied with a survey of plays and authors and practical advice for those who might be considering directing or acting in one.

presenting **one-act plays**

In 2000 the play *Faraway*, written by Caryl Churchill, was staged at the Royal Court Theatre and later transferred for a successful West End run. What was unusual about this production was that it ran for less than an hour. If the play had been presented a few decades earlier, theatre managers, producers, (and bar managers) would have demanded a second play for fear that audiences might have felt short-changed.

Most of Shakespeare's plays run to five acts and throughout the first six decades of the 20th century a full-length play was expected to have three acts. But, possibly as a result of the influence of television viewing habits, the recent trend has been for new full-length plays to be shorter, often playing without an interval. Very few modern playwrights emulate such authors as Eugene O'Neill whose *Mourning Becomes Electra* runs over four hours. At the same time the trend is for *longer* one-act plays so now the boundary between the full-length and the one-act script has become blurred; often there is little clear distinction between the two.

There is enormous diversity and variety in the one-act play catalogues, with some scripts playing for just a few minutes with others lasting well over an hour; the subject matter may cover any aspect of life in a variety of genres and styles, so the play may be a raw hard-hitting piece of 'In-Yer-Face' theatre or a gentle whimsical comedy. Clearly selecting the right play – or combination of plays – for your group, the audience, the playing space and the time available is ultimately vital in making for a successful theatrical experience.

Some companies may still consider it a risky enterprise to present a 45-minute play as the sole theatrical event, so how and where can the short play be presented?

places and occasions for the one-acter

the amateur drama festival
Many one-act plays are presented at the hundreds of amateur drama festivals which are held annually throughout the UK and beyond. Indeed, it has been claimed that the amateur theatre has continued to provide the most fertile territory for one-act playwrights, the number of productions presented at festivals each year running well into four figures. The next chapter gives more details of the festival scene.

the double (or triple) bill

Theatre companies may consider it best to present a double bill. In recent years there have been professional touring productions coupling *Black Comedy* (Peter Shaffer) with *Talent* (Victoria Wood), *The Browning Version* (Terence Rattigan) with *The Twelve Pound Look* (JM Barrie), and Harold Pinter's *The Dumb Waiter* has played alongside some of his early sketches. *Green Forms* and *A Visit From Miss Protheroe*, two stage adaptations of Alan Bennett's television plays, were presented under the umbrella title *Office Suite*. Various combinations of Bennett's *Talking Heads* monologues have also be presented on the same bill.

Creating a double bill where the plays chosen can be linked in some way, will give some cohesion to the whole programme and help with the marketing. The connection might be purely in the title as when Peter Shaffer linked *The Private Ear* with *The Public Eye*, and *Black Comedy* with *White Liars*. The choice of play may have a seasonal link – *There's Always Spring* (Arthur Lovegrove) with *Too Long an Autumn* (Jimmie Chinn); a time link – *Shadows of the Evening* (Noël Coward) with *A Night Out* (Harold Pinter); a mealtime link – *Lunch Hour* (John Mortimer) with *The Long Christmas Dinner* (Thornton Wilder). There are wide opportunities for imaginative creative linking of play titles.

The type of plays will often be contrasted in style. It is interesting to note that for its original production Terence Rattigan wrote the farcical *Harlequinade* to go alongside the poignant *The Browning Version*.

The double bill may comprise plays by the same author – for example, *Laundry and Bourbon* with *Lone Star* two linked plays by James McClure. The several volumes of short plays by Tennessee Williams provides fertile territory for building interesting double – or indeed – triple bills (The Young Vic presented a successful quintet of his plays). The brief vaudevilles of Chekhov, such as *The Bear* and *The Proposal*, can be built into an entertaining programme.

the pick and mix bill

Some playwrights have written series of short plays which have created a full evening's entertainment, but the individual scripts can be selected as time, space, casting or inclination dictate. Back in the '30s under the title of *Tonight at Eight Thirty* Noël Coward wrote ten one-act plays presented in three separate programmes in varying combinations. Among the ten are the ever-popular *Red Peppers*, *Still Life* and *Fumed Oak*, but all ten plays are still available for individual presentation. Forty years later, Alan Ayckbourn wrote five loosely-linked plays under the umbrella title *Confusions* and they have proved enormously popular especially in amateur drama festival circles where *Gosforth's Fête*, *Between Mouthfuls* and *Mother Figure* are regularly seen. More recently Richard Harris has written a series of short plays set in a hospital ward; these were presented as an evening's bill titled *Visiting Hour*.

the themed evening

The plays presented might have a common link. In 1969 eight leading playwrights, including Pinter and Ayckbourn, wrote short playlets on the subject of marriage under the title *Mixed Doubles*. The choice of linked themes is endless, for example attitudes to old age – *Say Something Happened* (Alan Bennett) with *Parcel* (David Campton); disability – *Effie's Burning* (Valerie Windsor) with *Touching Tomorrow* (Gillian Plowman). The link might be the location which could aid a solution to the setting problems. *Seaside Postcard* (Terence Frisby) could play with one or more of Jean McConnell's *Deckchairs*.

the shared double bill

Two local theatrical companies might combine each presenting one half of a double bill which might provide a social occasion and break down the insularity of some societies. If this becomes an annual event the venue for the presentation could alternate each year.

building round the chosen one-act play

If a company does opt for just one play in the evening it might be augmented with songs and/or poems on the same theme or by the same writer. For example, a Noël Coward play could be surrounded by some of his prolific output of verse and song. Or the theme of the play might be expanded by related poems and songs – and possibly dance.

the supper evening

Some companies have found theatre/supper evenings combined with a short play to be popular. The play is either preceded or followed by a light meal with drinks which allows time for the director to talk about the play and perhaps for the audience to discuss the production with the players, as well as amongst themselves.

undiscovered talents

Where does a budding new playwright go to get an opportunity to get their work staged? Few companies will risk presenting a full-length untried play, but they might well take the exciting chance with a short play. This could be followed by discussion among the cast, audience and the playwright. Similarly where do new directors find their first opportunity to flex their directorial skills or actors, new to a company, find a place to expose their talents? An evening of one-act plays could provide the ideal vehicle which could well see whole theatrical careers gather momentum. The fact that the talents are new and hitherto yet undiscovered add to the excitement and frisson of the occasion.

the play reading

Some drama groups enjoy play-reading evenings; full-length plays allow little or no time either for discussing the play or socialising, so the one-act play may well provide the better vehicle.

touring the play

For companies which like to tour their production round village halls or to local hospitals or old people's homes, where timing is important, the short play probably provides the more practical option.

one-act plays performed outdoors

There are two spaces which are often overlooked as places to present plays – churches and in the open air – and both venues can add enormously to the theatrical experience. The possibility of an outdoor production is often over-looked by many groups, but it can have a magical quality – the fact that the presentation is open to the elements adds to the excitement of the occasion, if sometimes nerve-wracking for the director!

Where can plays be staged? Do not despair if you do not have a natural amphitheatre close at hand; it is much better to start in a small way. The lawn of a house may be much better than a vast field where voices can be scattered to the four winds. Ideally, the actors need something to play 'against'; shrubbery or a bank of trees may serve the purpose, or alternatively the façade of a house, especially when the building fits the style and period of the play. A really impressive façade might well influence the choice of play.

It is important when selecting a site to keep an alert ear for the possibility of extraneous noises – whether this be motor traffic, railways, or the regular chiming of a church clock. The audience needs good sightlines, especially if the actors are performing at the same level as those who attend, but two or three rows of chairs or benches will give a reasonable audience size, especially if the front row is lower in seat height. As with all theatre, it is important to create close audience/actor contact, and that can be better achieved if, in the outdoors, the area for staging and audience is relatively compact.

Having found a suitable space, what short plays might be performed? It may be better to opt for pieces which include visual interest and colour, rather than drama which rests primarily on complex text. So period plays, where costuming adds an extra appeal, are certainly worth considering. Christopher Fry's *The Boy with a Cart*, set in early English history, with many outdoor scenes, has remained a popular script for outdoor production for many years. Many companies have adapted scenes from Shakespeare (the scenes involving the mechanicals from *A Midsummer Night's Dream* being an obvious example) while others have taken two or three of the short spoof Shakespeare plays written by Michael Green and played them together. It is also worth considering the short plays of Molière (*Sganarelle* is a particular favourite). The well-known melodrama *Lady Audley's Secret* is set in a Victorian garden.

Harold Brighouse, one of the Manchester school of dramatists, who wrote many plays in the first years of the 20th century, published several volumes of short plays written specifically for outdoor performance. Two delightful plays written in jokey rhyming couplets by Dorothy Carr on sporting themes are also fun to play outdoors; *Ace King Queen* is set on the Centre Court at Wimbledon and *Willow Woe is Me!* on a cricket field.

Contemporary plays should not be overlooked as many have an outdoor setting. The American author Jack Heifner has written a pair of one-act plays *Porch* and *Patio* whose titles describe their stage locations. A corner of a park is the setting for most of the five short plays in the collection *A Seat in the Park* by Cherry Vooght. An allotment is the setting for *Albert's Plot* by Bob Hartwell and unsurprisingly for *The Allotment* by Gillian Plowman. A garden location is desirable for *But Yesterday* (by Jimmy Chinn) and *Smile* (by David Campton), while *Roman Fever* (Hugh Leonard) and *Terrace Talk* (George McEwan Green) take place on a terrace outside a house. *Winners* by Brian Friel and *No Picnic* (George MacEwan Green) have a hillside setting.

If a suggestion of beach can be achieved then *Footprints in the Sand* (Colin Crowther) and *And Go to Innisfree* (Jean Lennox Toddie) are possibilities. Other plays to consider with outdoor potential include *One Was Nude and One Wore Tails* (Dario Fo), *Deckchairs* (Jean McConnell), *Day of the Dog* and *Hyde Park* (Graham Swannell), *Singing in the Wilderness* (David Campton) and *Zartan* (Nick Warburton).

With the modern trend for socialising on patios, terraces and decking, many plays originally set in living rooms can be easily transported to an outdoor location, and that opens up a huge new range of plays for selection for alfresco performance.

Where possible, rehearse in situ, rather than turn up at the location on the afternoon or night of the performance and hope for the best! Several specific problems in outdoor playing may need to be resolved: for example, can the off-stage actors hear the on-stage players from their hidden locations? Undoubtedly lighting adds to the magic of outdoor evening performances, especially where trees form part of the scenery. Rather than have recorded music, there may be a case for having live music before, after and perhaps during the performances to add atmosphere. The interval, if you have one, or the post-production refreshments can add greatly to the atmosphere of the evening. Fairy-lights in the trees, wine served on the lawn, strawberries and cream, a string quartet playing quietly in the background are all features which can delight those who come to watch the play. Depending on the production, you might even end up with a well-timed cascade of fireworks.

Throughout the rehearsal period, there will be some who doubt the weather, but it is reassuring to recall that annually the average number of cancelled (rained-off) performances at the summer open-air Minack Theatre in Cornwall is only three.

As there are likely to be no overheads (literally) in the form of theatre or scenery hire, the outdoor production should be a financial success, but more importantly it can make an exciting, atmospheric, theatrical experience for both players and audiences on a summer afternoon or night.

one-act plays in churches

Drama and the church have been closely linked since mediaeval times, when the dramatisation of Easter and Christmas stories were played out within the liturgy, but there are many reasons why short plays might be used in a church setting, both within and outside formal worship.

Some one-act plays are specifically designed to be played in churches, for example, see the stage directions of Christopher Fry's *A Sleep of Prisoners*, in which four soldiers are susceptible to visions whilst resting in a church at the battlefront. Philip Turner's *Christ in the Concrete City* has been a recurring favourite for church performance since its was first written in the 1950s, with its echoes of Henri Gheon's poetic mediation *The Way of the Cross* cleverly mixed with modern allusions and swift changes of scene to contemporary situations.

Other plays, with 'neutral' set backgrounds are very suitable for playing in churches because of the religious aspects of their content, e.g. Edward Murch's *No Name in the Street*, TC Thomas's *Mirage*, TB Morris's *Night on the Hill*, Charles Williams' *The House by the Stable*. Many examples of one-act plays with Biblical and/or religious themes are given in the biography secion. Some plays may be surprisingly enhanced and given added meaning by a church context, e.g. NF Simpson's *The Hole*, and Norman Holland's *Happiness my Goal*.

It would not be true to say that the subject matter of all one-act plays can be suitable for church performance, but there are few churches which operate a 'narrow' policy these days, providing that the subject-matter of the play is not seen to be offensive or blasphemous. For more information about plays suitable for churches (there are literally hundreds available) contact RADIUS (The Religious Drama Society of Great Britain, see Appendix 3) which has a comprehensive library of such plays and publishes lists and catalogues for members; there is also an excellent quarterly magazine.

If a company wishes to play in a local church, it is essential to seek the co-operation of the local priest or minister at the outset and also, usually, of the church council. When seeking permission to play in a space used for worship it is good practice (and good manners) to indicate the nature of the play and to supply a copy of the text in advance. If church officials have the chance to know what is involved in detail, they are much more likely to be supportive.

In some cases, a one-act play might be staged as part of a church service, or as an adjunct to it, if its subject-matter is attractive or relevant to the church community in which they are being played. Quite apart from this, the church may be available for hire separately as a performance space. When a suburban hall burnt down in Mill Hill, London in 1992, the Anglican church next to it offered its space for the performances of the local drama society which used the hall, and for the next two years they carried out a full programme of plays using the chancel of the church. Several theatre companies have acquired chapels or churches which have fallen into disuse or are no longer required for worship and have converted them into permanent performance spaces for their own purposes.

Churches and chapels offer interesting performance spaces. Anglican churches may have a rood screen separating chancel from nave, but some have installed platforms in front of the rood screen for nave altars. Nave altars and communion rails are usually movable and the platform can thus become a very usable stage area.

There are often side chapels, entrances from behind pulpits and organs, long aisles suitable for procession and movement which gives a church great potential for the imaginative producer. However, large Anglican and Roman Catholic churches may be very suitable for music, but offer a considerable acoustic challenge for the performance of the spoken word. Similarly, the presence of pillars may make viewing from side aisles an unsatisfying experience, unless this is carefully taken into account when the production is planned.

Some churches may allow performances if the sanctuary and altar are screened off. Modern churches (post-1945) often have movable seating and the flexibility of this may permit or encourage performance in the round.

Churches may be more available for rehearsal than the average hall! But it is important to note that there are differences relating to licensing and safety regulations when playing in churches, and the local fire and council officers need to be consulted if a public performance is planned.

Church communities are a ready-made audience for plays. A congregation may be very pleased not only to welcome the offer of a play (say on a topical or social theme) from a local group, but also to publicise it, attend it and to discuss its content afterwards. Faiths other than Christianity may also respond to an offer.

drama festivals

Over the past century, a particular haven of the one-act play (indeed, perhaps its vital base) has become the drama festival. Here, at a neutral venue, usually over a period of several evenings, drama groups congregate to present a varied menu of one-act plays in the presence of not only an audience but an independent and qualified adjudicator. In each session two or three plays are presented, and then, at the end of the evening an adjudicator provides a final 'act' by going on stage to present a public assessment of what the audience has just seen. The adjudicator will also usually meet the teams informally afterwards to explain and amplify his or her comments and to hear the team's views on the judgements given.

Most of the festivals are competitive – in North America these events often go by the name of competitions or tournaments. The event may last one day or up to a fortnight (for many years the festival at Woking in Surrey, UK, has run for two weeks). At the end of the event there is usually an award ceremony with trophies for the best production, best actors, best stage presentation and other notable achievements by individuals or the groups. While a few people deplore this competitive element in the arts, it has to be said that most societies enjoy the edge that the 'Oscar' ceremony brings, realising that competition is an enjoyable way of pacing each other on the way to excellence. And that is one of the most important functions of the drama festival.

Drama festivals vary considerably, not only in their venues but also in their style and atmosphere, and so teams who are thinking of entering for the first time are well advised to do some judicious reconnaisance to sample a festival's flavour.

The smaller festivals are often based in community or church halls where the conditions for performance have to be created specially for the event. The stage may be relatively small and equipped only with the basics. A team of local volunteers will form the back-stage crew and bring in extra lighting and staging to give the teams as much help as possible. The auditorium may well be flat-floored and be in use as a general hall at other times and so audience viewing may not be perfect. Teams need to take account of the limitations when both choosing and preparing their productions for venues such as these. Creative flexibility needs to be the order of the day and teams with over-ambitious lighting plots or scenic demands may come to grief. On the other hand, it is surprising what can be done imaginatively in quite unpropitious venues. One of the oldest one-act drama festivals in Britain, in Letchworth, Hertfordshire, has operated for many years in a historic building known as The Settlement which has only a postage-stamp of a stage, less than 20 feet wide between the two pillars of the proscenium arch.

Larger festivals may well have the use of a purpose-built theatre, where there is a well-equipped stage, where the auditorium seating has a 'rake' and where professional stage staff are there to augment the efforts of the festival volunteers. These theatres may range from those which are the regular home of a large amateur company to those which usually host professional performances but which are willing to mix their fare. Here, though the technical conditions are enviable, the very size and scope of the theatre may be daunting, and companies may need to 'expand' their original plans in order to cope.

why enter a one-act festival?

The extra pressures of time and financial resources needed to present a play in a drama festival are considerable commitments but many forward-thinking drama groups realise the considerable value to be attained from these events.

- Festivals provide an exciting learning experience. The helpful constructive comments from the adjudicator should give considerable food for thought and discussion – even if the company not agree with every point that has been made. Friends and family *tend* to heap praise on a production and performances whereas the well-qualified adjudicator is completely independent.

- In addition to hearing the assessment of their own production, much will be learned by watching the other festival entries. Facets of production, stagecraft, staging, lighting, sound effects, acting technique, new theatrical genres – all provide ideas which can be called upon in future productions.

- By entering the event, each company becomes part of the festival, which means meeting other enthusiasts who share the same love of theatre. The insularity which can be a regrettable feature of some local drama societies is broken down. Within a short time companies often become friends rather than rivals, and from such accord mutual practical help may well emerge.

- Most societies have a regular programme of home productions which must, of financial necessity, largely be box-office winners. That is understandable but to grow artistically actors and directors need to keep fresh and extend their range by trying new, unusual or less accessible work. This is where the festival comes into its own. Here there is no need to present a lightweight boulevard comedy, perhaps chosen only because of the taste of a company's regular home audience. Festivals provide an opportunity to try a play by Beckett, Pinter, Dario Fo or Tennessee Williams; maybe present an unknown play or a compilation of poetry, word and music. There are so many possibilities. Drama festivals are places where theatrical risks can be taken.

- Playwrights are often looking for places to present their new work. Few companies will risk presenting an original work as part of their main home programme – but might well be willing to present a new script at a festival. To create and stage a completely new work, knowing that no other company has taken this journey before, can be a very exciting experience. Moreover, hopefully the playwright will be delighted to see the work transfer from the page to the stage.

- Maybe within a drama group there are those who wish to direct for the first time or the company has an influx of new untried members. The drama festival could be just the place for them to flex their creative muscles. Much could be learned which could be of great benefit to the company in the future.

- For personal reasons some actors cannot commit the time to either a full-length play or to a long home run and they may prefer the one appearance in the one-act festival entry.

- The word festival suggests *celebration* and that is what should be evident at such an event – a joyful meeting of drama companies to share, and strive for an ever-improving standard of theatre. Clearly, companies will want to achieve success but the overriding reason for entering the competition should not be to win! Those companies desperate to carry off all the trophies rarely succeed; a sense of frenzied angst is apparent and the production is nervous, tense and uneasy. However, should the production win some of the silverware then the success can be used in publicity material through the local media – all adding to the kudos of the group.

Presenting the short festival play on stage is a challenge in itself. In almost all drama festivals, there are restrictions on the time allowed for setting and striking the scenery (so that evenings do not become too long), as well as limits on the overall running time of the production.

the adjudication

An essential part of every one-act drama festival is the adjudication. Seated in the audience, a professional adjudicator makes notes on each play they see, and then, at the end of the evening, goes on stage to offer public comment. In addition, the adjudicator is marking the plays on a generally-agreed structure, so that there will be a basis for making awards at the end of the festival.

In most cases, the adjudicator will not just be a well-meaning volunteer, but a member of a professional body who has trained and who is skilled in adjudicating. Some have come through the ranks of professional theatre and other have had long experience as directors and performers in drama festivals.

In England and Wales, a body known as the Guild of Drama Adjudicators (GODA) provides the adjudicator for most one-act festivals, and there are similar organisations based in Scotland (SASDA) and Ireland (ADA; see Appendix 4). Members of these organisations have undergone a rigorous training, selection and mentoring regime before being allowed to claim full membership.

GODA seeks to ensure that whoever is appointed adjudicator for a festival has the ability to evaluate accurately, to structure a judgement coherently (and instantaneously) and to speak clearly and resonantly from the stage – a challenging trio of attributes, which not all those who work in the theatre may be presumed to have. Audiences also like an adjudicator to be entertaining to listen to. Perhaps most importantly, adjudicators need to couch criticism in a constructive way, and at an appropriate level so that teams do not recoil from their festival experience with a vow never to subject themselves to such indignity again.

the marking system

Most festivals operate with a scheme of marking which has won general approval over the years. It allots particular amounts to different aspects of stagecraft as follows:

Stage Presentation (Set, Lights, Costumes, Props, Effects, Sound, Make-up, etc)	**15 marks**
Acting	**40 marks**
Production	**35 marks**
Endeavour, Originality, Achievement (or, simply, Dramatic Achievement)	**10 marks**
	Total 100 marks

The adjudicator allocates marks on this basis when considering the play but does not usually announce the actual marks in public. On the last night of the festival, after the awards have been announced and trophies presented, the adjudicator hands the mark sheet to the festival organiser backstage, and this is then circulated by post for the teams to digest in the privacy of their own group meeting. A mark of over 80 generally signals very good work, whilst a mark of under 50 should be seen to be cause for concern about the group's standards.

Experienced adjudicators are usually able to mark within three or four marks of each other; an important criterion, since the marks a team gets at a particular festival may determine whether or not they receive an invitation to the National Drama Festival Association (NDFA) All-Winners Festival at the end of the season (see below).

the festival network

Drama festivals take place throughout the UK; in Ireland the emphasis tends to be on the full-length festivals rather than the one-act variety.

The National Drama Festival Association (NDFA) has 50 members who each present an annual event comprising a number of one-act plays. Founded in 1964 the association is dedicated to the advancement of live theatre, and to encourage and support community theatre particularly drama festivals. Each year NDFA hosts a prestigious All-Winners Festival, in a different part of the UK which includes about eight one-act productions which have won a member festival in the previous year. The festival includes both one-act and full-length productions.

Completely separately, each of the four British countries organises a progressive knock-out one-act competition. The All-England Theatre Festival has more than 40 festivals from which successful productions can progress through two further rounds to reach the English Final where the national winner is selected. For more than 70 years the Scottish Community Drama Association has organised a similar event which attracts a large number of entries from around Scotland. In Wales the event is organised by the Drama Association of Wales, with the initial rounds taking place in about six centres throughout the principality – all assessed by the same adjudicator. Although somewhat eclipsed by the major full-length festivals in Ireland, the Association of Ulster Drama Festivals presents a one-act event each year. In the Irish Republic a national one-act festival is organised by the Drama League of Ireland.

Each year the four winners from England, Scotland, Wales and Northern Ireland compete for the blue riband award at the British final, usually in July, and held in each of the four parts of the UK in turn.

Looking to further horizons, every four years Monaco hosts an International Festival of One-act Plays presented through the auspices of the International Association of Amateur Theatre. Another well-known European event is the annual one-act Festival of European Anglophone Theatre Societies (FEATS) which, as its name implies, is open to any English-speaking drama company operating in continental Europe.

In addition to adult festivals, one-act youth competitions are also popular. Some are held as part of a wider community festival but others are entirely separate. A notable example is the Welwyn Garden City Youth Festival, which has been running for well over 60 years. Many secondary schools and colleges hold their own internal drama festival of short plays. The NDFA All-Winners Festival introduced a separate youth category in 2005.

When you add together all the productions presented at these hundreds of festivals each year, clearly these events provide fertile territory for the one-act play.

For addresses of organisations, see Appendix 4.

one-act plays for young actors

When people speak of youth drama the term can cover a wide spectrum of ages. The players may be as young as four and range up to the early 20s. In many cases, working in a youth or school drama group may be the first taste of the theatre for a young performer. Short dramatic pieces often feature in the work that young companies do, through time constraints and the abilities of the performers. Clearly the scripts selected must be chosen to reflect the age and experience of the actors.

Educational drama is often used to help young people to look at life and make their own decisions. It can give them opportunities for playing out situations and developing life skills. Good stories from any age, country or culture provide material for stimulating imagination and creativity in an enjoyable way.

In recent years there has been an increasing move towards developing improvised and devised pieces of drama as part of examination work in schools. Improvisation can lead on to short scripted plays that are expressions of the student's own thoughts and concerns. Whilst this has its particular place in fostering creative skills and self-confidence in the students, there is also much value in working on a well-honed and polished script from a professional playwright. This usually makes for a more satisfying theatrical experience for an audience, whilst giving the students an opportunity to study the rich and wider world of dramatic literature.

Here we confine ourselves to scripted and published plays for young performers. For convenience we have divided it into three sections although these are fairly arbitrary and companies will often span across these loose groupings.

under eleven

There are several specialist writers for the under eleven age group: Nick Warburton has written several plays for primary school classes. *Round the World with Class Six* is an exuberant and entertaining script for a large cast, but needing imaginative direction. His other plays include *Domby Dom* and *Ghost Writer.*

Alan Ayckbourn originally wrote *Ernie's Incredible Illucinations* for schools to produce and it has proved one of his most widely performed scripts. As the fantasies all take place in young Ernie's fertile imagination, the piece is a director's dream as it can be presented in any number of inventive ways.

Pete Meakin has dramatised three of Hans Christian Anderson's haunting stories: *The Little Match Girl, The Tin Soldier* and *The Snow Queen,* while more than a dozen of Grimm's stories have been cleverly written and dramatised by Carol Ann Duffy and Tim Supple to provide excellent material for enchanting productions full of theatrical wonder. The stories appear in two volumes entitled *Grimm Tales* and *More Grimm Tales* and include such favourites as *Hansel and Gretel, Asputtel, The Golden Goose, Snow White,* and *Rumpelstiltskin* as well as other lesser known stories such as *The Lady and The Lion* and *Iron Hans.* AA Milne's version of *The Ugly Duckling* is also worth seeking out.

There are several versions of scenes from classic children's stories such as *The Wind in the Willows* and *Alice in Wonderland,* many drama groups choosing to create their own adaptation of these well-loved tales. *Aesop's Fables* can be similarly mined for dramatic presentation, as can religious texts. Colin and Mary Crowther's delightful *Noah's Ark* has been written especially for 7–10 year olds to practice their acting skills. There are numerous scripts with a Christmas theme ranging from Richard Tydemans's unusual Nativity play *Dawn on our Darkness* to *The Real Spirit of Christmas* by Wes Magee which has a cast of 48 children. *The Last Leaf* and *Papa Panov's Magic Christmas* are adaptations of stories by O Henry and Leo Tolstoy, respectively.

The old Pied Piper story is the basis of Graham Walker's lively *The Hamelin Incident,* while there is a strong sense of theatrical magic in Tony Edwards' *The Day they Lost Raggety Ruth* where the inanimate objects in a girl's playroom act out a funny, tender and original story. Toys also come to life in *Teddy Bear's*

Picnic by Paul King. Simple to stage, the comedy of errors *Perkin and the Pastrycook* by David Foxton, has a warm fairy-tale quality. For those looking for more unusual fairy tales, seven by Oscar Wilde have been adapted by the American playwright, Jules Tasca under the umbrella title *Telling Wilde Tales*, which includes **The Nightingale and the Rose**, **The Happy Prince** and **The Star Child**. Judith Johnson's colourful **The Willow Pattern** is based on the Chinese legend of the ancient Willow Pattern. David Wood had adapted two of Enid Blyton's well-loved stories in *More Adventures of Noddy* comprising two one-act plays. Still in print are more than a score of plays by the specialist children's writer Brian Way whose scripts include **Magical Faces**, **The Bell** and **The Clown**.

Recently the National Theatre has published five new 20-minute plays ideally suited for younger children; the titles are **The Willow Pattern** (Judith Johnson), **The Gift of the Gab** (Christina Reid), **Daffodil Scissors** (Philip Ridley), **Jeremy and the Thinking Machine** (Janet Neipris and Barbara Greenberg) and **Alice in the News** (Charles Way).

eleven to eighteen

For several decades there appeared to be a dearth of plays for this age-group, so well-tried scripts such as **In Need of Care** (David E Rowley) and **Dreamjobs** (Graham Jones) were given numerous productions. Although the young people depicted in these scripts may now seem to lack contemporary veracity these plays are still frequently seen.

One of the most important initiatives which has enlived this area of youth drama has been the National Theatre Shell Connections project. This unique and exciting venture unites some of the most important and significant contemporary playwrights with the talents, enthusiasm and experience of youth companies throughout the UK. The scheme, which began in 1995, provides about a dozen one-hour plays each year for schools, colleges and youth drama groups to present initially in their own area. A few of these are then selected for performance at the National Theatre. These play scripts – now about a hundred and published jointly by Faber and Faber and the National Theatre – are then available for production.

Many of these Shell Connections plays have proved highly popular with youth companies. One of the best known is *Sparkleshark* by Philip Ridley, which is set on a (metaphorical ivory) tower block where a group of teenagers are trapped into playing roles that have been fashioned by their background and circumstances until, though the magic of storytelling, their façades are stripped away. In *Cuba* poet Liz Lochhead writes from personal experience about being an impressionable 15-year-old schoolgirl at the time of the Cuban Missile crisis. With a period Japanese setting, the powerful *More Light* by Bryony Lavery contrasts a highly-wrought and oblique dramatic poetry with sex, cannibalism and survival. In the introduction to another of her Connections plays, the baroque freewheeling **Discontented Winter – House Remix**, she writes, 'I encourage you to go mad with invention and sane with caution'. Writer of the popular television comedy series, *Drop the Dead Donkey*, Andy Hamilton contributed *The Exam*, which takes a wry focus on three teenagers and their families as they face the dreaded examination.

Mark Ravenhill's *Totally Over You* examines the cult of modern celebrity and boy bands, while his bitter-sweet *Citizenship* explores with great sensitivity a teenage boy exploring the confusion of his sexuality.

Other notable scripts in this series include *The Musicians* (Patrick Marber), *Brokenville* (Philip Ridley), *Friendly Fire* (Peter Gill), *Taking Breath* and *Dust* (Sarah Daniels), *After Juliet* (Sharman Macdonald), *The Devil in Drag* (Dario Fo), *Gizmo* (Alan Ayckbourn), *The King of the Castle* (Christina Reid), *Can You Keep a Secret* (Winsome Pinnock), *Bedbug* (Snoo Wilson), *17* (Michael Gow), *Lunch in Venice* (Nick Dear), *Mugged* (Andrew Payne), and *The Actor* (Horton Foote).

As the title suggests *Sepia and Song* by David Foxton is a collection of plays with music based on historical events so we have *Titanic*, *A Memory of Lizzie*, concerning the axe-wielding Ms Bordon, and the suffragette play *I Was a Good Girl Til I Met You*. The same playwright wrote the popular all-female *After the Picnic*, a reworking in effective theatrical terms of the incident at Ayers Rock in Australia where a party of schoolgirls mysteriously disappeared. His perceptive *Rabbit* has a distant echo of *Lord of the Flies* as a group of lone teenagers struggle to make sense of a world desolation without adults.

The actor Bill Owen wrote several short scripts about life in working-class Victorian London, notably *The Laundry Girls*, set in a washhouse, and *Them Boots Ain't Made for Walking*, which is based on the strike in the Bryant and May match factory.

Several one-act plays by the prolific dramatist David Campton make suitable vehicles for young actors, especially as many of them are gender flexible. Probably the most popular scripts are *Us and Them*, *Cagebirds*, *Can You Hear the Music?* and *Singing in the Wilderness*.

Rob John's *Living for Lady Macbeth* is a fascinating and very original youth play and one which many young people will find pertinent. It tells how overlooked, dull, unfulfilled Lily sees in Lady Macbeth a woman of burgeoning power and overriding ambition so she auditions for the role in the school play with a surprising result. The central character in *The Terrible Fate of Humpty Dumpty*, by David Calcutt, is a teenage boy who is dared to climb a dangerous electrical pylon. For those looking for comedy rather than plays of adolescent angst, then *Lashings of Ginger Ale*, by Stuart G Smith, is a deliciously funny parody of those Enid Blyton children's stories of yesteryear.

The notable dramatist, Willy Russell, has written several short youth plays including *Boy with a Transistor Radio*, *I Read the News Today* and *Terraces*, but his best known script, *Our Day Out*, concerned a school visit by a group of under privileged school children.

Mark Wheeler has written several plays on social issues relevant to young people. *Missing Dan Nolan* is based on the real case of a teenage lad who disappeared from home, *The Gate Escape* concerns truancy, *Why did the Chicken Cross the Road* and *Legal Weapon* tackle road accidents, *Hard to Swallow* addresses anorexia, *Sweet F.A.* has the central schoolgirl character seeking to represent her country at football. In *Too Much Punch for Judy*, based on a true incident, a young girl kills her sister in a drinking and driving incident. As the titles implies *Arson About* has the theme of arson at schools.

Several leaders of youth companies write their own scripts, tailor-made for their actors. In recent years Andra Bishop from Bedfordshire and Coral Watson from Welwyn have written and produced their own plays with considerable success. Many of Andra Bishop's are now published by Schoolplay Productions including her most popular script *Why Can't I be a Teenager in Love?* For those with some skills writing your own play can be an exciting and, because there is no royalty to pay, money saving venture. Another way of cutting the costs is to adapt some scenes from copyright-free classic plays or stories so that, for instance, the mechanicals' scenes from *A Midsummer Night's Dream* could be re-worked into a short presentation.

The Scottish playwright Harry Glass has enjoyed considerable success with *The Dust of the Street, Fireflies* and *I Thought Cabbage was Green*, published by the Pederson Press. The catalogue of Spotlight Publications includes several scripts aimed at the teenage market, including plays by Ron Nicol and Mark Rees.

In the 1970s various collections of more than 40 one act youth plays by acclaimed writers were published by Hutchinson. The umbrella titles *Playbill*, *Prompt*, *Terraces*, *Wordplays* and *Act* each ran into several volumes. Among more than 20 titles in the *Playbill* series there are works by Tom Stoppard (*A Separate Peace*), Alan Plater (*Excursion*) and Ann Jellicoe (*The Rising Generation*). *Prompt* includes works by Willis Hall (*They Don't All Open Boutiques*), Barry Hines (*Speech Day*) and Peter Terson (*The Ballad of Ben Bagot*). *Act* has plays by Alan Bleasdale (*Love is a Many Splendoured Thing*), Susan Hill (*On the Face of It*) and two plays by Barrie Keeffe (*Two Men From Derby* and *Here comes the Sun*).

In more recent years a series of upfront plays have been published under the revealing title *Plays with Attitude*, where titles include *Twisted*, *Much Ado About Clubbing* and *Dragon Chaser*. Each is described by the publishers, Hodder Wayland, as a 'ground-breaking play for today's teenagers'. Another recent addition to the collections of plays is *Theatre Centre Plays for Young People* which includes *Listen to Your Parents* by Benjamin Zephaniah and *Souls* by Roy Williams.

eighteen plus

When the players reach their late teenage years then most of the broad range of adult drama is within their capability, although if there is a youth element in the theme then it should have a stronger resonance for those taking part. (A play where all the senior citizens are confined to an old people's home might not be the best choice.) Each year the *Sunday Times* hosts a Student Drama Festival reflecting a wide rich variety of theatrical work presented largely from this age group.

It is clear that there is an ever-increasing demand for worthwhile material for the excitement and energy that youth drama offers and the burgeoning number of scripts in print is answering much of that demand. Schools, colleges and those involved in youth theatre know that drama instils discipline, commitment and teamwork – and a greater understanding of the human condition in personal development. The best youth drama makes bold, exciting stimulating theatre and bodes well for the future of this art-form.

some licensing and copyright issues

paying a royalty

If a one-act play is going to be performed before a public audience, just as with full-length plays, the group first needs to obtain copies of the play to rehearse with. If the play is published, the author will automatically be rewarded with royalties when copies are bought, as long as they have retained the copyright of the play. These royalties from the sale of the play book are calculated as a proportion of the price of each copy.

However, a drama company also needs a licence to perform the play, however informal the occasion. It is a matter of right that an author is rewarded for the actual performance of their work, whether in full-length or shorter forms. The administration of the performance rights of the play are usually handled by the publisher of the play or by an agent of the author. The play copy usually indicates to whom application should be made on the copyright page. Some of this performing rights licence fee (often also confusingly known as a royalty) may go to the person or company handling the performance rights to defray administrative costs of licensing, but most will go to the author. If, on the other hand, a play is unpublished, any remuneration for performance is only a matter between the performing group and the author or the author's agent, if there is one.

Most drama groups are honest in declaring their performances to publishers. If they do not do so, they may find that, sooner or later, news of their performance (even in the most out-of-the-way locations) filters back to the holder of the performance rights; if that happens, the group's future performances may be vigilantly policed.

That a licence fee or a royalty has to be paid is common knowledge and is invariably investigated by drama festival organisers before allowing companies to perform in their festivals. Usually the festival asks for written evidence that a performing licence has been obtained.

You do not necessarily need to pay a licence fee, however, if the original version of the play is out of copyright (i.e. if the author **died** more than 70 years before the performance you are giving). So, you are quite safe with Shakespeare and Sheridan, but not yet with George Bernard Shaw, who died only in 1950. Note that the crucial date is the date of the playwright's death, not the year when the play was written.

Also note that if there has been a new translation or adaptation of the play of an 'historic' author, a new copyright may have been created. So, for instance, the copyright of a new and modified version of an Oscar Wilde play may well rest with the adaptor, who could be very much alive and kicking, and hopeful of receiving some reward for their work. If in doubt, consult the copyright page.

sticking to the script

Having obtained a licence, groups are much less certain about how necessary it is for them to stick to the absolute letter of the script when it comes to performing the play. This is a question often asked of adjudicators by festival teams who feel that, for various reasons, they want to change (or often shorten) a play which otherwise suits them.

Such adaptations make take major or minor forms. Major incisions or omissions in a text may be sought by a drama group because the script, as written, runs perilously close to the maximum or minimum time limits of the drama festival they wish to enter, or because the company cannot cast one small part and want to cut it. Changing or losing particular lines or words may be desired because a theatre group feels that the language used is too strong for their audiences, or because it is otherwise deemed inappropriate. A character cast might, by necessity, be much older than the one described in the play, and so certain lines of physical description may need to be altered.

In this latter case, there is usually little hesitation about making such changes, since a director usually assures him/herself and the cast that this is in the best interests of the play and a matter of common sense, but as the amount of change rises, so too does the concern about 'would the author/publisher' allow this? Then comes the difficult decision about whether or not the changes are major enough to require consultation with the publisher to seek permission for the cuts or changes which are proposed, and the risk that the publisher may say no.

The key point to recognise here is that the author is the legal owner of the play and that no changes of any description should be made without their permission or the permission of the holder of the performing rights to whom the author may have delegated their authority. It is not up to individual drama companies to decide what is 'reasonable' but to the author, and as publishers well know, some authors are more liberal about this than others. Some authors categorically refuse to allow their work to be shortened or bowdlerised and the licensing agent has to take this into account when meeting the requests made by groups.

For some years Samuel French Ltd (which controls the amateur rights of the plays of many British playwrights and which has been ceded the decisions on cuts by many playwrights) have had a policy of allowing a company to make one major cut, but not multiple cuts. This can be justified as a common-sense policy which allows some flexibility for groups without acquiescing in the dismemberment of a text, but it removes the possibility of judiciously filleting a play by taking out lines here and there in order to shorten it.

However, the policy of the single cut can be retrograde. A company which recently reached the final of the NDFA All-Winners' Festival in Britain performed Jim Cartwright's *Two*, a play which, in its entirety, runs a little over an hour. This two-hander has a central story concerning a pub landlord and his wife, but the two actors also play all the pub customers. It needed cutting to fit festival requirements, and the decision was made to make the single cut that of the opening scene and start five minutes in to the play. This helped to preserve the internal unity of the dialogue but removed a scene of dialogue between the pub landlord and his wife which was unimportant in content, but crucial for setting up the relationship of the basic 'two' and the context of the characterisations which were to follow. The company, having had the honesty to consult the publishers, thus baffled some of their audience and were caught between the devil and the deep blue sea by the 'one cut' rule.

the views of the playwright

The views of playwrights differ considerably. Some (such as Samuel Beckett) are very possessive about their plays and wish them to be performed without any change whatsoever; others are much more relaxed about drama groups adapting their material. Tom Stoppard says in the introduction to one of his one-acters, 'feel free to change or omit lines in order to make it work in the theatre for you'. John Godber, writing in the introduction to *Bouncers*, one of his most popular short plays, goes further:

> ... flexibility can be applied to the script ... the play can run from forty minutes to an hour and a half. Keep it alive for today. Make it work for your particular actors in your particular space.

This is a clear invitation to 'cherry-pick' from the text provided, with the full agreement of the original author. Those companies entering *Bouncers* in festivals clearly need to make a selection of scenes from the text, and the choice will vary from company to company. It is not stated and it cannot be presumed that there is an 'approved' best script from the material provided by Godber.

Another established English playwright, James Saunders, in the preface to the published acting edition of his play *Games* says,

This script is not the final version, but the raw material from which the actors, the director and I worked out a more or less finished production. There is therefore nothing definitive or sacrosanct about any of the script...

An interesting example of another playwright's attitude to changes in the script comes from Fay Weldon in an introduction to one of her recent one-act plays (*The Reading Group*). She describes how she was asked to write a one-act play for a Townswomen's Guild of a small town in Wales, with a cast of five or six, so that they could enter a drama festival. She decided to write a play about a group of women who gathered weekly to talk about novels they were reading.

I was talking about the project to an actress friend ... and she said, 'but you have to have a couple of men in the play, so everyone can go down the pub after rehearsals'. So I added two men. And I wrote it, loving every minute of it. I sent it off to Wales thinking that the group would be pleased. World Premiere and all that. They weren't at all pleased. They were polite but definite. No, thank you. They wanted five women. Hadn't they said that they didn't want men? And it was ten minutes too long. I wrote and said actually you COULD do it as an all-women piece, if you wanted. A simple matter of writing the Tom and Harry parts off stage, as it were ...

Here we have an eminent playwright offering a group the chance to alter a given text with full permission. If you don't have men for the parts, Fay Weldon is saying find a way round it, and that clearly will involve major surgery to the text.

A little later in the introduction Weldon confirms her liberal approach by specific giving permission for such substantial re-writing:

So here it is, published in the form I originally wrote it, but the all-female version remains an option available to anyone who wants to undertake it.

And she goes on to give a second power of discretion :

If members of the cast have novels that they want to talk about, rather than the ones I have (given characters to talk about in the text) – *Vanity Fair*, *Madame Bovary*, *Jane Eyre* – they should feel free to interweave them, so long as it doesn't jar with their stage persona.

In the page of copyright information which accompanies the play, published in 1999, the publishers (French) say that 'licences are issued subject to the understanding that ... the integrity of the authors' work will be preserved' – a statement which seems to leave unresolved the question of whether lines (or even characters) may or may not be changed by the wish of cast or director. Presumably in this case, as in others quoted above, the publishers will be sensitive to the expressed wishes of the author in the words of introduction when making their decision. Publishers have an interest in having their plays performed are and are likely to agree to reasonable requests wherever authors give them latitude to do so. It should be remembered that it is not in the interests of publishers to prevent performances.

The attitude represented by the quotation about maintaining the 'integrity of the author's work' in the preceding paragraph (a quotation which is replicated in almost all of the preliminary notes in the current editions of French's acting editions) seems to signal a more relaxed view about the adaptation of play texts. (It is widely suspected that such adaptation is routinely done by some companies in a more clandestine way, with passages conveniently being 'forgotten' night after night, or with the assumption that what the publishers don't know, they won't worry about.) But bigger problems arise when authors are possessive about their texts. Some authors will not agree to any changes, however small, in the belief that their text will not benefit from being altered. This still, however, allows plenty of discretion for the imaginative director in design, style and sub-text.

It is, of course, true that a considerable set of alterations could substantially change the meaning or the rhythm of a play. But what is a trifling change and what is a major one? For instance, does changing the sex of a walk-on part (say, a policeman, doctor, postman, or vicar) constitute a violation of the 'integrity of the text'? How and when that boundary line is crossed is a difficult matter to assess.

The best policy is to have faith in the good sense and understanding of publishers. It is best to set out a case for changes in full and in writing when applying for a licence, and then be prepared to negotiate carefully about changes which may be desired. Fay Weldon, Tom Stoppard, James Saunders and John Godber are a powerful quartet of names to quote in finding examples of established authors who seem to understand the practicalities of performance and who not only allow but welcome change and adaptation. Their words may be quoted to advantage when similar liberality is being sought with other texts. Only if an author (or their estate) has been very specific about not allowing change will a 'hard line' policy be likely to be applied.

photocopying and downloading

A separate issue concerns the photcopying of scripts. Some drama companies are in the practice of buying a copy of a script and then photo-copying it, on the grounds that this is cheaper than buying a set of published scripts. This is illegal. Most printed plays contain an explicit prohibition of this and reasonably so, since if a group only buys one copy of a play, the income of both the author (who receives a royalty from the sale of each play copy, quite separate from a royalty on performance) and the publisher is severely diminished and the publisher may eventually go out of business, to the detriment of the theatre as a whole. Buying a set of scripts for all the relevant members of the company should be part of the production budget.

There are, however, an increasing number of authors who are anxious to have their work performed and who see the cost of the publishing process as an unnecessary hindrance to this; thus the texts of some plays can now be legitimately downloaded (and subsequently photo-copied) from web-sites on the internet. Authors who work in this way will still expect a royalty payment for a performance, but in these cases, the existence of photo-copies does not necessarily mean that the company using them are subverting copyright and/or avoiding buying a full set of play-texts.

If a published play is out of print, there are numerous ways to lay hands on a copy. There are local and national libraries (notably the library of the Drama Association of Wales, see Appendix 2) which have large numbers of out of print plays on their shelves. Copies may be hunted down on internet sites such as doolee.com or amazon.com. The original publishers may still have copies in their archives. Several of the larger play publishers (notably, Samuel French) maintain their archive in good catalogue order knowing that such requests will be made. They will usually allow a single script to be photocopied for a specified number of members of a group. They may even provide a photocopy of the script itself if one has not proved obtainable anywhere else. This is usually done for a small fee, between £10 and £20 based on current (2006) practice but note that the usual licence fee still has to be paid.

Companies entering drama festivals should be warned – most festival organisers know the law well, wish to protect the rights of authors and will reject photocopied scripts if they know the play to be currently in print. Not to do so would eventually reduce the number of scripts which are made available in published form.

writing **the one-act play**

by Nick Warburton

It is hard to suggest ways of tackling the one-act play because it is such a diverse form. There are so many *kinds* of one-act play. I have written several that have little in common with each other except their length. In fact, at one time I began to wonder whether I'd ever write anything beyond the 30- to 50-minute barrier.

Then I had the good fortune to meet David Campton, doyen of one-act playwrights. I asked him a rather naïve question: how do you make the step from writing a one-act play to writing a full-length play? David's succinct answer was, 'Somebody asks you to do it. Then you do it'. I suppose that's another way of saying 'necessity is the mother of invention' and I am sure it works the other way round as well. You write a one-act play because there is a demand for a one-act play: somebody asks you to do it.

Of course, you do not have to sit around waiting to be asked. You can create your own demand. If your local group presents one-act plays, you can ask them if they'd like to try something new and different (yours). If they have never done a one-act play before, you can suggest that now would be a good time to start (with yours). You can also suggest that the group might broaden its horizons and learn from others by entering a one-act drama festival. You can recommend that they try an evening of supper and entertainment (your one-act play). And so on.

If you are not a member of your local group, become one. One of the best ways to learn how a play – any play – works is by helping to put one on. You can do this by performing or by helping backstage. And if you do not have a local group, start one. One-act plays can be comparatively easy to present. You do not need a vast organisation: three or four willing souls might be enough. And if you cannot get three or four together, write a monologue. The important thing is to get your work on, to try it out, to see how it works when you put it on its feet.

Before all this, however, you must have a script you can show to people. You need an idea, and then – big step – you have to turn it into a play.

finding an idea

Spotting ideas is not unlike spotting birds. If I sit at a window long enough and wait for a bird to turn up, one probably will. But if I go to the places where birds are known to gather, a lot more than one will turn up, and the chances of spotting something rare are greatly increased. So it is with ideas. I do not just wait for ideas to come to me, I go to good idea-spotting locations – good for me, anyway.

I take note of dreams (when I can remember them) and, even more so, daydreams, idle thoughts: 'I wonder what would happen if …'. My play *Zartan* came from just such an idle thought: 'I wonder what would've happened if Tarzan had been found by some creature other than an ape. If, in fact, he'd been found by an ant'. I also listen to anecdotes and stories told by aunts, uncles and strangers. I tune in to snatches of conversation heard on trains and in shops. Sometimes I might look at newspaper headlines for inspiration (just the headline, not the story: I want to provide that myself).

It is not difficult to gather ideas. I have notebooks filled with fragments that might or might not turn into a play one day. Here is one taken at random from the notebook nearest to hand: 'a character from a dream – the seemingly amiable car park attendant'. That has possibilities – plenty of conflict, certainly – but you can see that it is actually little more than a fragment. It is a bit of broken-off thought and does not have much of a shape.

Ideas have a growth cycle – from seed to shoot to flowering shrub – and most of these fragments are the seeds. The majority will wither and perish, a few will grow and flourish. In my case, I am looking for ideas that turn into stories. I am interested in narrative.

It is very rare, incidentally, that an idea comes to me fully-formed and complete with a structure. *The Last Bread Pudding* was one of the exceptions. The idea for this came to me when I was being given a lift by a friend and we were talking about plays we might like to do. I thought it would be interesting to write a play about someone who had written a play which a committee was discussing. As the committee talked about what they did and did not like to see in plays, those things came to pass in the play in which they were appearing. That was both the idea and the fulfilment of the idea in one thought. Most of the time, however, these seeds of ideas are much smaller and need to be cultivated. That thought about Tarzan being discovered by ants needs to be developed into a proper story.

It is at this stage, the cultivation of the idea, that I consider what it might turn into. If it is to be a stage play I have to start thinking of it as a stage play. I have to think not just in terms of the characters and what they say to each other, but also in terms of the stage pictures, the way it will look and move and have its being. This might sound like an obvious thing to say, but people often tell me they have written a play and, when I ask them what kind of play – is it for stage or film or radio? – they do not know. They have not thought about it. Well, they need to have thought about it. Otherwise what they end up writing will not be a play at all; it will just be dialogue. A stage play must have action and stage pictures as well as dialogue.

shaping the play

A writer friend once told me that, in his opinion, people sometimes spoil good ideas by turning them into the wrong thing. They try to hammer an idea into a full-length play when it should really be a one-act play; or vice versa. Or they have a good idea for a radio play but, having told themselves they are writing a stage play, struggle endlessly with staging problems. (Famously, in *Educating Rita*, Rita is asked how she would solve the staging problems of *Peer Gynt*, 'Do it on the radio,' she says. It is funny but Rita has a good point. Perhaps Ibsen was writing a radio play before radio had been invented.) Or, more drastically, people might have an idea for a short story which they try to crush and twist into the form of a full-length musical. You have to be critical of your ideas.

There are ideas which, in length and scope, are much more suited to a one-act play than to a full-length play. The one-act play is, broadly speaking, the equivalent of the short story. It offers the opportunity to examine single strands of narrative in close focus and in telling detail. It usually deals with a smaller number of characters and, because of this, it can often seem more intimate than a full-length play. A full-length play, on the other hand, is likely to be more complex and multi-layered, to offer sub-plots and sometimes minor characters. There are, as always, exceptions to all this – intimate full-length plays with close focus (*Old Times* by Harold Pinter, for example) and one-act plays with large casts and 'public' themes. (*Our Day Out* by Willy Russell, for example.)

Of course, a lot of plays for young people have large casts – they must very often provide opportunities for whole classes – and a fast pace with a broad narrative sweep, but I wonder if they can be counted as true one-act plays. Are they not, in a sense, full-length plays that just happen to be short? All these thoughts about ideas tell me why my question to David Campton was so naïve. If I have an idea for a play, the chances are that the idea will itself dictate whether or not it is to be a one-act or a full-length play.

writing the play

Having developed my idea and decided that it should become a one-act play, I can set about writing it. How do I do that? Well, there are no fixed rules though there is plenty one can say. There is not really room to say it here so I will limit myself to three points about writing.

● There are good books which explore the writing process and, more specifically, the writing of plays. On writing in general, Stephen King's *On Writing* is good – thoughtful and practical. For the writing of plays, you should read and re-read *The Crafty Art of Playmaking* by Alan Ayckbourn. Stuart Griffiths has also written a very useful little book called *How Plays Are Made*.

- Learn to write by writing. If you write a play and it does not quite work, you have discovered something in the doing of it; do not despair, and do not dismiss it. Write another one. Learn, also, by reading plays (and producing them in your head as you read) and, of course, by going to see them. Good and bad productions can teach you things. Listen to plays on the radio. The best of these are miniatures in the finest tradition of one-act theatre. You might not learn much about movement and stage pictures, but a good radio play can teach you about dialogue, character and structure.

- It is useful to keep one simple question in mind while you are writing: what's the story? It is very easy to get bogged down or side-tracked when you are writing a play; to ramble off in unexpected and unhelpful directions. This little question will help you keep to the straight and narrow. It works best like this: imagine you have just met yourself in the pub and you are telling yourself the story of your play for the first time. You do not want yourself to become bored and wander off so you keep it simple and direct. By doing this you will soon learn what is most important to the plot, what is extraneous or unnecessary, and, most usefully, what really does not work at all.

make time to reflect

When you have written your play, you will want to rush out and get it read by someone. Don't. Rather than do that, put it away for a while, then read it again later – a month later if possible. The time lapse between reading it and reading it again should help you to view it more objectively. When you do that, you will probably want to rewrite it, or bits of it. Do not show it to all and sundry: there are some very nice, very sweet people out there who cannot read plays properly and should not be asked.

If you can find a director you trust, give it to them to direct. Do not do it yourself if you can avoid it. And do not be in it if you can avoid it either. (If you cannot avoid it, if the choice is 'be in it or it won't go on' then be in it.)

If you have good actors in your play, be very thankful. Good actors may also have interesting things to say about the script. Listen to them, think about what they say, but do not be bullied into making changes. Do not be tempted to be democratic about it or your script might end up looking as if a committee has written it. It is your play and it has to have your mark on it. Make changes, yes, but only because *you* think changes are needed.

Beware of people who say, 'Your play would work well on radio'. What this often means is, 'Your play is wordy and undramatic'. Wordy and undramatic plays will *not* work well on radio.

So listen to people, and then make up your own mind.

some one-act plays I remember

The first one-act play I recall with fondness was *It Shouldn't Happen To A Dog*, a lively re-telling of the Jonah story by Wolf Mankowitz. It is chirpy and absurd and, sadly, the first time I saw it also turned out to be the last. Shortly after that I enjoyed another absurd one-act gem – NF Simpson's *A Resounding Tinkle*. Perhaps there is something about the one-act play that provides good growing conditions for absurdity and philosophical pondering. I was also attracted to Tom Stoppard's little firecrackers, *After Magritte*, *Albert's Bridge*, *If You're Glad, I'll Be Frank* and so on. More recently I've come to appreciate the acute and tender plays of Gillian Plowman and Harold Pinter's beautifully enigmatic shorter plays – I think particularly of *Victoria Station* and *Family Voices*.

Both Pinter and Plowman are playwrights whose work has also been presented on radio. Others include Samuel Beckett, Giles Cooper, Barry Bermange, Don Haworth, James Saunders and, of course, Tom Stoppard. The link is clear. A senior BBC producer was once asked if he could think of any leading modern playwrights who started in radio. 'Yes,' he said, 'all of them.'[1]

short or long?

There is a second reason why my question to David Campton was naïve. The question assumes that I would *prefer* to write a full-length play. It assumes that in the scheme of things full-lengthers are more worthwhile that one-acters, that there is some kind of natural progression or hierarchy. I *ought* to be moving on to the full-length play. That is not necessarily so.

There are good plays and bad plays: a longer running time does not automatically bestow superiority on a script. A writer does not necessarily start by writing sketches, then move on to short monologues, then one-act plays and so on before finding true fulfilment as a writer of huge spectaculars with large casts and massed orchestras.

I have written full-length plays now but I keep returning to the one-act play – both for stage and radio – because I love what can be achieved with the form. A full-length play is perhaps like a symphony – a one-act play is like a string quartet. (Or a duet. Take a look at David Mamet's brilliant *Duck Variations*.)

A one-act play can also do what some paintings can do: offer us a glimpse into a space, a room where something is happening or has just happened and where some kind of meaning continues to reverberate. It is a matter of concentration – concentration of character and theme; things condensed to an episode, an encounter, a moment. The one-act play is best suited to explore a single revelation – an epiphany James Joyce might have called it – in the most economical way. Of course, they're not all like that but the one-act play is nothing if not diverse.

[1]*British Radio Drama* edited by John Drakakis (CUP, 1981)

biographies **of playwrights**

introduction to the biographies

Biographies and short discussions of the work of about 250 playwrights are included in the following section, specifically in relation to their work in the one-act play. We have limited our survey to plays written (or translated) into English so it is not surprising that the list includes many playwrights from Britain and the USA, but there are also a considerable number of writers from other parts of the world.

General biographical listings of playwrights exist in other publications, but in compiling this one, we have been struck by the fact that few of the acknowledged one-act 'specialists' appear in supposedly comprehensive listings elsewhere.

We have sought to include playwrights who have written a considerable number of one-act plays and whose work has been performed regularly on both professional and amateur stages whether such productions are contemporary or have been in the past (stretching back to 1850). We have not included plays which never appear to have been performed in public or never intended for stage performance.

A key consideration for inclusion was whether or not the playwright had a significant number of one-act plays published. Though many one-act plays may not be currently in print (and indeed the publisher may no longer exist) in many cases, it is possible to obtain copies of these plays, by paying a fee to the present copyright holder, if you can locate them. Usually, a single copy of the script will then be sent and permission given for photo-copies to be made. (We have indicated in Appendix 3 which firms have been subsumed by others in the course of time.)

We have also included, exceptionally, biographies of authors who may have only written a single one-act play, if we believe the play to have been an interesting or significant contribution to the genre. Other single plays are listed in a separate section beyond the biographies.

guide to the entries

In the opening line of each biography we have indicated the author's name, and date of birth and death where applicable and known. In the same line we have indicated their nationality and whether or not they have claims to fame beyond being a dramatist (e.g. poet, actor, film director). A short description and comment on each author's work follow, drawing attention to one-act plays of particular significance. Plays mentioned in the text are dated where possible; the date given is (as far as can be ascertained) the date of first public performance. Publication of the play may have been in the same year or, perhaps a year or two later in most cases.

At the end of the entry, we list alphabetically by title some of the author's other published plays which are worth consideration. This final list is not necessarily an exhaustive one; in some cases, there are simply far too many plays to list. In the final line we list the principal original publishers of the plays. (It should be noted that the publishers listed are those who first published the plays; some of these publishers may have since been amalgamated or taken over by another company (see Appendix 3 where we also list the addresses and contact details of publishers who are publishing one-act and/or short plays in 2005.)

In some cases, we have included a writer whose career or plays (or both) are representative of a particular set of circumstances (e.g. a writer primarily of plays whose origins are in radio but which might be adapted for the stage; a writer working from local historical material; a writer who produced many plays but who published only a small number). In these cases we have added an asterisk (*) in front of the name, to indicate that a generic point about sources of one-act plays is being made in this entry, quite apart from the merits of the individual playwright.

Inevitably, our choices must bear elements of subjectivity, and are related to the extent of our researches and experience. We hope that there are no notable omissions but also that readers will be surprised and heartened by the extent of what is available in this genre. We do not mean to imply inferiority to those whose work may not be noted here, and, with the help of readers, hope to expand this list in subsequent editions

a note about adapting scripts from other media

Though theatre was the dominant medium for drama at the beginning of the 20th century, the related media of film, radio and television developed as the century progressed. Writers, who would have thought only of producing plays for the stage in 1900, thus had increasing opportunities for their work to be produced in other contexts.

Radio drama flourished (both in Britain and the USA) in the inter-war period, and remains today, in the UK at any rate, a major source of short plays. In Britain, Val Gielgud's tenure as Head of Radio Drama at the BBC led to the commission of both short and longer plays from many major playwrights. The tradition continues today through series such as *Afternoon Theatre*. Similarly, the frequent presentation of plays on television since the 1940s has meant that some writers (who in an earlier age would have sought primary outlet for their work on the stage) – Dennis Potter is a good example – have directed their output almost exclusively to that form. The BBC's *Play for Today* and ITV's *Armchair Theatre* were a prime source of new drama in the 1960s and 1970s, and since then there have been many stand-alone new plays presented in prime-time viewing.

Radio, film and TV scripts are frequently reproduced in book form, or may be obtained from the authors or authors' agents. More recently, there has also been the practice of reproducing scripts from situation-comedies or drama series in print. A recent (2005) check of one town bookshop's shelves revealed complete scripts from the following TV series available: *Blackadder, Dad's Army, Monty Python's Flying Circus, Fawlty Towers, Dinner-Ladies, The Office, Porridge, Phoenix Nights, Little Britain, Only Fools and Horses, Alan Partridge, Frasier, The West Wing*. Many of these scripts are of pieces which range from 30 to 60 minutes in length, and with a little imagination and enterprise they can be transformed into the stage one-act form. They represent an important extra resource for potential directors and performers of short plays on the stage.

The difference in origin may mean that adaptation and simplification of setting needs to be made, and this must be negotiated with the copyright holders, but the potential of this growing resource of material is high and may itself not only re-invigorate work by stage playwrights but also bring new audiences to the theatre.

the biographies

Edward Albee (1928–) American dramatist

Adopted as a child by a well-to-do American theatrical family, Edward Albee's first job was writing continuity dialogue for radio stations. On his 30th birthday he resigned from this post and wrote the short play, *The Zoo Story* (1959), a two-hander set in New York's Central Park. Rejected by American producers, the play was first staged in Berlin in a double-bill along with Samuel Beckett's *Krapp's Last Tape*.

Gradually it was realised that Albee's was a new dramatic voice, a theatrical innovator who jumped boundaries and challenged his audience both mentally and emotionally. *The Zoo Story*, which won awards when first produced in America, is still successfully making demands on audiences – and the two actors!

Another of his earlier short plays which is still popular is *The American Dream* (1961), a vicious parable which Albee describes as 'an examination of the American scene, an attack on the substitution of the artificial over the real values in society; a condemnation of cruelty and emasculation'. As such, it as relevant today, decades after its first performance.

After *The American Dream* he wrote his first full-length play, the hugely successful *Who's Afraid of Virginia Woolf?*, after which he rarely returned to the one-act form. However, two more of his early plays worth seeking out are *The Death of Bessie Smith* (1960) and *The Sandbox* (1960).

It has been said that if it *is* possible to categorise Albee, he might fit into a school of Anti-Complacency. With his sharp hard-edged dialogue, he has continued to challenge audiences on both sides of the Atlantic.

Other plays to consider: *Fam and Yam*; *Finding the Sun*; *Listening*
Publishers: Samuel French; Dramatists Play Service

Arthur Aldrich English dramatist

Based in Leicester, Aldrich has produced several effective one-act plays which have won a place on the drama festival circuit in recent years. Most interesting of these is *The Road to Northborough*, which deals poignantly with episodes in the life of the family of the peasant poet, John Clare. While he is confined to a mental institution Clare's wife struggles to bring up a family, only to discover that he has gone off to search for his first love. *Shindig* (1990), by contrast, has a contemporary setting and explores some of the darker sides of the office party.

Other plays to consider: *The Housewarming*; *The Guest of Bedlam*
Publishers: Samuel French

Woody Allen (1935–) American dramatist, director, actor

The multi-talented Woody Allen always brings his highly personal sardonic view of life his work.

If a drama company is looking for a large cast play then *Death* (1975), with a cast of over 20, is an extraordinary screwball madcap black comedy with element of nightmare and melodrama. Beneath the almost comic-strip humour there is an allegorical undercurrent reflecting the authors view of death. A companion piece, the farcical *God* (1975), has an even larger cast.

More recent work includes three short plays collected in one volume – *Riverside Drive, Old Saybrook* and *Central Park West* (1995) – all set in and around New York where unexpected things happen to an innocent man from that city – the archetypal Woody Allen character.

Publishers: Samuel French; Random House

Jean Anouilh (1910–1987) French dramatist

Jean Anouilh was the prominent French playwright of the mid-20th century, but in recent years his work, which some critics have deemed lightweight, has declined in popularity.

One of his best-known short plays is *The Orchestra* (1967). Adapted from his television script, the curtain rises on a charming café orchestra but once the music stops it is clear that disharmony and jealousy is rife among the sextet of ladies and the lone beleaguered male pianist. There are great opportunities here for full-blooded performances from the largely female cast.

Other plays to consider: *Augustus*; *Cecile*; *Episodes in the Life of the Author*; *Madam de*; *Medea*
Publishers: Samuel French

* B Douglas Arnot English dramatist and director

Douglas Arnot was a journalist (in later years the editor of the *Edgware Post*) and a talented theatre writer whose amateur company in Hendon in north-west London (The Motley Crew) performed his own material exclusively for over 40 years between the early 1930s and the 1970s. He wrote a stream of full-length plays, musicals (with Eric Nash as composer) and revues but was, perhaps, at his best in the one-act form.

He often entered more than one original play in local drama festivals in north London, and his entries would almost invariably be in deliberately contrasting moods and styles. He won scores of awards in the years either side of World War II, as he skilfully tailored the demands of the parts he wrote to members of his group. His dramatic style was mostly naturalistic (often using topical events as a focus) but he also wrote delightful comedy fantasies.

Sometimes in October (1946), a play about servicemen in an occupied country saying farewell to the café where they had congregated in their leisure time, was a gentle and poignant piece published by Deane in 1947, but he was so prolific (writing five or six plays or musicals each year) that, regrettably, he never bothered seeking further publication. One of his festival-winning one-acters, *Shadows Quietly Waiting* (a tense drama about an escaped mental patient and his visit to an isolated farm) was exhumed, revised and published for the first time in the 1990s.

His work is a good example of an unpublished oeuvre of fine one-act plays which were written for a particular company, but which deserve wider knowledge and performance. Theatre companies, both professional and amateur, may, with a little research, be able to unearth and use similar work in their own district.

Publishers: Deane; Cambridge Publishing Services

Geraldine Aron (1951–) Irish dramatist

Geraldine Aron has spent 15 years in central and southern Africa, but she was born in Galway and most of her plays reflect that Irish background. Perhaps her best known full-length is *Same Old Moon* but she has written several other scripts – including a screenplay for Franco Zefferelli's *Toscanini*. Now London-based, she also writes for television and radio.

Among her list of one-act plays probably the most popular is *The Donahue Sisters* (1990) in which three sisters return to their old Irish family home to re-enact in a ritualistic way a terrible event from their childhood days. It makes a powerful and demanding play with three strong and contrasting roles for the actors.

Geraldine Aron writes about close relationships. In *Bar and Ger* (1975) she focuses on the developing relationship over several years between a young girl and her newly-born brother. In the tragi-comedy *A Galway Girl* (1979), a married couple reminisce about their life together until death looms for one of them. The couple in *The Stanley Parkers* (1990) are middle-aged and gay, and here, as in the other plays, their story is told with warmth and compassion. Interestingly the script of *The Stanley Parkers* is written in blank verse with each actor speaking directly to the audience.

Joggers (1981) is a play about superficial envy and a realisation that the grass is not always greener beyond one's own domestic fence, while *Olive and Hilary* is a whimsical play about alternative lifestyles.

Other plays to consider: *Mickey Kannis Caught My Eye*; *On The Blue Train*
Publishers: Samuel French

Fernando Arrabal (1932–) Spanish dramatist

The Spanish playwright Arrabal has been much influenced by Beckett and the Theatre of the Absurd. His father (whom at one time he thought dead) was away in his youth, fighting in the Spanish Civil War and his first one-acter, *Picnic on the Battlefield* (1952), is a powerful pacifist plea, its title self-explanatory of its theme. It is his best-known short play in English and an occasional festival choice by teams who are searching beyond the mainstream. *Guernica* echoes the same theme as an old Basque couple descend into stranger and stranger behaviour, reflecting the madness that war brings.

Other plays to consider: *The Condemned Man's Bicycle*; *The Labyrinth*; *An Orange on the Mount of Venus*; *Orison*; *The Solemn Communion*; *The Two Executioners*
Publishers: Calder and Boyars; Samuel French

Alan Ayckbourn (1939–) English dramatist

Since the late '60s Alan Ayckbourn has produced an amazing succession of plays which have won critical and popular acclaim both in Britain and on the international scene. In this vast output there have been comparatively few one-act scripts; however his quintet of loosely-linked plays under the title *Confusions* (1974) has regularly appeared on the menu of drama festivals for decades.

In *Mother Figure* the comedy arises from a mother only able to communicate in baby talk while in the next play, *Drinking Companion,* we see her absent husband's hapless attempts to chat up two bored girls in a bar. The best known of the five plays *Gosforth's Fête* and *Between Mouthfuls*, both demand superb timing and technical expertise. In the first, the village fête proves a disastrous event for all involved, while the couples dining at a restaurant in the second play becomes equally fraught. In the final piece, *A Talk in the Park*, five lonely people try to communicate only to be met with complete disinterest. This sense of loneliness, a need to form relationships, runs beneath the comedy of all the plays.

Originally written for a BBC schools' television programme in 1984, *A Cut in The Rates*, has been successfully adapted for stage presentation, while another schools' play, *Ernie's Incredible Illucinations* (1969) has proved to be one of the most popular plays for children in recent years. *Countdown* (1970) was Ayckbourn's funny/dark contribution to *Mixed Doubles* where eight notable playwrights wrote short plays on the subject of marriage. In spite of their great popularity Ayckbourn plays do not 'play themselves'. They are deceptively difficult both for directors and for actors, who need to give skilled truthful comedy character performances.

Other plays to consider: *Gizmo*
Publishers: Samuel French; Faber and Faber

Harley Granville Barker (1878–1946) English dramatist and director

Described as 'the most complete theatre artist of the twentieth century' by his biographer Eric Salmon, the enigmatic Barker's reputation in the British theatre is generally high, though his contributions as a writer relatively sparse. His major full-length plays, *The Madras House* and *The Voysey Inheritance*, have been revived by the National Theatre, but his three one-acters are much less well known.

Farewell to the Theatre (1917) is a beautifully crafted two-hander (never produced on stage in his life-time but well worth considering for production today) in which an ageing actress and her lawyer jointly come to a decision that she should leave the stage; some of the profound insights in the play reflect Barker's own ambivalence about continuing a stage career as he was moving to a second marriage. *Vote by Ballot* is about an MP who loses his seat at an election by one vote – the vote of his best friend, whom he had assumed was a political supporter. It raises some political themes which have modern resonances, despite its 1914 origins. *Rococo* (1911) is a light trifle and begins with a comic and baffling near-tableau (reminiscent of Tom Stoppard's opening fashioned for *After Magritte*); it turns out to be a farcical family dispute over a huge (and supposedly valuable) vase – which inevitably gets smashed as the curtain falls.

Publishers: Sidgwick and Jackson

Peter Barnes (1931–2004) British playwright

Described by *The Times* as 'one of the most original and biting comic writers in Britain', Peter Barnes' most famous works are his sprawling gothic large cast plays *The Ruling Class* and *Red Noses* but he also wrote some notable short plays and a series of monologues. He often wrote about nightmare visions of historical moments. For instance, **Leonardo's Last Supper** (1969) shows the artist, prematurely declared dead, achieving resurrection in a filthy charnel house. The author has said that he has always wanted to write roller-coaster drama of hairpin bends, a drama of expertise and ecstasy balanced on a tightrope between comedy and tragedy – which he achieved in **Noonday Demons** (1969) which veers from pained soliloquy to slapstick and song.

He often wrote about people on the margins of society as in **Nobody Here But Us Chickens**, **More Than a Touch of Zen** and **Not as Bad as They Seem**, a trilogy of short plays which take a refreshing view of aspects of disability.

In lighter mood he wrote new versions of outrageous comedies: **The Purging** by Feydeau and the **The Singer** by Wedekind which played together under the umbrella title *The Frontiers of Farce* (1976) at the Old Vic. A further quartet of short plays entitled *Corpsing* (1996) comprises **Acting Exercise, Humour Helps, Waiting A Bus**, and **Last Things**. Companies might choose to mix and match these plays to present 'An Evening with Peter Barnes' with other short plays such as **The Real Long John Silver**, a battle of supremacy in a suburban living room or **The Right Time and Place** where a Samaritan counsels a suicidal woman. Peter Barnes wrote extensively for radio including a whole series of trenchant monologues which took the title *Barnes People*.

Other plays to consider: **Bye Bye Columbus**; **Dancing**; **The Spirit of Man**; **Revolutionary Witnesses** (four monologues concerning the French Revolution)
Publishers: Samuel French; Methuen

Alec Baron British dramatist

Alec Baron has written scripts for *Coronation Street* and had his plays staged at the Edinburgh Fringe Festival.

His themes and styles are wide-ranging, for instance **The Big Cats** (1984), which focuses on an old lady facing the demolition of her home, is told with a sensitive charm while **Asylum** (1990), set in a German sanatorium in 1970, is a powerful exploration of suppressed memory.

Chimera (1987) is a thoughtful three-hander for women, while **The Push** (1987) is a delightful comedy concerning money and marriage.

Other plays to consider: **Company Come**; **Dress Rehearsal**
Publishers: Samuel French

JM Barrie (1860–1937) Anglo-Scottish dramatist and writer

It would be a mistake to judge Barrie's dramatic output solely by the well-known whimsy of *Peter Pan* (1904). He was a thoroughly competent dramatist who worked in both the full-length and the one-act field, and some of his short plays show a mastery of the form which makes them playable and watchable nearly a hundred years after they were written. In the National Festival of Community Drama of 1929–1930, out of 935 one-act plays entered, 46 were productions of Barrie plays, more than by any other single dramatist.

One of his best known one-act plays (and still often found as part of a double-bill in the touring professional repertory) is *The Twelve-Pound Look* (1910), a well-structured piece in a which a prosperous and pompous politician renews his acquaintance with his former wife, when she comes to his house from a secretarial agency to type his letters for him. Far from being depressed about her loss of status, she tells him that she revels in her new-found independence, bought at the cost of £12 (the price of a typewriter), a state which the politician's timid second wife also comes to admire. As the curtain falls, the second wife is found musing about where to get the money for a typewriter.

In *The Old Lady Shows her Medals* (1917) an impostor is provoked to act out the role of a son to an old lady who wishes she had a son in the Great War. The pair develop a touching though temporary friendship. *Shall We Join the Ladies?* (1921), supposedly intended to be the first act of a three-act play, is nevertheless a masterly piece of false-trail laying in its own right in which a dinner-party of 16 people gather. They are all suspects to a previous murder, all have secrets and expect one of their number to be poisoned.

Other plays to consider: *Barbara's Wedding*; *Half-an-hour*; *Seven Women*; *A Well-remembered Voice*; *The Will*
Publishers: Samuel French; Constable

Sam Bate (1907–?1995) English dramatist

Working from his base in Cornwall, Bate has produced a stream of sturdily-constructed comedies, dramas and thrillers over the years, most of which are in cosily domestic contexts. Many of his plays are written for all-women companies. *Head of the House* (1958) deals with the strict regime of Amelia over her spinster sisters in a country house; *Playback* (1974) features a mysterious visitor whose motives are unclear – he may have lost his memory, or is it something more? *Murder at Eight* (1977) is a thriller set in a farmhouse kitchen.

Two of his mixed-cast plays have theatrical contexts. *Decline and Fall* (1977) is centred around the proposed demolition of an old theatre which is saved at the last moment by a visit from a former actress. It transpires she has become the wife of the chairman of the firm who plan re-development. *Stage Door Murder* (1979) is based on the true story of the murder of William Terris.

'I write to entertain – to give the audience some good laughs. I don't believe in preaching in plays', says Bate.

Other plays to consider: *A Mouse! A Mouse!*; *Anniversary Day*; *Christmas Cheer*; *Christmas Cracker*; *Christmas Spirit*; *Escape to Fear*; *Flora McDonald's Mission*; *Grannie Takes the Helm*; *Her Husband's Harem*; *Hit or Miss*; *Honeymoon for One*; *Legacy of Ladies*; *Love and Lavender*; *Mandy's Washing Day*; *Mrs Dooley's Table*; *The New Choirmaster*; *A Question of Colour*; *The Quiet Places*; *Royal Carpet*; *Rugs and Pewter*; *Rumour*; *Shelley and Mary*; *South Seas Sighting*; *Tarzan's Mother*; *They Wanted a Leader*; *Unscheduled Stop*; *Wedding Crisis*; *Wishing Day Welcome*
Publishers: Bakers Plays; Kenyon-Deane; New Playwrights Network

Clifford Bax (1888–1962) English writer and dramatist

Heavily influenced by WB Yeats in his younger years, Clifford Bax was an English writer who tended to concentrate on serious historical and mystical themes in his stage work. He wrote some well-known full-length historical pieces (notably *Rose without a Thorn*) as well as short-stories, poems, and books on the theory of the theatre.

Of his one-act plays, *The Cloak* (1924), a modern morality play written in rhyming couplets, is perhaps the best known. Three characters meet at a rocky place; an Angel, the Unborn, and the Dead. The Dead is persuaded to divest himself of a cloak (pride?) before going off to heaven, but the Unborn falls to the temptation of picking up the cloak and entering the world with it. *Tragic Nesta* (1937) is set in 12th-century Wales and is a melodrama in which a son unwittingly slays his father; the powerful play ends with high rhetoric of sorrow. *Square Pegs* (1920) was a two-hander in different style with Hilda, a modern girl, meeting Gioconda a 16th-century Venetian.

Of his *Twelve Short Plays*, a collection published by Gollancz in 1932, all but one were in verse.

Other plays to consider: *The Apricot Tree*; *Aucassin and Nicolette*; *Nocturne in Palermo*; *The Play of St Lawrence*; *The Poetasters of Ispahan*; *Prelude and Fugue*; *The Quaker's Cello*; *The Rose and the Cross*; *Silly Willy*; *The Summit*; *The Unknown Hand*; *The Volcanic Island*; *The Wandering Scholar*
Publishers: Samuel French; Victor Gollancz; Penguin

Paul Beard (1954–) British dramatist

Paul Beard has been involved in both the amateur and professional theatre, both as an actor and a director, since he was a teenager when he was a member of the National Youth Theatre. He became a dramatist writing full-length plays, musicals, pantomimes and youth plays but enjoys particular success with his one-act scripts, his range extending from humour to gritty hard-hitting dramas.

His most widely produced scripts have been comedies – such plays as *Cliff's*

Edge (1998), a very amusing black comedy set on Beachy Head which is visited by such quirky characters as a suicidal actor, a maniacally depressed landlord and a schizophrenic. The setting of another of his comedies, *Piste Off* (1990), is a cramped ski chalet in which two couples are confined as there is no snow. Full of sparky dialogue, *Meat and Two Veg* (1999) begins with light domestic badinage and, taking a route through broad-humoured sexual innuendo, veers toward a black comic conclusion.

By contrast, **Waiting for Pierrepoint** (1991) is an in-depth psychological examination into the mind and emotional state of the serial killer John Christie as he faces his hangman, using fact, fiction and mime to makes a theatrical impact. Another powerful drama is *Death of a Clown* (1993) which has two estranged brothers fighting over the future of their family circus. Other dramas include *Lavender Years* (1995) and *Where the Heart Lies* (2003). *Shadows in Red* (1992) is a musical drama while *Rose Tinted Glasses* (2001) is a play for young actors.

Other plays to consider (all comedies): *Come the Resolution*; *A Pain in the Neck*; *Strangeways*; *Swingers*; *Up the Garden Path*
Publishers: Samuel French; New Theatre Publications

Samuel Beckett (1906–1989) Irish writer and dramatist

Beckett is unquestionably one of the great dramatists of the 20th century but his work, even in one-act form, needs tremendous application and study to be performed successfully. He has written for a variety of media, and in his later years has tended to contribute 'fragments' rather than full-length plays. Some of his work for radio and television has been adventurously performed in the theatre.

Of his one-act plays, *Endgame* (1964) is described as 'a vision of the end of the world' and involves two characters: blind, paralysed Hamm and his servant Clov, who discuss the implications of the apparent catastrophe whilst Hamm's parents, apparently incarcerated in dustbins on stage, offer a raw commentary. Some think that the play may represent the dissolution of a single personality in the face of death; others that it is a morality play about the death of a rich man. In *Play*, three characters speak about an apparently trivial comic story that has lead to three suicides, and then repeat this a second-time round, only faster and softer. As they start on the round a third time the play ends, though we may conclude that the recital is to be 'unending'.

In *Krapp's Last Tape* (1958) a man sits alone with a tape-recorder reviewing the events of his life, more concerned with his love-affairs than the 'work' he has produced. Other solo pieces in play form include *Rockaby* (notably performed by Billie Whitelaw on the professional stage) and *A Piece of Monologue*, also known as *Solo*. For those tempted to distil the essence of Beckett's most famous play as a short piece, it is worth noting that the Beckett estate does not allow either of the two acts of *Waiting for Godot* to be performed on stage without the other (a prohibition which applies equally to amateur and professional companies).

Other plays to consider: *Act without Words (I and II)*; *All Strange Away*; *All That Fall*; *Breath*; *Cascando*; *Catastrophe*; *Come and Go*; *Eh Joe*; *Embers*; *Ghost Trio*; *Not I*; *Ohio Impromptu*; *Ping*; *Quad*; *That Time*; *Words and Music*
Publishers: Faber and Faber

JJ Bell Scottish writer and dramatist

Publishing one-act plays among other material from 1913 onwards, the Scottish writer John Joy Bell was the author of many one-act plays which were performanced by amateur groups through to the 1950s. The thriller *Thread o' Scarlet* (1923) was the most performed, but Bell's more frequent style was farcical comedy in Scottish settings, as in *The Laird's Lucky Number*, *Exit Mrs McLeerie*,(1927) and (for children) *Wee McGregor's Party*, the dramatisation of an episode in the life of a boy whom he had already made popular through children's story books.

Other plays to consider: *All Ages*; *Breaking Point*; *Courtin' Christina*; *Good Morning Sir John*; *The Pie in the Oven*; *A Relapse in 'Consols'*; *Those Class Distinctions*; *Wolves*
Publishers: Gowans and Gray; Repertory Plays (Nelson)

Saul Bellow (1915–2005) Canadian-American novelist and dramatist

Winner of the Nobel Prize for Literature for his novels, Canadian-born Saul Bellow rarely wrote for the theatre but in 1966 three of his short quirky one-act comedies were staged on Broadway under the collective title *Under the Weather* (1966). The most popular of the three, *Orange Souffle*, centres on the regular monthly meeting between 'a very ancient millionaire' and a middle-aged prostitute and the culinary title takes on an increasing significance. The other two plays in the trio are *Out From Under* and *A Wen*.

Publishers: Penguin

*Alan Bennett (1934–) English writer and dramatist

Originally one of the team who created and performed the ground-breaking revue *Beyond the Fringe*, Alan Bennett has since risen to the forefront of British dramatists through his willingness to take on a variety of styles and themes, and through his gift for creating closely-observed dialogue and monologue.

In the one-act field, he has written a notable double-bill of one-act plays which played professionally under the title *Single Spies*. One of these, *An Englishman Abroad* (1989), was based on an actual visit by the actress Coral Browne to the double-agent Guy Burgess, living in poignant isolation in

Moscow and pining for a return to his English roots. Burgess's conduct is not excused by Bennett, but his humanity is vividly brought out and the play abounds with good lines. The second play, *A Question of Attribution*, concerns another of the 'Four Apostles' who worked for Russia, Sir Anthony Blunt.

Bennett also produced some popular one-act plays about office-life (*Green Forms* and *A Visit from Miss Protheroe*) and domestic situations (*Say Something Happened*). One of his greatest stage successes in has been a succession of long monologues, which, under the title *Talking Heads* (1988), are often put together in twos and threes to form an evening of entertainment. Seen both on television and in the professional theatre, these are pieces of great humanity as well as golden opportunities for good performers to develop a character and hold a stage on their own for 35–45 minutes. The characters vary from an naive young actress telling the story of her audition for a risque film, to a lonely unmarried son, describing life with his mother; from a unfulfilled vicar's wife, resorting to an affair with an Asian shopkeeper to a lady sitting at her sitting-room window and putting all the world's affairs to rights.

Publishers: BBC Books; Faber and Faber; Samuel French

Steven Berkoff (1937–) English dramatist, actor

An actor as well as a dramatist, Steven Berkoff is widely known for the power and physicality of both his performances and his writing. His highly successful adaptation of Kafka's *Metamorphosis* (1969) is typical of the sinewy element running through his work. That script – as with his *The Fall of the House of Usher* (1974) – can play uninterrupted in the one-act form.

His plays are both actors' and directors' pieces in that they allow wide scope for creativity. Mime, movement, body language, plus imaginative use of sound and light can produce a sense of Total Theatre. He has said of *Usher*, 'When this plays works one lives on the crest of a wave when all the elements fuse into a dynamic whole'.

In the Penal Colony (1968) is a frightening, black comic moral adaptation of another story by Kafka, while his *Agamemnon* (1973) is a modern look at the great Greek tragedy.

Plays with a contemporary setting include *Lunch* (1985), *Massage* (1997), *Brighton Beach Scumbags* (1991) and *Bow Of Ulysses* (2001). Subtitled *Confessions Of a Cad*, *Sturm und Drang* (1994) is a comedy of manners written in blank verse.

Steven Berkoff has also written a series of monologues which include *Dog* (1994), *Actor* (1994), the tragic/comic *Harry's Christmas* (1985) and *The Tell-Tale Heart* (1996), a further adaptation of an Edgar Allan Poe short story. His short television script, *Dahlings You Were Marvellous* (1994) which is a large-cast play set in a theatrical 'luvvies' watering hole during a first night party, has been successfully adapted to the stage. By complete contrast *Requiem for*

Ground Zero (2002), originally staged on the Edinburgh Festival Fringe, presents the playwright's ruminations on that fateful day in New York in September 2001.

Publishers: Faber and Faber; Calder and Boyars; Amber Lane

Barry Bermange (1933–) English dramatist

Bermange is a London-based author whose economical style has a tinge of the Theatre of the Absurd. Several of his plays have been broadcast on radio or TV and then adapted for the stage.

In *No Quarter* (1962) a quiet man and a fat man seek lodging in a mysterious hotel, which collapses around them and renders them totally immobile. *Nathan and Tabileth* (1967) (a proven drama-festival winner) is an agonisingly poignant study of old age: an elderly couple feed pigeons in the park, return home and are then visited by Bernie, a young man who says he is their grandson, though they don't remember him. As he leaves 'darkness comes'.

In *Oldenberg* (1967), another play which deals with the discomfort of 'invasion', a couple furnish a room for an unknown stranger but are disturbed by the fact that he may turn out to not be English. When he arrives their expectations are confounded and they are even more discomforted to find he is blind. *The Interview* (1968) is about a group of men waiting in an outer office, who regard each other uneasily, as they wait for a job, the nature of which is never revealed to the audience

Publishers: Methuen

* Andra Bishop English dramatist and director

Andra Bishop is a Bedfordshire secondary schoolteacher who has developed many effective plays for young casts in the last 20 years by taking the improvised work of her pupils and skilfully kneading it into a finished scripted form for performance. In her experienced hands this irons out some of the unevenness of improvisation, whilst retaining its fresh and innovative qualities.

Her *Bermuda Tangle* is a hilarious piece in which a couple of ordinary present-day holiday-makers find themselves mixed up with Sir Walter Raleigh, his cabin boy and Guy Fawkes as they sail unsuspectingly into that mysterious triangle of waters in the Caribbean. *Romeo Loves Juliet – OK?* is, as its title suggests, an amusing modern take on the famous Shakespearean story, but seen from the point of view of the disappointed swains.

Some of her plays have large casts – *Trouble with Brother* (which has a circus theme) has a potential cast of 26, though it can be played with some doubling; *The Show's the Thing* (an in-joke skit on amateur theatre) can involve 28. Some of her plays such as *Christmas is Cancelled* (a mock-heroic adventure tale involving the kidnap of Santa Claus) are designed for 9–13 year-olds, but most of her plays suit mid-teenage players very well.

Other plays to consider: *Growing Pains*; *Happy Ever After*; *Staying Alive*; *Three Bags Full*; *Why Can't I Be a Teenager in Love?*
Publishers: School Play Productions

Edward Bond (1934–)   British dramatist

The fame – or some would say the notoriety – of the prominent British dramatist Edward Bond rests largely on his full-length plays, but several of his shorter works are worth seeking out.

Passion (1971) was commissioned by the Campaign for Nuclear Disarmament in the early '70s while *Stone* (1976) was written for the Gay Sweatshop. By no means a 'gay play', it is a fascinating piece: part allegorical fable, part parable of oppression, it carries recurring telling images and themes.

Grandma Faust and *The Swing* (1976) are both anti-racist plays, whilst *Black Mass* (1970) is part of the *Sharpeville Sequence* written at the height of intensity of the apartheid movement in South Africa.

Edward Bond has written several plays for young people. *Derek* (1982) appeared as part of the RSC Youth Festival while *At the Inland Sea* toured schools in 1995.

Publishers: Methuen

Anthony Booth   British dramatist

Anthony Booth is one of the small group of playwrights who are known chiefly for their one-act plays. A resident of Jersey, he was particularly popular in the '60s and '70s when many drama festivals included at least one of his scripts. His subjects and styles are varied ranging from farces such as *This Desirable Cottage* (1960) and *Costa del Packet* (1975) to powerful plays about human relationships caught in extreme situations.

These plays often afford strong roles for women. Set in a city – which might be Belfast – *The Trial* (1972) concerns the harsh interrogation of an informer, while the setting of *Deadline Dawn* (1977) is a Middle Eastern country where tension is heightened among the four women trapped in an attic room. Both these powerful, uncompromising plays are still seen regularly on the festival circuit.

But there are several other Anthony Booth plays for women which are worth seeking out. *The Living Hell* (1960) is set during the Second World War in a steamy jungle hut in the Far East as the Japanese approach, while South America is the location for *Quake* (1978) in which five women are isolated by an earthquake. In all these plays the unseen forces bring out strengths and weaknesses in the characters while the relationships are explored with understanding.

Other plays to consider: *The Band Wagon*; *The Boy is all Yours*; *Dangerous Twilight*; *El Campesino*; *Element of Doubt*; *First Stop Paris*; *Forty Minutes*; *The Gentle Rain*; *House Party*; *How Little We Know*; *Incident at Dago Creek*;

The Island; The Italian Girl; It Could Happen to You; Men!; Never Let Go; The Ninth Day; Nitre; None the Wiser; Ride a Tiger; Rip Off; Satellite Story; See You Rome Sometime; The Sky is Overcast; Smithy; This Boy Connor; This Isn't My Scene Man; Yesterday the World
Publishers: Samuel French; Evans; Kenyon-Deane

John Bowen (1924–) British dramatist, novelist and TV script-writer

In addition to writing plays for the theatre, John Bowen has written numerous television and radio scripts as well as novels both for adults and children.

As a dramatist he first came to the fore in the '60s with such full-length plays as *After the Rain* and *The Fall and Redemption of Man*. He followed these successes with a double bill entitled *Little Boxes* (1968) both plays taking place in contrasting flats in very different parts of London where the inhabitants have withdrawn from mainstream society. *The Coffee Lace* is set in seedy Kennington and concerns a sad, poverty-stricken elderly vaudeville troupe who have refused to go out since their performance was ridiculed a decade before. *Trevor* is set in smart Kensington where a lesbian couple try to hide their relationship from their parents by inveigling an actor to play their boyfriend. The plays have a warmth and a humour which shows the playwright's understanding of the human condition. The same might be said of *The Waiting Room* (1970), which tells with great sensitivity of a newly-widowed young woman who gradually discovers that the other person in the waiting room is her husband's male lover.

John Bowen contributed to *Mixed Doubles*, the collection of short plays on the marriage theme, with *Silver Wedding* (1969), which is often staged separately. *Which Way are You Facing?* was commissioned by the National Theatre for the opening of its new building in 1976.

Other plays to consider: *Alarm; Bondage; Cold Salmon; Diversion; Roger; Young Guy Seeks Part-time Work*
Publishers: Samuel French; Methuen; Arnold

Sydney Box (1907–1983) English writer and dramatist

Box was a man of many parts (perhaps best-known for his award-winning film-scripts of *The Seventh Veil* and *The Golden Girls*) but together with his wife, Muriel (1905–95), he was a prolific writer of one-act plays in the '30s. They produced scripts both separately and together from their meeting in the 1930s until their divorce in 1969. Sydney Box contributed a chapter on 'The experimental play in the one-act theatre' to William Kozlenko's 1939 book dealing with the genre and also wrote about drama festivals.

Some of Box's own plays, *Bring Me My Bow* (1938), an anti-war fantasy set at a girls school prizegiving, *Symphony Pathetique* (1933), in which diners chatter is set to music, and *Not This Man* (1937) demonstrated this interest in experimental styles, though none have survived in publication.

One of his most frequently anthologised plays is *In Black and White* (1939), a four-hander with flashbacks and a neat final curtain-line. It concerns a proposed divorce in which the lawyer apparently adjudicating a case turns out to be an interesting player within it. Another of his plays, *Murder Trial* (1932), dramatises the real-life 1930s' cause célèbre of the trial of Dolores Smith.

Other plays to consider: *Anti-Clockwise*; *Beauty for Sale*; *Be Sure Your Sins Will Find You Out*; *Danse Macabre*; *The Government Regrets*; *Husbands Are A Problem*; *March Wedding*; *A Marriage Has Been Disarranged*; *Martha and Mary*; *Merry-Go-Round*; *My Kingdom For A* ...; *Number Ten*; *Peace in Our Time*; *Sing a Song of Sixpence*; *Slow Curtain*; *Self-made Man*; *Solomon's Folly*; *The Tree*
Publishers: Samuel French

Bertold Brecht (1898–1956) German dramatist and writer

Known for his life-long commitment to pacifist and socialist politics, Brecht has also been a major influence on world theatre in the 20th century through his pioneering work in developing non-naturalistic frameworks for the presentations of stories on stage. He is best known through his full-length plays *The Caucasian Chalk Circle*, *Mother Courage*, and *The Resistible Rise of Arturo Ui*. His use of 'distancing effects' (often known as 'Brechtian devices') in the plays he wrote for his Berliner Ensemble have created a distinctive form of theatre. These are as apparent in his short plays, as in his epic pieces. Songs of comment, placards, asides to the audience, open set changes, all emphasise the artificiality of theatre but are designed to highlight and reinforce political messages.

In *The Exception and the Rule* (1931), for instance, the actors assemble before the curtain at the start and tell the audience 'We hereby report to you the story of a journey, undertaken by one who exploits and two who are exploited. Observe the conduct of these people closely ... observe the smallest action ... with mistrust'. A merchant crosses a desert to seek new business in a far-off city and deals badly with both a guide and a carrier in his anxiety to get there first. The whole play is a commentary on capitalist principles and morals.

Just after World War I he wrote mainly one-act plays, whilst drama critic for a daily communist newspaper. Working in Munich he was much influenced by the comedian Karl Valentin at the time, and his plays took on something of Valentin's approach, mixing political messages with comic and farcical situations. The short plays written in this period include: *Lux in Tenebris* in which a man is ejected from a brothel and sets up a lecture-tent in opposition on the other side of the street, but then eventually goes into partnership with the brothel-keeper; *He's Driving out a Devil* in which a boy seduces a girl by trickery; *The Haul* in which a drunken fisherman nets both his wife and her lover and enlists help of other fishermen to drop them over the side at sea; *A Respectable Wedding*, in which the collapse of the wedding furniture mirrors the dismantling of conventional attitudes; and *The Beggar or the Dead Dog* in which an Emperor converses with a beggar in a surreal mixture of nonsense and logic.

Other plays to consider: *Dansen*; *The Elephant Calf*; *Fears and Miseries of the Third Reich* (27 playlets); *How Much is Your Iron?*; *The Informer*; *The Jewish Wife*; *Lindbergh's Flight*; *The One Who Says No*; *The One Who Says Yes*; *Senora Carrar's Rifles*; *The Trial of Lucullus*
Publishers: Samuel French

Howard Brenton (1942–) British dramatist

Howard Brenton has said that it took him a long time to get over being taught literature at Cambridge but since those university days in the '60s he has achieved a reputation for the eclectic independence of his work. He has written *Scott of the Antarctic* for an ice rink and *Wesley* (1972) for a Methodist chapel.

Told in eleven scenes the highly controversial and stimulating *Christie in Love* (1970) takes a unique perspective on the police search for the notorious London serial killer, and is often performed as a one-act piece. One of his first plays, *Gum and Goo* (1969), is an experimental and challenging script taking the audience on a journey through an autistic child's view of the world. *The Education of Skinny Spew* (1980) is a brash satirical political farce while *The Thing* (1982) is a 30–minute play for young people. First produced at Bradford University, *Heads* (1969) is a surreal farce.

Brenton's colourful large-cast full-length play *Epsom Downs* (about the 1977 Derby) is in two almost self-contained halves, either of which may be played separately to considerable theatrical effect.

Other places to consider: *How Beautiful with Badges*; *Iranian Nights*
Publishers: Methuen; Nick Hern Books; Arnold

James Bridie (1888–1951) Scottish dramatist

James Bridie was the pen name of OH Mavor, a Scottish doctor involved with the founding of the Glasgow Citizens Theatre. From 1928 onwards, he wrote many full-length and one-act plays full of a very personal style of humour. He is considered hilarious to some, and arch to others. *Tobias and the Angel* and *Mr Bolfry* are his best-known full-length plays and he often wrote of heaven/earth linkages, as in one of his best-known one-acters *Paradise Enow* (1944). Set firstly in a booth in front of Ali the Coppersmith's hut in Southern Syria and then in Paradise, it wittily shows how a discontented husband dies, but then becomes ill at ease with the pampering of all the female angels (known as *houris*) and longs to return to the more mundane company of his wife.

Bridie's biographer, Winifred Bannister, considers *A Change for the Worse* (in which the Devil orders a change of position between a goldsmith and a fisherman but both like the reversal) his best one-act play. Something of Bridie's style may be inferred from the introduction to a book of sketches and one-act plays published in 1944: 'Mr Bridie has pleasure in presenting to the public, for their entertainment and his profit, a number of parerga unearthed in a recent salvage drive … He notices in railway stations and trains that the reading public have nothing to read and that almost anything will do…'

Other plays to consider: *The Fat Women*; *Mrs Waterbury's Millennium*; *The Open-air Drama*; *The Pardoner's Tale*
Publishers: Constable

Harold Brighouse (1882–1958) English writer and dramatist

Harold Brighouse was one of the 'regional' dramatists fostered by Florence Horniman's work at the Gaiety Theatre, Manchester in the early years of the 20th century, though his work came to have national significance. He was one of those known as the 'Manchester School' (with Stanley Houghton and Allan Monkhouse) who sought to bring realism to the portrayal of urban working-class life of the time. Brighouse did this successfully in over 15 full-length and 50 one-act plays.

One of his first (and most famous) short plays was *Lonesome-like* (1911) which was set in a working-class cottage. It concerns a rough-tongued old woman threatened with the workhouse and unable to be helped by the local church. There is an unexpected solution of the problem: her young companion's rejected suitor adopts her as his mother to console him for the loss of his own mother who had similarly berated him and made his life a misery. Writing in 1953, Brighouse reckoned that it had had over 3000 performances by both professional and amateur casts.

The Price of Coal (1912) was similarly set in a working-class cottage with a young miner seeking an answer to his proposal of marriage before going off to work. News of a pit disaster creates drama, but there is a happy resolution and the young miner returns with no worse than a broken arm, potential tragedy turning to comedy.

Brighouse wrote at least a dozen short plays specifically designed for outdoor performance. These days his plays are best regarded as colourful Northern period pieces, evocative of their time and still exhibiting strong dramatic structure and earthy comedy.

Other plays to consider: *Albert Gates*; *Alison's Island*; *The Apple Tree*; *A Bit of War*; *British Passport*; *The Doorway*; *Followers*; *The Funkhouse*; *Ghosts of Windsor Park*; *The Happy Hangman*; *How the Weather is Made*; *Inner Man*; *Laughing Mind*; *Maid of France*; *The Man who Ignored the War*; *A Marrying Man*; *The Night of Mr H——*; *Oak Settle*; *Once a Hero*; *Oracles of Apollo*; *Passport to Romance*; *The Prince who was a Piper*; *Rational Princess*; *Smoke Screens*; *Sporting Rights*; *The Stoker*; *The Wish Shop*
Publishers: Samuel French

Lynn Brittney British dramatist

The range of Lynn Brittney's work extends from children's nativity plays to adaptations of Victorian classic novels. Her one-act plays are equally wide-ranging in theme and setting.

One of her most frequently directed plays, *A Different Way to Die* (1993), is a touching, compelling drama set in Israel five years after the Second World War and concerns the seething emotions and barely suppressed secrets of a female survivor of the concentration camps. By contrast, *Have a Nice Day* (1994), set in a studio, looks behind the superficial smiles in the plastic world of modern daytime television.

The four women in *Failed Investments* (1995), described as an adult social comedy, have all had unhappy experiences with men and their resulting conversation could well start heated arguments between the sexes.

Tudor England is the background to *The Last Wife* (1994) where Henry VIII, on his deathbed, is haunted by the ghosts of his earlier murderous marital actions. Death is also an important element in *Properly Processed* (1994) where the deceased main character causes considerable impact in a high-powered unsympathetic planning office.

Publishers: Samuel French

Rupert Brooke (1887–1915) English poet and dramatist

Widely known as an early 20th-century romantic poet who died tragically young, Brooke wrote a single one-act play. *Lithuania* (1915) (in prose), but it is of some historic interest. It deals with the melodramatic story of a peasant family who do not recognise their long-lost son who returns to the family home as a visitor, and who kill him through their own greed. Shortly after Brooke's death it was staged at His Majesty's Theatre at a special matinee performance that also included two other one-act plays of the period, Gordon Bottomley's *King Lear's Wife* and Wilfred Gibson's *Hoops*. The eminent young actress Lillah McCarthy played the daughter and John Drinkwater (q.v) the son; the play was also staged at the Chicago Little Theater in 1915.

Publishers: Sidgwick and Jackson

Patricia Brooks English dramatist

Patricia Brooks's plays were frequently seen on one-act festival bills in the 1950s '60s and '70s, particularly those she wrote for all-women casts. She usually worked on small-scale contemporary themes in everyday life, and some of her comedies such as *The Undiscovered You* (1954), middle-aged ladies in a beauty and keep-fit class, had real flair.

One of her best-known and most frequently-performed plays is a drama, *The Light we Know* (1958), in which a wife faces the question of whether to leave the comfort of her suburban home and join her husband in a dangerous spying mission in Russia. *Our Pleasant Vices* (1963) has the unhackneyed setting of a women's PE college, and *His Other Love* (1963) is a play about climbers, set in a Welsh mountain hotel.

Other plays to consider: *Celestial Error; Crisis in the Rag Trade; Find the Tiger; Fool; Missing Person; Only Prison; Operation Footprint; The Prodigal Daughter; The Time of the Rat; Venture All*
Publishers: Deane

Brian J Burton (1922–) British dramatist

An actor and a director, Brian J Burton's first published play was an English version of Ibsen's *Rosmersholm*. In 1962 he published *Sweeney Todd*, which became the first of a highly-popular series of re-workings of old Victorian melodramas. These included *Maria Marten, The Drunkard* and *East Lynne*.

Alongside these classic melodramas, he wrote a large number similar one-act scripts which have been frequently used to create double or triple bills and as part of a music hall or evening of Victorian theatre. These have included the frequently seen *The Gypsy Curse* (1979), *The Drunkard's Wife*, and *Foiled Again!* The titles of the plays reveal very clearly the subject matter – so we get *Save My Child* (1982), *One Month to Pay* (1979) and *Sold to the Gypsies* (1998). As with all melodramas, they need to be played with serious full-bloodied relish; played as coarse acting shows they fail.

Brian J Burton has written well over 50 plays, ranging from short sketches for women (*Ladies Only*) to a full-scale musical version of *Little Women*, but the majority of his writing has been in the one-act form, including several modern plays such as *Murder Play* (1981), *Sudden Death* (1983), and *Drink to Me Only* (1982). His re-working of the famous Chekhov farce is entitled *A Bear with a Sore Head*.

Other plays to consider: *According to the Formula; The Axe and the Rose; Being of Sound Mind; Between the Lines; Cry for Help; Dirty Work in the Garden; Double Dealing; Fanny's Prayer; The Flying Visit; Ghost of a Chance; The Knave of Hearts; Mayhem at the Mill; Tea in L.A.; Trouble Shared*
Publishers: Samuel French; Hanbury Books

Yves Cabrol Nom-de-plume of English dramatist TB Morris

TB Morris (q.v.) produced a stream of one-act comedies in the 1950s and 1960s which chronicled the amusing side of French village life. The romantic and domestic adventures of the Parpot and Plum families were presented with an elegant sense of fun, and there was also a gentle strain of philosophy and morality intertwined.

The Fish was one of the first and also one of the most popular of these plays, set on a river-bank and entwining a fishing expedition with misunderstandings and romantic entanglements. *The Calf Before the Hearse* was the follow-up to this, with a similar mixed cast. *The Affairs of Madame Parpot* was an all-women cast continuation of the village themes, and *The Parpot Assassination* and *Operation Parpot* (also with all-female casts) continued to mine the rich vein of comedy centred around a village shop.

Almost any of the Cabrol comedies will still bring audience enjoyment if a company tackles them with a sense of style and an appropriate lightness of touch. There are some forgotten jewels here awaiting re-discovery.

Other plays to consider: *The Elephant; The Lady from England; The Lovers of Madame Dulapin; Monsieur Bombel Breaks the Bank; One Marries the Property; The Parents Propose; Tapestry of Shades*
Publishers: Evans

George Calderon (1868–1915) English dramatist

Best known as an early translater and producer of Chekhov (q.v.) for the London stage, George Calderon (not to be confused with the Spanish playwright of the same surname) was also a writer of one-act plays. Eight of the plays, probably written as curtain-raisers for the professional theatre of the pre-1914 era, were collected in one volume and published after his death.

Of these, the best known is *The Little Stone House* (in Chekhovian style), which was premiered by the Stage Society in 1911, but others are of considerable interest. In *Derelicts* a middle-aged pair teeter towards marriage and away from it, in the midst of a quite profound discussion about the merits and disadvantages of the institution; in lighter vein *Peace* features a burglar's visit to a pacifist-advocating MP only for the burglar to find that the MP does not practice what he preaches and for the MP to find that the burglar is rather better at making rhetorical speeches than he is.

Other plays to consider: *Geminae; Longing; Parkin Bros; The Two Talismans*
Publishers: Grant Richards

David Campton (1924–) British dramatist

One of the most prolific playwrights of the late 20th century, David Campton is a rarity in that he best known for his one-act plays. His vast output of over one hundred scripts has long been regular features of drama festivals in the United Kingdom and beyond; indeed it has often been said that no short play festival is complete without at least one Campton play.

He has said that he objects to being pigeon-holed. His themes and styles are wide-ranging including the environment in *Singing in the Wilderness* (1986), married life in *Getting and Spending* (1960), the conflict between private and public morality in *Permission to Cry* (1996), prejudice in *Incident* (1967), old age in *Parcel* (1979) and *Resting Place* (1970).

A simple but powerful comment on how wars can develop, *Us and Them*

(1972) has a flexible cast making it popular with many youth groups. In the anthropomorphic, *The Cagebirds* (1972), he highlights the denial of many people to escape from their cosy familiar world, while in the similarly allegorical *Can You Hear the Music?* (1988) the characters may be mice but their yearnings are clearly human. In each of these scripts the cast gender is flexible which helps to make them three of his most popular texts. In most of his plays there are opportunities for imaginative staging which adds further to their appeal

The playwright has said, 'When theatre stops being fun I shall give up writing and grow turnips'. Many devotees of one-act plays are delighted that his turnip plot remains untended.

Other plays to consider: *After Midnight; Before Dawn; Cards; Cups and Crystal Balls; The Do-It-Yourself Frankenstein Outfit; The Evergreens; Little Brother Little Sister; Mrs Meadowsweet; Mutatis Mutandis; Now and Then; Out of the Flying Pan; The Right Place; A Smell of Burning; Smile; Soldier from the War Returning; Table Talk; Two Leaves and a Stalk; A View From the Brink; What Are You Doing Here? Who Calls?; The Winter of 1917*
Publishers: Samuel French; Garnet Miller; Campton; Evans; Methuen

John Lewis Carlino (1932–)   American dramatist and script-writer

John Lewis Carlino burst on the off-Broadway scene in the mid-60s with a number of remarkable short plays, since when he has moved into writing scripts for film and television.

The double bill *Cages* (1963), comprises the gritty but touching drama *Snowangel*, and the absurdist *Epiphany*, a powerful theatrical piece which has distant echoes of Kafka. Both these plays are still frequently performed in his home country and far beyond. Another brace of plays under the title *Doubletalk* (1964), is made up of *The Dirty Old Man*, the deeply affecting story of a chance meeting between an aged poet and a virgin, and *Sarah and the Sax* where the conversation is between an old Jewish lady and a black musician.

Subtitled *A Collage for Voices*, *The Brick and the Rose* (1959) has ten actors playing 47 characters to tell the poignant story of a young lad's desperate search for beauty in his bleak landscape. The search in *High Sign* (1962), a five-hander for men, is for personal identity.

Other plays to consider: *Junk Yard; Mr Flennery's Ocean; Objective Case; Used Car for the Job*
Publishers: Dramatists Play Service

Dorothy Carr   English dramatist

Some of Dorothy Carr's one-act plays from the 1930s stand out 70 years on as skilfully-sketched delicate period pieces which might, surprisingly, be well worth revival. She wrote distinctive light comedies in witty rhyming couplets and often added in (as optional extras) a cast of innumerable extras as crowd background.

Ace King Queen (1934) charts the titanic battle in a Wimbledon final between the tennis kings, dashing Harold Jones and the darkly handsome Carlo Platz. The hand of Julia (Queen of Hearts) hinges on a line call but the linesperson is found to be asleep at the time. As the argument reaches a climax, Alan, the aviator Ace, lands on the court, having just crossed the Atlantic solo, and sweeps Julia off her feet. In similar charming style, **Willow Woe is Me!** chronicles the trivia of a summer cricket match on a village green, with a delightful cast of characters. Both plays are suited to outdoor performance on a summer's evening and together or singly would provide a nostalgic and atmospheric evocation of an English sporting occasion.

Other plays to consider: *A Present from Saltsea*; *The Way to Norwich*
Publishers: Samuel French

Jim Cartwright (1958–) British dramatist

Best known for his full-length plays *The Rise and Fall of Little Voice* and *Road*, Lancashire-born Jim Cartwright has written two well-contrasted long one-act scripts. *Two* (1991) is set in a working class pub (perhaps reflecting the playwright's Bolton roots) where a whole series of customers are played out by the publican and his wife while hiding, until closing time, their own personal internal drama. This challenging script needs performances of great versatility from the two actors.

Seven elderly people reside in the vast *Bed* (1991) dreaming, reflecting on their long past. Originally staged at the National Theatre, this unusual play with a variety of themes is at times harrowing, hilarious, poetic and moving. *The Sunday Times* critic said that, 'Cartwright writes better about old age than anyone I know, except Beckett'.

Publishers: Samuel French; Methuen

Anton Chekhov (1860–1904) Russian dramatist

Chekhov wrote 'In one act plays one has to write nonsense – therein lies their strength'; however, he refused to accept that his short light-hearted pieces, which he termed vaudevilles, were anything but serious theatrical enterprises. It was said that he gained as much pleasure from these small comic curtain-raisers as he did from his major works.

Several of these plays are still regularly seen on international stages well over a century after their first performances in Russia. Their structure is made up of clearly defined characters quickly caught up in a complex situation in fast flowing continuous action. The comedy is often broad and there is more than a nod to traditional French farce (hence the term *vaudeville*).

His first success with 'a jest in one act' came in 1888 with **The Bear**, an explosive battle between the eponymous gruff creditor and a young widow. He followed this with the even more acclaimed **The Proposal** (1889), where the attempt of a nervous hypochondriac to become engaged to a neighbour's fiery daughter take a comic and unexpected route.

In most of these plays the humour emerges from the great gulf between the characters' intense aspirations and cold reality. This is also the case in his large cast play, *The Wedding* (1900). Based on a short story, *The Jubilee* (1903) is another script often revived, while *On the Highway* (1884) strangely ran into censorship trouble and was not performed until ten years after Chekhov's death

Other plays to consider: *The Night Before the Trial*; *Swan Song*; *A Tragic Role*; *Tatyana Repina*; and two comic monologues on the vicissitudes of marriage, *On the Harmfulness of Tobacco* and *A Tragedian in Spite of Himself*
Publishers: Samuel French; Methuen; Dramatists Play Service

Jimmie Chinn (1940–) British dramatist

Although he has enjoyed success with his full-length scripts, Jimmie Chinn has achieved a considerable reputation for his short plays which have proved hugely popular in one-act festivals. Before training as a professional actor and later teaching, he spent some time as a member of an amateur company in his native Lancashire. When he moved to London and became a playwright he wrote many of these short plays for local amateur companies. Several of these plays have been adapted for the radio

Many of his most popular scripts include excellent character roles for women. *A Respectable Funeral* (1985) concerns three feisty sisters returning from burying their mother; the central role in *Too Long An Autumn* (1987) is a sparky theatrical artiste facing life in an old peoples' home; *Interior Designs* (1987) focuses on three lonely women yearning for male a companion. In all these plays the playwright happily combines the human situation with warm understanding and a good humour. These qualities of sadness and comedy are also evident in *From Here to The Library* (1985), *In by the Half* (1994), which has a theatrical background, and the wartime reminiscence *In Room Five Hundred and Four* (1998) whose title is based on an evocative popular song of the Second World War. He demonstrates a different mood in *But Yesterday* (1989), an enigmatic atmospheric play where the characters and the relationships are more complex.

In *A Different Way Home* (1999), he returns to his Northern roots with two very moving linked monologues. The first delivered by *Leslie* tells of the events leading to the death of his mother while in the second, his sister, *Maureen*, reveals the strength of her emotion at her apparent rejection by her family.

It seems likely that the plays of Jimmie Chinn will continue to delight and amuse audiences on radio and, particularly, on stage, as theatre has always been his first love.

Other plays to consider: *Pity About Kitty*
Publishers: Samuel French

Agatha Christie (1890–1976) English novelist and dramatist

Though Christie has almost iconic status as a writer of detective novels she took a hand in dramatising several of her stories for the stage. She also produced a trio of one-act plays which were presented briefly on the professional stage, and which have since been frequently taken up by amateur companies.

Afternoon at the Seaside (1963) is a dramatised detective story about a theft of a necklace and is set amongst a party of holiday-makers a beach; *The Rats* (1963) is about a group of people tricked into coming to an empty flat and a non-existent party and then framed for murder by one of their number; *Patient* (1963) presents a rather contrived situation in which a women who has fallen off a balcony is left unable to speak or move except through the fingers of one hand. Through this she indicates that she has been the victim of an attempted murder and then thwarts a second attempt by recovering the power of speech just in time.

These are competent thrillers but do not have the distinctiveness or attraction of the author's most successful novels.

Publishers: Samuel French

Caryl Churchill (1938–) English dramatist

Churchill has been one of the most influential playwrights of the later 20th century and has experimented with a great many different styles of drama. She has pioneered a notation in print for the deliberate overlapping of speeches in plays. In her collection called *Shorts*, she describes some of her shorter pieces as 'radio plays that could possibly be done in a theatre'. Not all of them have been given stage performance. Her work often makes a radical critique of society (from both socialist and feminist perspectives) and it usually calls for a bold and imaginative approach from both directors and performers.

Three More Sleepless Nights (1979), was an early one-act attempt which did not please the critics at the time but which has proved popular since; it is set in three different bedrooms, but easily stageable and charts marital tensions with a clever variation of acting styles. *Hot Fudge* and *Ice Cream* (1989) make a challenging double-bill (for both performers and audience); and the two halves of *Blue Heart* (1997) (*Heart's Desire* and *Blue Kettle*) both call for virtuoso and highly-skilled playing. Churchill allows the first act of her well-known full-length play *Top Girls* to be played separately. This dinner-party scene in which a group of high-achieving women battling againt the odds makes a most effective self-contained piece, with many rich acting opportunities.

Other plays to consider: *Abortive*; *The After-Dinner Joke*; *Faraway*; *Hospital*; *The Hospital at the Time of the Revolution*; *The Judge's Wife*; *Not Enough Oxygen*; *Schreber's Nervous Illness*; *Seagulls*

Publishers: Samuel French; Cambridge University Press; Nick Hern Books

George Coleman (1732–1794) British dramatist

A complete man of the theatre, George Coleman was one of the first managers of Haymarket Theatre in London. He noticed that in the mid-18th century plays and novels had an increasingly strong streak of romantic sentimentality so with such plays as *The Jealous Wife* he pricked this high-flown bubble with barbs of humour.

In his still-popular short comedy *Polly Honeycombe* (1760) he satirises the heroine who believes that real life will be a reflection of life in the latest successful romantic novel. It is said that the title role inspired Oliver Goldsmith to create Lydia Languish in *The Rivals*. To work, the play needs period style and full-bloodied comic performances to capture the mood of those vibrant times.

This amusing play, which still appears in modern drama festivals is, of course, copyright free and can found in a collection of 18th century short plays published by Oxford University Press in 1970.

Stewart Conn (1936–) Scottish dramatist, poet, broadcaster, producer

Stuart Conn has written more than 20 theatre scripts, including the fascinating short play *The King* (1967), a strange mix of lyricism and Pinteresque menace. It is a play containing many conflicting elements and is heavy with symbolism. The playwright has said, 'My plays are explorations. I pose questions, not wishing to impose a set of values on audiences but like to think that they will be induced to reassess their own'.

Other plays to consider: *Fancy Seeing You Then*
Publishers: Penguin; Hutchinson

H Connolly (1955–) British dramatist

A somewhat self-effacing playwright, H Connolly premiers most of his scripts with his own local Berkshire amateur theatre company, Compton Players, where he is simply known as 'H'.

Most of the plays combine humour with a wry and telling observation of life – and death. In *Overtime* (1994), one of his most popular plays, the jocular farcical mayhem of a retirement party gives way to surrealism and a surprisingly touching climax. There are similar violent shifts of mood in the tautly-written *Daddy's Gone A-Hunting* (1994) which moves from comedy to terror in what becomes a deadly game of jealousy and attempted murder. In *One Careful Owner* (1997) confusion reigns when an advertisement lures a purchaser into thinking a wife, rather than a car, is on offer. Here, as in most of this author's work, there are good opportunities for broad character playing.

H Connolly's most recent play *Bill and Bob* (2004) starts with jokesy banter between two forklift drivers but it soon becomes clear that the badinage is a façade to hide the heartache in their personal lives. Once again H Connelly has created a powerful little drama which at times is very funny.

Other plays to consider: *Bluey is the Colour; Forgive Us Our Trespasses; Murdering at the Vicarage*
Publishers: Samuel French; New Theatre Publications

Mabel Constanduros (1880–1957) English writer, dramatist and actress

Born in Chichester, West Sussex, the versatile Mabel Constanduros was a considerable figure in several of the performing arts throughout the first half of the 20th century. She created the melancholic Buggins family for radio (and played all the parts in the sketches about them) and also wrote novels and TV and film scripts (notably, post-1945, *The Huggetts*) as well appearing on stage as a comedienne and character actress, and in films.

But one-act plays were a consistent part of her writing output throughout her life, and she penned over 50 of them, some written alone and others with Howard Agg, Michael Hogan and her nephew Denis Constanduros. Most of them were vignettes of working-class life, both comic (e.g. *The Ogboddy's Outing* (1936), about preparations for a choir supper; *Shepherd's Pie* (1946), in which a visiting cookery lecturer is mistaken for a murderer; and dramatic, e.g. *The Shadow Passes* (1939) and *Far Above Rubies* (1944). Many of them offer a wry but loving commentary on domestic life, as it was in the 1930s and 1940s, and were comfortably within the compass of small amateur groups.

Her approach was clearly stated in a preface to a 1939 collection of her work: 'These plays have not been written to exploit any pet dramatic theories nor to point any morals; they are purely an attempt to provide the many Amateur Societies and Women's Institutes throughout the country ... with a good evening's entertainment. They may be performed in the smallest village hall ... for which, indeed, they are written and intended'.

Other plays to consider: *And So They were Married; Beauty and the Beast; Before the Morning; Between the Lines; Birds of Prey; Breaking Point; Companion to a Lady; Cream of Tartar; Cuckoo Time; The Curse of Cairo; Family Occasion; The Gentle Shade; A Gift from the Gods; Goose Chase; Lady from Abroad; The Life and Soul of the Party; Man from the Sea; Mrs Carter; A Nod A Sneeze and a Goat; Nothing Ever Happens; Open Your Eyes; Peacock for Two; Sentimental Ladies; A Snake on Sunday; The Spider Ring; Spies in the Cellar; Uncle Gabriel; White Russian*
Publishers: Samuel French

*Giles Cooper (1918–1966) English dramatist

Giles Cooper's major play written for the stage was the full-length *Everything in the Garden*, but he is best known as a prolific and notable radio dramatist of the 1950s and 1960s. He wrote nearly 50 radio plays between 1950 and 1965, though many remain unpublished. He often focussed on 'the malice and avarice simmering beneath comfortable bourgeois existence', as one critic put it, but this was usually done in a clever and subtle way.

For some years, as a memorial to his work, the BBC offered the Giles Cooper Award for the Best Radio Play of the Year. A selection of his best radio plays has been collected and published by the BBC. In both length and quality these plays provide material full of potential for enterprising theatre companies which welcome the challenge of translation of context.

The gripping *Unman Wittering and Zigo* (1958), especially suitable for youth casts and also published separately, is a disturbing piece about the way in which a class of school pupils decide to murder their unbearable teacher and then maintain an unshakeable collective alibi. By contrast, *Under the Loofah Tree* (1952) is a delightful comic daydream in which the reclusive Edward conjures up images whilst in his bath and, in doing so, provides an oblique commentary on aspects of society far removed from the domestic setting.

Other plays to consider: *Before the Monday; The Disagreeable Oyster; Mathry Beacon; The Object; Without the Grail*
Publishers: BBC Publications; Nelson

Joe Corrie (1894–1968) Scottish dramatist, poet, journalist, short story writer

Scottish born Joe Corrie left school at the age of 14 to work in the mines, yet with little formal education he became a popular playwright, poet, and journalist. The themes of his writing often reflected the harshness of working class life, and the popularity of his plays with his audiences came through the recognition of their everyday existence.

His fervent socialist view of life emerged strongly from a background of poverty; indeed his first short plays *The Shillin'-a-week Man* and *Hogmanay* were staged in 1926 to raise funds for the miners' soup kitchens. The theatrical establishment tended to frown on the political stance in Corrie's plays so, facing this rejection, he continued to write one-act plays which found an enthusiastic appeal among the many amateur theatre companies throughout Scotland.

The drama for five men set in the depths of a mine, *Hewers of Coal* (1937), proved his most popular play and is still presented frequently both in his home country and beyond.

By the time of his death in 1968 Joe Corrie had written more than 50 short plays including many light comedies and romances. Many of these are still in print including *Salmon Poacher, The Tinker's Road* and *A Plumber and a Man,* all reflecting his warm understanding of common humanity. It is said that he set out to give audiences a good cry and a good laugh, and over many decades audiences of his short plays would agree that he succeeded in that objective.

Other plays to consider: *Billy Shaw; A Bride for Featherhill; Colour Bar; The Darkness; The Domestic Dictator; The Favourite Lass; Hikers; The Income; John Grumlie; Madam Martini; Martha; The Miracle; The Mistress of*

Greenbyers; The Poacher; Queen of the May; Red Roses; The Theft; Up in the Mornin'; What's Good for the Goose; When The Old Cock Crows
Publishers: Brown Son & Ferguson; Samuel French

Noël Coward (1899–1973) English dramatist

By the time of his death in Jamaica in 1973, Noël Coward had written more than 50 plays and revues, but comparatively few fall into the one-act category. His greatest success in this area came in 1936 with *Tonight at 8.30*, ten short plays designed to be played in various combinations as a showcase for himself and Gertrude Lawrence. One play – *Star Chamber* – was dropped and the remaining nine played in repertory to great popular acclaim.

Of these, three are still produced regularly. *Red Peppers*, a struggling music hall act is seen both on and off-stage as they wrestle with poor material, dropped props and backstage vicissitudes. This theatrical comedy is contrasted with *Still Life*, the story of a chaste affair between a respectable woman, caught in a loveless marriage, and a doctor. Nine years later the film version of this play, directed by David Lean and entitled *Brief Encounter* became one of the most successful films of its age. In the comedy *Fumed Oak*, Coward moves down the social class ladder to tell of a hen-pecked man who finally cracks and makes a bid for freedom.

When Lord Mountbatten saw *Hands Across the Sea*, a gentle send up of his socialite family, he said, 'Absolutely outrageous and certainly not worth the six free tickets'. The other plays in the set are *We Were Dancing, The Astonished Heart, Shadow Play, Family Album* and *Ways and Means*.

After this great success – six of the plays were filmed – it is strange that Coward did not write another one-act play (apart from many revue sketches) until 1965. His final plays have a common theme: a failure to live life to the full. *Shadows of the Evening* features a dying man, his wife and his lover accepting a mutual dependency, whilst *Come Into The Garden, Maud* deals with the subject in lighter terms. The valedictory tone of this suite of plays suggests that 'The Master' knew that this might be his last work.

Publishers: Samuel French; Methuen

Constance Cox (1915–1998) British dramatist

Constance Cox acquired a considerable reputation for her stage adaptations of major classic novels into full-length plays. Her short play catalogue includes versions of such famous Victorian melodramas as *Lady Audley's Secret* (1976) and *Maria Marten* (1969), and such gothic pieces as *The Vampire* (1978).

She has written a modern English version of the medieval morality play *Everyman* (1967) as well as plays with a contemporary setting such as the comedy *What Brutes Men Are* (1980).

Publishers: Samuel French

David Cregan (1931–) English dramatist

Cregan's one-act plays often exhibit a witty, wry style in which the lives of 'outsiders' are put under sympathetic scrutiny. He works best as a miniaturist, and his characters often offer droll asides to the audience in the midst of the action.

Most performed is *Arthur* (1969), an episodic fable (with echoes of Ayckbourn's *Ernie's Incredible Illucinations*) in which the immature 21-year-old anti-hero burns down his aunt's house (with her complete acquiescence), falls in love with the policewoman who has come to arrest him, and then involves the fire-service, the mayor, the police force, and the Boy Scouts of the town in a wild mixture of improbable and eccentric situations, before finishing up as mayor himself. In *Tina* (1975), a primary-school teacher tries to deal with a disaffected pupil in various ways, even donning motor-cycle leathers in her anxiety to identify with her interests and pre-occupations. *Poor Tom* (1976), is another play which highlights the plight of an outcast who so desperately wants to 'belong' that he is driven to murder the owner of a boarding-house to prevent its sale. *Transcending* (1966), features a teenager who seeks to escape the conventional world (and school examinations) by taking the veil and reappearing as a nun.

Other plays to consider: *The Dances*; *George Reborn*; *If you Don't Laugh You'll Cry*; *Jack in the Box*; *Liebestraum*; *Pater Noster*; *The Problem*
Publishers: Hutchinson; Samuel French; Methuen

Martin Crimp (1956–) British dramatist

One of the most innovative of modern English dramatists, Martin Crimp has influenced many of the new generation of 'In-Yer-Face' playwrights, yet his work appears to be more appreciated overseas than in his own country. His very short play *Face to the Wall* (2002) includes many elements typical of his work. There is no plot in the conventional sense; the emphasis is on the words and the seething unspoken tensions and menace behind the façade of text and situation.

In his longer work, *Attempts on Her Life* (1997) which is often played without an interval, the central character does not appear and the dialogue is not assigned to any actor. Clearly his plays make the audience work – as well as the company.

Martin Crimp has won acclaim for his translations of modern European classic one-act plays notably Ionesco's *The Chairs* (1997), which was staged at the Royal Court Theatre and Genet's *The Maids* (1999) which was first presented at the Young Vic in London

Other plays to consider: *Fewer Emergencies*
Publisher: Faber and Faber

Rachel Crothers (1878–1958) American dramatist

Often considered as the first major American woman playwright, Rachel Crothers was among the first to attempt to write problem plays (such as *A Man's World* (1915) in the style associated with Ibsen). She was born in Bloomington Illinois, and taught there for a number of years before becoming a full-time writer in 1906. She often directed and staged her own work, even on occasion starring in it. Her plays were well-crafted rather than innovative, but she introduced the 'New Woman' to the American theatre; none of her heroines seemed to find a satisfying alternative to eventual marriage, however.

Her one-act plays were collected into a single volume, published in 1925 and included four which drew their titles and inspiration from Oscar Wilde's classic – *The Importance of Being Clothed*; *The Importance of Being Nice*; *The Importance of Being Married*; *The Importance of Being a Woman*. The volume also included *What they Think* and *Peggy*.

Publishers: Bakers Plays; Samuel French

Colin Crowther (1950–) English dramatist

Colin Crowther writes with depth and understanding about old-age and the approach of death, yet his plays are shot through with a life-affirming hope. *Footprint in the Sand* (2001), set on a beach, has an affecting lyrical quality and *Till We Meet Again* (2003) uses the device of a dying man revisiting and reassessing scenes from his life.

In the affecting *Tryst* (1999), a popular festival piece, an ailing husband seeks a way to create a tangible personal memory for his caring wife.

Publisher: Samuel French

Richard Curtis (1956–) English dramatist and film and TV script-writer

A prolific writer of television comedy shows, Richard Curtis has made several of the scripts of these available in published form. The published book of *Blackadder* scripts, for instance, which he wrote with Ben Elton, is a fruitful source of material. Each of these covers a half-hour episode in the colourful life of Sir Edmund Blackadder (played by Rowan Atkinson in the TV series) and his forebears, and the periods range from 1547 to 1918. When played on stage, the characters do not need 'impersonations' of their TV creators to make them work.

Publisher: Methuen

Gordon Daviot (1896–1952) Scottish novelist and dramatist

Best known for her sweeping historical dramas and especially for the big West End success, the drama, *Richard of Bordeaux*, Gordon Daviot also wrote a number of shorter pieces especially for the Little Theatre movement in the inter-war years. Best-remembered of these is the comedy *The Pen of my Aunt* which can still occasionally be seen in present-day drama festivals and a popular religious short play about the life of Joseph, *The Stars Bow Down*. The pen-name hid the persona of Elizabeth McIntosh, who also wrote historical and detective novels under the pseudonym Josephine Tey.

Other plays to consider: *Clarion Call*; *Leith Sands*; *The Mother of Mase*; *Mrs Fry has a Visitor*; *Rahab*; *Remember Caesar*; *Three Mrs Madderleys*
Publishers: Duckworth; Oxford University Press; Samuel French

Doris M Day (1920–) British dramatist

In the '70s English writer Doris M Day – sister of the playwright Ted Willis – produced several one-act scripts which proved popular with all-female companies. Probably the most widely seen was *A Gathering of Doves* (1974), which shows the effects of a brutal civil war in the lives of seven very different women. Tension and drama also feature in *A Will of Her Own* (1983) but here the period is Edwardian England. The playwright's other all-female plays include *A Crowing Hen* (1978), *Ruins*, and the comedy *Ever been Had?* (1977).

One of her plays still often seen on the festival circuit is the enigmatic mixed-cast *Audition for a Writer* (1979) in which a playwright appears to have a mental block; unsuspecting characters are called up to play a role in someone's imagination.

Other plays to consider: *Finishing Tape*; *The Mystery Unravelled*
Publishers: Samuel French; Hanbury Press; Kenyon-Deane

RF Delderfield (1912–1971) English novelist and dramatist

Worm's Eye View, a full-length comedy about life in an RAF servicemen's billet ran for over five years in the West End in the years following World War II. It was the first of several major successes for RF Delderfield, who later went on to write TV blockbusters such as *A Horseman Riding By* and *To Serve Them All Their Days*, scripts derived from some of his many novels.

A fluent writer with an easy style and a gift for both character and story, Delderfield grew up in the London suburbs (where several of his full-length plays and novels are located) before going to Devon to run a local paper. Writing plays took up all his spare time until he became a full-time writer after 1945. His one-acters have never had the same fame as his full-length plays and novels but they are similarly well-constructed and crafted pieces. Several are comedies with historical contexts, such as *The Old Lady of Cheadle*, set in the time of the 1745 Stuart rebellion and *Sailors Beware*, about the wives of the officers of the fleet facing the Armada (and in which Queen Elizabeth makes a surprise appearance). *Home is the Hunted* (1954) is a 'Cockney comedy' about a convict mistakenly thinking that his former home will be a haven of peace when he is on the run.

Other plays to consider: *Absent Lover; And Then There were None; The Bride Wore an Opal Ring; The Guinea Pig; Made to Measure; Miaouw! Miaouw!; Prophet in Jeopardy; The Rounderley Tradition; Smoke Across the Valley; The Testimonial; This Happy Brood; Wild Mink*
Publishers: Deane; Evans; Samuel French

W Dinner and W Morum English dramatists

In the 1930s and 1940s there was a great appetite for one-act plays for amateur societies and Dinner and Morum fed this with a series of comedies and dramas each of which lasted 20–30 minutes. Twelve of these were gathered together in a single volume and published by Samuel French.

A typical (and once-popular) example of their work is **All My Juliets**, an female comedy in which a group of actresses meet in a solicitor's office following the death of a famous actor who has made love to each of them when they played Juliet to his Romeo. The actor has jotted down in his diary what each of them said at his declaration of love, and conceitedly has left a sum of money to any of them who can remember exactly what they said to him at the time. As a time-limit approaches one actress makes a derisory remark to another, and so accidentally pockets the reward, to the disgust of the others.

The contexts of their plays varied widely: from a police-post in the Yukon (*The Bluffing of Gaston Leroux*, 1949) to a workhouse garden (*The Old Wives' Tale*, 1946). Their themes had similar breadth: from deciding the future of a blind and deformed child on a lonely island (*Behind My Skull*, 1948) to averting a suicide in a chain-store (*Nothing Ever Happened to Millie*, 1947).

Other plays to consider: *All This and Jumble Too; Art and Craft; Bargain Business; The Cat and the Cream; The Eternal Buy Angle; The Fair and Lovely; The Gentle Comedy; Ladies' Bar; Ladies' Knight; The Leaning Shepherdess; Miracle for Edward; Mr Worm Gets the Bird; The Old Man Shows His Medal; Old Soldiers Never Lie; Out Out Damned Plot; Play Without End; Postman's Knock; Private Drama; The Proctor's Dilemma; Scarlet Petals; Shall We Leave the Ladies?; Ticket to Springtime; Wedding Breakfast; What's in a Name?*
Publishers: Samuel French

Charles Dizenzo (1938–) American dramatist

Charles Dizenzo came to prominence in 1965 with his television play, *The Drapes Come*, which was subsequently adapted as a highly-successful stage play. Boldly imaginative and absurdist in style, this two-hander examines a mother–daughter relationship with lightning changes in personality as, by turn, each dominates the other.

Three years later the Lincoln Center staged a successful double-bill of his plays. Although the *New York Post* claimed the writer of **A Great Career** (1968) had 'a gift for the humour of the absurd of comic lunacy', there is a more serious

Kafkaesque undercurrent in this tale of life in a modern office. The play was coupled with *An Evening with Merlin French* (1968), a lethally funny dissection of suburban family life. In these plays, as in most of his work, he distorts reality and thus illuminates the darker emotional shadows which separate human existence.

Other one-act Dizenzo plays include the acerbic comedy of manners, *Sociability* (1970) and *Big Mother* (1970), another of the writer's zany comedies. He has also written his own adaptation of Kafka's *Metamorphosis* (1972).

Publishers: Dramatists Play Service

John Drinkwater (1882–1937) English dramatist and poet

Nurtured in his dramatic interests by working at the Birmingham Repertory Theatre under Sir Barry Jackson, John Drinkwater is known to many for his multi-scene stage biographies of historical figures such as Abraham Lincoln, Robert E Lee and Oliver Cromwell.

Of his one-act plays, *X=O; a Night of the Trojan War*, written in 1917, is best known, using a heightened blank-verse style to present the lives and subsequent deaths of individuals from each side of the war, within a highly-charged and dramatic night setting. The one-act *Cophetua* was his earliest writing for the theatre (1911), a play in rhyming verse about a king who chooses an unconsidered serving-maid to be his queen. A few years later Drinkwater wrote some other one-act verse plays. *The Storm* (1915), centred on the anxiety of waiting at home for a loved one in danger on the mountains, and *The God of Quiet* (1916), had, at its centre, a silent figure who is killed by a vainglorious and victorious king after a battle.

Publishers: Sidgwick and Jackson

Christopher Durang (1949–) American dramatist and actor

A prolific writer of one-act plays, the American writer Christopher Durang is best known for the comedy *The Actor's Nightmare* (1981), in which a hapless actor finds himself wandering in and out of plays by such diverse writers as Shakespeare, Noel Coward and Samuel Beckett. That play often appears as part of a double bill with *Sister Ignatius Explains it All for You* (1980), where the author makes some pertinent points about his Catholic boyhood – a recurring theme in his work.

Twenty-seven of his short plays have been assembled in one volume which reflect his penchant for parody where his frequent targets are cinema, theatre and books. So we have bizarre re-workings of *The Glass Menagerie* in *For Whom the Southern Belle Tolls* and Sam Shepard's *Lie in the Mind* becomes Durang's *Stye of the Eye*. The remarkable *Desire, Desire, Desire* manages, in ten pages, to combine elements of *A Streetcar Named Desire*, *Cat on a Hot Tin Roof*, *The Iceman Cometh* and *Harvey!* No doubt the playwright's experience as a professional actor gave him an added insight into the writing of many of these plays.

He has sometimes been criticised for his undergraduate-style humour but his best writing shows a strong gift for satire and farcical situations. He has also written serious plays, notably *Not My Fault* (1991), a provocative play about alcoholism.

Other plays to consider: *An Altar Boy Talks to God; Cardinal O'Connor; Death Comes to Us All; 'Dentity Crisis; Funeral Parlour; Gym Teacher; John and Mary Doe; Medea; Mrs Sorken; The Nature and Purpose of the Universe; Nina in the Morning; Phyllis and Xenobia; Titanic; Under Duress; Wanda's Visit; Women in a Playground*
Publishers: Dramatists Play Service; Samuel French

Marguerite Duras (1904–1996) French novelist, film-script writer and dramatist

Duras often re-worked material from one form to another. Concerned more with perceptions, language and the fragility of conversational exchange, her stage plays feature brief encounters between individuals on the brink of change. In *La Musica* (1966), the best of her short pieces, a delicate and rewarding work for two performers, former lovers meet again by chance and wonder if they should re-kindle their relationship.

Other plays are written without an intended interval but tend to run well over an hour in performance. She was fascinated by the 1950s' episode of a French couple, Claire and Pierre, who murdered their deaf and dumb companion and dropped her pieces one by one over a railway embankment into goods trucks going all over France. Duras dramatised it in two different ways as *The Viaducts of Seine-et-Oise* (1960) and *The Lovers of Viorne* (1975)

Other plays to consider: *Days in the Trees; The Square; Suzanne Andler*
Publishers: Calder; Calder and Boyars; Penguin

David Edgar (1948–) British dramatist

One of Britain's highly-regarded contemporary playwrights, David Edgar has been variously described as the theatrical equivalent of a photo journalist and a secretary of our time. His output has been huge with a wide range of themes and styles, varying from the sprawling multi-cast epic adaptation of *Nicholas Nickelby* to small chamber pieces.

His best-known short plays for stage and television have been collected under the title, *Edgar Shorts*. The most popular of these, *Ball Boys* (1975), set in the locker room of a tennis star, has many themes, notably the corroding emotion between the 'haves' and 'have nots'. The powerfully moving *Baby Love* (1973) explores a woman's reasons for snatching a baby, while *The Midas Connection* (1989) takes an ironic look at gold dealing and *The National Theatre* (1975) sets *The Three Sisters* in a seedy strip club. *Blood Sports* (1975) consists of five sketches on sporting subjects including beaters, cricket, and shot-putting – along with the aforementioned *Ball Boys*.

Other plays to consider: *The National Interest*
Publishers: Nick Hern Books; Methuen

Les Ellison (1956–) English dramatist

Lancashire-based Les Ellison couples his work as a scientist with being one of the leading contemporary exponents of the short religious play. His first play, *East and Twenty-Third* (1987), was a Chicago-gangster adaptation of the Book of Hosea. *New Nativities* (later re-worked and expanded as *Do the Kings Still Wear Curtains?*) has an intriguing opening as the performers in a traditional Nativity play break out of tableaux and resign their roles. Then follow a series of thoughtful and amusing duologues in which the old hands discuss the nature of their part with newer and younger performers who they are recruiting to carry on. The titles of *First Easter* (winner of the 1999 Nimbus award for new writing) and *Away from the Manger* make their contexts self-evident and they are written in the same accessible and humorous style.

Ellison's most recent one-act play, *Red Star*, was the winner of the short-play category in the 2004 Radius playwriting competition. It is a thoughtful and theatrically effective exploration of the deeper effect of fame and celebrity on Yuri Gagarin, the Russian cosmonaut, using non-naturalistic settings.

Publishers: Samuel French, Radius

Elaine Feinstein (1930–) and the Women's Theatre Group British poet, biographer, novelist and dramatist

Elaine Feinstein has written more than a dozen plays for radio and television. Her sole venture towards specific stage work so far was in 1987, when she suggested to the Women's Theatre Group the idea of a prequel to the King Lear story. Through workshop and improvisation the company devised the play *Lear's Daughters* (1987) which has subsequently found both national and international success. Using just the three daughters, the nurse and the queen from Shakespeare's original script, the play uses ritual, fairly tale imagery and music hall humour to tell a devastating, highly theatrical story of daughters growing up within a severely dysfunctional family where a father rules supreme.

In the Sheffield University Press version, the play appears in an anthology called *Herstory*: it is also published by Faber in a collection titled *Mythic Women, Real Women*.

Publishers: Faber and Faber; Sheffield Academic Press

Georges Feydeau (1862–1921) French dramatist

Feydeau has the deserved reputation of being one of the masters of domestic farce. His brilliant ability to manipulate story-lines so that the wrong people are caught in the wrong place at the wrong time (and usually with their skirts or trousers down, metaphorically or even literally) has contributed to the continuing success of his relatively limited number of full-length plays, of which *A Flea in Her Ear* and *Hotel Paradiso* are, perhaps, the best-known. Though these plays are centred around the amorous adventures of the bourgeoisie of Third Republic France, they have an international reputation and appreciation.

What is perhaps less-known to English-speaking audiences is that Feydeau was also a continuing experimenter in the one-act form. Many of his shorter plays (which reflect the same themes and style of his longer ones) were originally designed to be played as 'salon entertainments' (*Amour et Piano* (*Romance in A Flat/The Music Lovers*)) (1883), assumes that a grand piano can be provided on the set), though they later were used as curtain-raisers in Parisian theatres. A 1982 book by the American critic Norman Shapiro (*Feydeau: First to Last*) brought these one-acters to notice, as well as providing acceptable English translations of eight of them. The earlier one-act plays have happy endings, but the later ones (e.g. *Dormez, je le Veux!* (*Caught With his Trance Down*; 1897), *Hortense a Dit 'Je m'en fous'* (*Tooth and Consequences*; 1916) provide a bleaker final outlook, in which return to marital bliss is not posited as a solution, perhaps reflecting Feydeau's own increasing marital difficulties.

Other plays to consider: *C'est une Femme du Monde (Mixed Doubles)*; *Feu la Mere de Madame (Madame's Late Mother/Night Errant/Better Late)*; *Gibier de potence (Fit to Be Tried)*; *Leonie est en Avance (One Month Early)*; *Les Paves de L'ours (The Boor Hug)*; *Mais n'te Promene donc pas Toute Nue! (Don't Walk Around with Nothing On!/Put Some Clothes on Clarisse!)*; *Notre Futur (Ladies Man)*; *On Purge Bebe (We're Giving Baby a Laxative/Take your Medicine Like a Man/The Purging)*; *Par la Fenetre (Wooed and Viewed)*. NB The alternative English titles indicate different translations of the original French text.
Publishers: Samuel French; Cornell University Press

Harvey Fierstein (1954–) American dramatist and actor

Brooklyn-born Harvey Fierstein used his early experiences as a drag artist to write *The International Stud* (1978), which proved so popular off-off Broadway that it soon transferred to a larger theatre. It also created a demand to know what happened to Arnold and Ed, the main characters, so the author wrote two further short plays – *Fugue in a Nursery* and *Widows and Children First* (1979). Together these plays made up *The Torch Song Trilogy* (1982), which won huge success on both sides of the Atlantic and was subsequently filmed with the playwright in the central role.

Perhaps the reason for his success lies in the fact his recurring theme is the need to find warmth and genuine love in a human relationship, and that need is not bounded by a person's sexuality; hence his plays have a wide appeal far beyond a ghettoised gay audience. He also writes sharp witty dialogue, a talent which was further displayed in his lyrics for the musical *La Cage Aux Folles*.

Under the title *Safe Sex* (1987), Fierstein wrote another trilogy of one-act plays which deal with aspects of life in the Aids era. The title play, **Safe Sex** was originally presented along with **On Tidy Endings** and **Manny and Jake**, but each can be staged separately.

However, his most frequently seen short play remains **The International Stud**, a script which is further enhanced by the songs from a night-club blues singer which comment on the emotional journey of the central character. It is a bitter-sweet play which demands great commitment and integrity in performance and production.

Publishers: Samuel French

Tim Firth (1964–)   British dramatist and scriptwriter

Scriptwriter for film (*Calendar Girls*) and television (*The Preston Front*), Tim Firth's best known full-length stage play is *Neville's Island*. *A Man of Letters*, one of his rare short plays, was written for Alan Ayckbourn's theatre at Scarborough. It is a comedy set on a roof, where a commercial letterer juggles his alphabet with hilarious and unexpected results.

Publishers: Samuel French

Lucille Fletcher (1912–2000)   American dramatist and novelist

A writer of radio plays and short stories, Lucille Fletcher's fame rests largely on two taut thrillers – **The Hitch-hiker** (1941), and **Sorry Wrong Number** (1943), which she adapted from one of her earlier novels.

Orson Wells appeared in the hugely popular original American radio version of **The Hitch-hiker** where a lone traveller is faced with a nightmare situation as he drives across America. The equally lonely distraught figure in **Sorry, Wrong Number** is a bedridden woman who becomes involved in a frenetic cross-wired telephone situation. A masterpiece of suspense, it was later filmed starring Barbara Stanwyck and Burt Lancaster.

Publishers: Weinberger; Dramatists Play Service

Dario Fo (1926–)   Italian dramatist and actor

The son of an Italian socialist railway worker and amateur actor, Dario Fo started his theatrical life by writing satirical revue sketches and songs. In 1957 he and his wife, Franca Rame, set up their own company, which staged many of his own short plays, often featuring the playwright in a leading role.

Gradually audiences and critics recognised that his was a unique voice – an ability to express strong political opinions through highly enjoyable farce. Full of volatile high-octane energy, his plays found a relevant echo far beyond Italy and in 1997 he received the Nobel Prize for Literature.

Although he is now best known for such full-length plays as *The Accidental Death of an Anarchist*, several of his short farces are often revived. In *The Virtuous Burglar* (1958), the hapless thief gets involved in convoluted extra-marital intrigue while in *One Was Nude and One Wore Tails* (1962) a roadsweeper finds that different clothes give a different aspect on life and divinity. In *The Open Marriage* (1983), which has been said to be based on his own marital relationship, he displays the broadest comedy whilst making a biting socio-logical comment.

All Dario Fo plays demand tremendous drive, energy and invention as the actors take audiences on a frenetic roller-coaster ride which should produce reactions not just in the belly but also in the mind.

Other plays to consider: *Bodies to be Despatched*; *The Boss's Funeral*; *Corpse for Sale*; *A Day Like Any Other*; *The Loom*; *Marcolfa*; *The Three Suitors*; *When You're Poor You will be King*; and many monologues, notably *Obscene Fables*, one of four pieces which were presented at London's Young Vic
Publishers: Samuel French; Methuen

Horton Foote (1916–) American dramatist

A doyen of the American drama scene, Foote began his career in the theatre as an actor. In his writing, he is mainly a chronicler of life and he skilfully evokes the ambience of the Southern states of the USA where he spent his childhood and where he has now returned to live. His writing exhibits a restrained humanism with a care and belief in positive moral and spiritual values. Though his contexts are sometimes reminiscent of Tennessee Williams, he is much more positive in his portrayal of the predicaments of his characters.

One of his best known short-plays is *A Nightingale*, set in 1924, a story about a young woman who visits friends but is strangely vague about her family, and her purposes in life. Her anxious husband visits to collect and puts her on a streetcar home, but she wanders back again in the same state of mental disarray, to the anxiety of her friends. This is the first of a trilogy of plays (published as *The Roads to Home*) about the same characters and is followed by *The Dearest of Friends* and *Spring Dance*.

Some of his TV work for Kraft Theatre and Playhouse 90 was collected and published by Harcourt in a volume entitled *Harrison, Texas* (the title taken from the mythical small-town where he set many of his stories). There was a late flowering and gathering interest in his work towards the end of the 20th century. A set of his one-act plays were collected into one volume and introduced by Gerald C Wood and published by the Southern Methodist University Press in

1988. He won the Pulitzer Prize for drama (1995) with *The Young Man from Atlanta*. He is to be found among the contributors to the 2002 International Connections series of plays for young people sponsored by the National Theatre, with *The Actor*, a one-act period piece set in the US in 1932.

Other plays to consider: *Blind Date*; *The Dancers*; *The Death of the Old Man*; *John Turner Davis*; *The Land of the Astronauts*; *The Man who Climbed Pecan Trees*; *The Midnight Caller*; *The Old Beginning*; *The Oil Well*; *The One-Armed Man*; *The Prisoner's Song*; *The Road to the Graveyard*; *The Tears of My Sister*; *A Young Lady of Property*
Publishers: Dramatists Play Service; Harcourt; Southern Methodist University Press; Faber and Faber

David Foxton (1937–) British dramatist

Yorkshireman David Foxton has written several plays which have a strong appeal for young actors. Many have an historical background; his collection of short plays *Sepia and Song* (1990) includes *Titanic*, set on the doomed liner, while *The Memory of Lizzie* tells the story of the infamous Lizzie Borden whose axe-wielding led to an untimely end for her parents. Also in this popular volume is a suffragette play entitled *I Was a Good Little Girl 'Til* and *The Godmother*, a spoof of the prohibition era. As the title of the collection suggests the texts include evocative songs to add to the period atmosphere.

Popular with female casts is the theatrical *After the Picnic*, which is set against the mysterious disappearance of a group of Australian high school girls at Ayers Rock on Valentine's Day 1900. By contrast the powerful drama *Rabbit* (1989) is set in the future where 15 young people are facing life after surviving a nuclear explosion alone. *Card Play* and *The Crowns, The King, and the Long Lost Smile* (1980), two longer plays for children, are sometimes played without an interval.

David Foxton also writes for adult companies. *Breakfast for One* (2002) is a raucous fast-moving comedy set in 1895, whilst the very amusing *Caught on the Hop* (1993) has a similar French style and Parisian setting.

Other plays to consider: *Perkin and the Pastrycook*; *Unsung*
Publishers: Samuel French; Nelson; New Plays Network; Macmillan

Mario Fratti (1927–) American dramatist and theatre critic

When Mario Fratti arrived in New York in 1963 he had already achieved some success as a playwright in his native Italy and since that time he has produced scores of new plays in his adopted country. His scripts are often staged in fringe theatres off-Broadway, a tribute to his originality and readiness to expose uncomfortable truths about modern society.

Four by Fratti (1965), a collection of his short plays, includes *The Suicide*, a three-hander with themes of guilt and transferred cruelty, and the fascinating mystery drama, *The Return*. *Races* (1972) is the title of a further collection of seven literate and intriguing Fratti one-act plays displaying a mix of murder, mystery and social significance. The titles: *Fire, The Refusal, Rapes, The Other One, The Bridge, White Cat* and *Dialogue with a Negro*. The mystery *Porno* has won awards not just in the States but in Europe and beyond. It is published along with the moving *A.I.D.S.* and *Brothel* (1972). In a totally different style *The Academy* (1963) is a delightful satire.

Other plays to consider: *Her Voice*; *The Piggy Bank*
Publishers: Samuel French

Michael Frayn (1933–) British dramatist, novelist, and translator

Michael Frayn's best-known and most popular full-length play *Noises Off* had its origins in one of his earlier one-act scripts, **Chinamen**, which was part of a quartet of two-handers entitled *The Two of Us* (1970). The plot of **Chinamen** concerns a dinner-party, where the hosts and all the guests are played by the same two actors. Watching the play backstage – as Richard Briers and Lynn Redgrave exited stage left, dashed round frantically changing costumes and character to re-appear calmly stage right – gave him the idea of the theatrical joke which later became the modern classic farce *Noises Off*. **Chinamen** proved the most popular of those four plays, but **Mr Foot** and **Black and Silver** are sometimes seen at drama festivals.

More recently, in *Alarms and Excursions* (1998), a series of eight short plays, Michael Frayn has turned his astute eye on the way modern technology has added to the complications of our everyday life. The plays vary in length, with **Alarms** and **Doubles** being the more substantial pieces. These formed the first half of the London production, while the other six were played after the interval. In most of the plays the humans are left frustrated, dancing to the tuneless vagaries of these so-called life-improving gizmos. All eight comic pieces can be played separately. Although his full-length *Look Look* failed in the West End, he adapted the first act into *Audience* (1990) which takes an amusing look at a collection of mindless, insensitive theatregoers – a play written from the heart, one feels!

Michael Frayn has also adapted eight short Chekhov plays and stories under the title *The Sneeze*. Each of these plays can be staged separately or as part of an evening of one-act plays: *The Alien Corn*; *The Bear*; *Drama*; *The Evils of Tobacco*; *The Inspector General*; *The Proposal*; *Swan Song*; and the overall title play, *The Sneeze*.

Publishers: Samuel French; Methuen

Brian Friel (1929–) Irish dramatist

The prominent contemporary Irish playwright Brian Friel has produced comparatively few short plays but in the late 60s his double bill of **Winners** and **Losers** was presented under the title of *Lovers* (1967) and won acclaim on both sides of the Atlantic. Both are still seen, both together and separately, but of the two, **Winners** – a poignant tale of adolescent love and death – has proved the more popular.

In completely different mood and style, **London Vertigo** (1992) is a delicious satire on Irish Anglophiles in the 18th century. The two-hander, **Afterplay** (2002), one of his most recent short plays, has as its conceit the meeting of Uncle Vanya's Sonya with Andrey Prozorov, brother of the Three Sisters, in a Moscow café 20 years after the end of Chekov's plays.

Other plays to consider: *Performances*
Publishers: Faber and Faber; Gallery Books; Samuel French

Christopher Fry (1907–2005) English dramatist, poet and writer

Fry was a leading figure in the 'poetic revival' which briefly flourished in post-war Britain. His view of poetry is that it is 'the language with which man explores his own amazement' and his plays sparkle with brilliant phrasing yet have no pretentiousness. He is best-known for his full-length plays, notably *The Lady's Not for Burning* and *The Dark is Light Enough* but he wrote a number of important one-act plays which exhibit his distinctive style.

Fry's early dramatic life was in amateur theatre in Tunbridge Wells and Oxford University and much of his work has reflected his Christian (Quaker) faith. *The Boy with a Cart* (1939), about the young Sussex saint, Cuthman, was originally written for open-air performance; *One Thing More* (about the poet Caedmon isolated and silenced for 30 years by immense personal grief) played first in Chelmsford Cathedral; and *Thor with Angels* (1949) (about the crucifixion of a young Christian Roman soldier and its effect on others) have similar 'early Britain' scenarios. In 1946 he wrote *A Phoenix Too Frequent*, a comedy of manners overflowing with *joie de vivre*, though set at the tomb of a dead lover. To celebrate the Festival of Britain in 1951 he wrote the powerful and atmospheric *A Sleep of Prisoners* (designed for church performance) a verse drama in which a group of soldiers reflect on war and its aftermath in a kind of modern Passion Play.

Even in his 90s, he produced a short and effective play about John Bunyan to celebrate the Millennium, *A Ringing of Bells*.

Publishers: Samuel French; Dramatists Play Service; Oxford University Press

Jean Genet (1910–1986) French dramatist and writer

Though relatively sparse in output, Jean Genet has contributed one or two major short plays to the stage, which continue to have great impact today wherever they are staged. The orphaned and homosexual Genet spent much of his early life in jail and later wrote of prison life and prostitution in terms of beauty and fantasy as well as of abhorrence and despair. The essence of his work is that man is caught up in a maze of distorted reflections of himself and that life is inevitably a matter of desperation and loneliness. His work is one of the bleaker aspects of the Theatre of the Absurd.

The Maids (1952) is a chilling yet enthralling piece in which two servants dress up to role-play servant and mistress while the real mistress is absent. Her bed becomes an altar on which they immolate themselves: her premature return leads to a bizarre climax. *Death Watch* is a powerful piece set in a death-cell in which three condemned prisoners indulge in daydreams and dangerous erotic fantasies about each other as they discuss their plight.

Genet's work is strongly theatrical, but it needs skilled direction and performance to bring out fully the multiple themes which are implied.

Publishers: Faber and Faber

Peter Gill (1939–) British dramatist, director and actor

Peter Gill was born in Cardiff where several of his personal plays are set. He writes with great sensitivity about human emotion often trapped in difficult or complicated relationships. Although strong feelings of love and desire might be prevalent, his plays are often quietly understated which serves to make them all the more touching.

Presented at the National Theatre, *Kick for Touch* (1983) tells in jumbled fragments the story of two brothers who are loving, jealous and incredibly close; they form two sides of a emotional vice with the wife of one brother trapped at the centre. Originally written for radio, *Lovely Evening* (2001), set in 1950s' Cardiff, is a stage adaptation of his radio play which beautifully encapsulates the morals and frustrations of that dull restricting decade. It has recently played in a double bill with *In the Blue*, a play of gay love which had been first staged at the Cottesloe Theatre in 1985.

Another recent Gill revival has been his 1968 one hour play *Over Gardens Out*, a low-key but beautifully textured rites-of-passage play set in his native Cardiff in the '60s. The same city is the backdrop for *A Look Across the Eyes* (1997) which was another of his adapted radio scripts looking back to family life in the 1940s.

For the National Theatre Connections series of plays for young people, Peter Gill wrote *Friendly Fire* (1999). This has a cast of ten, but the focus is on three people in love – but with the wrong person.

Publishers: Faber and Faber; Oberon Books; Calder and Boyars

Frank Gilroy (1925–) American dramatist, novelist and film director

The often bitter-sweet comedies of Frank Gilroy deal with man's loneliness and insecurity in dealing with his fellow man. In 1965 he won the Pulitzer Prize for his elegant full-length play, *The Subject was Roses* but it in his one-act plays that display his simple descriptive style by focusing at the heart of the human condition. For example, *The Next Contestant* (1978) features a telephone conversation between a game-show contestant and the girl-friend he had jilted. The underlying themes are manipulation, deceit and, ultimately, painful disillusionment.

Frank Gilroy's work in Hollywood is reflected in his collection of short comedies entitled *A Way with Words* (1991), which includes *Fore* concerning the golfing diversions of two screenplay writers, while *Give the Bishop my Faint Regards* also has as it main characters two film scriptwriters. In the same volume are *Match Point* and *Reel to Reel*.

In contrast, the drama, *Contact with the Enemy*, is set at the Washington Holocaust Museum where two men meet with very different recollections of their sight of the concentration camps. The New York critic described this affecting play as 'packing a wallop that implicates us all'. It appears in a volume along with *Getting In*, in which the central character is a GI finding civilian life difficult after returning from the war in 1945. These plays may have risen out of his experiences in the infantry during World War II.

Another collection entitled *Present Tense* (1972) includes *Come Next Tuesday, Twas Brillig, So Please be Kind* and *Present Tense*. *Dreams of Glory* (1979) is another of Gilroy's popular bitter-sweet comedies.

Publishers: Samuel French

Jean Giraudoux (1882–1944) French dramatist and writer

Not until he was 44 years of age, did the French writer Jean Giraudoux turn to the theatre, but in the remaining years of his life he wrote a number of major plays, many of which reflected his belief in the close relationship between the seen and unseen worlds.

He wrote about half-a-dozen one-act plays, not all of which have been published or translated into English. However, one of them, *The Apollo de Bellac*, has become a classic. A mysterious young man sitting in an office foyer convinces a young woman that the way to succeed in life is to see the best in her colleagues and help them towards greater self-esteem. The dialogue is handled with sparkling wit and lightness, and the play is a delightful light comedy which richly rewards sensitive playing. Bellac was the village in which Giraudoux spent his childhood. The play was first seen in Rio de Janeiro in 1943, but not presented in France until after the author's death.

Other plays to consider: *The Gracchi*; *The Impromptu of Paris*; *Song of Songs*; *The Virtuous Island* (also known as *Supplement to the Voyages of Cook*)
Publishers: Samuel French

Susan Glaspell (1876–1948) American dramatist and novelist

One of the founders of the Provincetown Players, which produced many of Eugene O'Neill's (q.v) early plays, Susan Glaspell also had some of her own plays produced by the company. Born in Iowa, she first worked as a journalist before marrying George Cram Cook and becoming part of the Greenwich Village artistic community in New York. Her full-length play *Alison's House*, a semi-documentary of the life of the poet Emily Dickinson, won a Pulitzer Prize in 1930, but it was her last piece of theatre writing and she produced only novels subsequently.

In the one-act field she is chiefly remembered for the influential *Trifles* (1916), in which two women are sent to collect clothes for the arrested Mrs Wright, while men search for clues which will incriminate her of her husband's murder. However, it is the women who uncover the true story – a sterile marriage and a lonely, isolated wife – a story which the men seek to cover up. Her earlier *Suppressed Desires* has also remained a popular piece for performance: it has many witty exchanges and, despite its early 20th-century origins, holds up well today as a satire on both psycho-analysis and attitudes to marriage.

Other plays to consider: *Close the Book; The Outside; The People; Tickless Time; Women's Honor*
Publishers: Bakers Plays; Cambridge University Press; Maynard

Harry Glass (1926–) British dramatist and actor

Born on Clydeside, Harry Glass was a keen amateur actor and director before moving into the professional world firstly as an actor and then as a playwright. Since 1985 he has written almost 40 short plays which have proved hugely popular in his native Scotland and, increasingly so, beyond his homeland.

The majority of his plays have warmth, humour and a touching insight into human relationships. Among his prolific output, the most widely performed have included *Murphy's Law* (1991), a wonderful mix of pathos and comedy, *Swings and Roundabouts* (1992), a wartime reminiscence, and *A New Interest in Life* (1994), a powerful family drama. All three of these have won awards for the author, with a translation into Welsh of *A New Interest in Life* winning a special award from the Drama Association of Wales.

Harry Glass has a particular personal affection for the trilogy *Chips with Vinegar* (1994), *A Brief Period of Rejoicing* (1996) and *After Enola Gay* (1996) which tell the story of a typical Clydeside family during World War II.

Typical of the playwright's work is the award-winning *Agnes* (2000) which has strands of humour, drama, nostalgia all suffused with a warmth and a keen understanding of the emotional side of family relationships. He has also written plays for all female casts – notably *Simpson's Tragedy* (1993) – and for young people where the disturbing enlightening *Fireflies* (1995) has been given numerous productions. One of his most recent scripts is *A Glimpse of Camelot* (2004).

Other plays to consider: *Daylight Robbery; Falls the Shadow; Is Your Engagement Really Necessary?; Kelly's Eye; Legge's Eleven; The Last Supper; Match of the Day; Not Only for Christmas; The Process of Elimination; Soap Gets in Your Eyes; To Make up his Jewels; Uncle Jimmy*
Publishers: Pederson Press; Drama Association of Wales

John Godber (1956–) British dramatist

John Godber burst on the theatrical scene in the mid-'80s with his unique punchy style. His up-front comedies with an undercurrent of sadness have made him one of the most popular contemporary playwrights.

In *Bouncers* (1985) and *Shakers* (1986), two of his best-known scripts, he looks at young people as they seek hedonistic pleasure in plastic, superficial night-clubs and cocktail bars. In 1991 he updated these two hugely popular plays under the titles *Shakers Re-stirred* and *Bouncers – 1990's Re-mix*. In *Teechers* (1987), he used his experience as a teacher to turn his focus on the under-achievers in a comprehensive school. *September in the Rain* (1983) shows Godber in gentler and more nostalgic mood as he dramatises anecdotes retold by his grandparents concerning their annual family holidays in Blackpool. In similar vein, *April in Paris* chronicles a married couple rediscovering romance on a weekend trip.

His plays run for barely 90 minutes – 'No longer than a soccer match' as he comments – and are constructed in a series of sharply-pointed episodes. He has said, however that several of his scripts are flexible and may be abridged to run for 40 minutes if required. As he writes in one of his introductions, 'Make it work for your actors and your space'.

The staging demands of his plays are apparently simple. He has said that when he sees a settee on stage he knows the play will be boring! He feels that the most underused element in the theatrical experience is the audience's imagination. So all his work needs invention from the director and versatility from the actors, who often have to play a wide variety of characters. Strong lighting and sound plots will further stimulate the audience and drive on the energy of these very physical scripts This simplicity of staging stems from John Godber's days as a teacher when his set, lighting and costumes all had to fit into his estate car. When he moved to his post as theatre director at Hull he was able to expand his transportation – hence the name of his theatre company, Hull Truck.

Publishers: Samuel French; Weinberger; Penguin

* Michael Gow (1955–) Australian dramatist, director and actor

Notable contemporary Australian director and actor, Michael Gow has also written plays which have become increasingly well-known beyond his native country. In 2005 his script, simply entitled *17*, was included in the 2005 Shell Connection series of plays for young people for London's National Theatre. This strangely affecting, enigmatic, rites-of-passage allegorical play concerns a young girl facing up to a scary journey into adulthood. In *Furious* (1991), the focus is on a family secret, a terrible betrayal and an obsession to re-write the past which combine in a terrible tale of fact and fiction.

Other plays to consider: *The Fortunes of Richard Maloney; The Kid; Sweet Phoebe*

Other modern one-act Australian plays appear in a series of collections entitled *Popular Short Plays for the Australian Stage*, selected and edited by the playwright Ron Blair and published by Currency Press. These anthologies include scripts by Timothy Daly, Philip Ryall, Michael Cove, Gordon Graham, John Mulligan, John Summons, Mil Perrin and Ron Blair.

Publishers: Faber and Faber; Currency Press

Publishers of other collections of Australian one-act plays include:
Best Australian One-act Plays – Angus and Robertson, 1937
Six Australian One-act Plays – Mulga Publications, 1944
Australian One-act Plays – Rigby (Adelaide) Book 1 – 1962, Book 2 – 1962, Book 3 – 1967
Six One-act Plays – University of Queensland Press, 1970
Seven One-act Plays – Currency Press, 1983

Ronald Gow (1897–1993) English dramatist

Stage-struck in his youth, and learning his trade whilst working with the well-known amateur Garrick Society at Altrincham, Ronald Gow wrote a number of one-act plays before going on to write the libretti for a couple of West End musicals, *Jenny Jones* and *Ann Veronica*.

Gow (who was married to the well-known actress Wendy Hiller) wrote many plays for young casts and his *Under the Skull and Bones* (1933), a rousing pirate fantasy, has often been anthologised. Working a similar theme, *Scuttleboom's Treasure* (1938) features a school expedition which encounters pirates on a desert island and finds their lost treasure for them; the pirates are so impressed that they sail off with the headmaster of the school, seeking education.

Gow's plays were often written to appeal to boys' schools and youth groups, and his later *The Vengeance of the Gang* was specially written for Scouts and Rovers. He specialised in writing large-cast short plays: *The Golden West* (1933), for example, calls for 20–30 young male actors.

However, he also wrote for other age groups, and probably his most famous and most-performed one-act play is *OHMS* (1934) an all-female comedy set in a village post office. The postmistress takes her duties 'On His Majesty's Service' so seriously that she regards herself as moral guardian of the community. A manipulation of telegrams arriving ensures that a young lady who is eloping is safely guided out of the hands of the village gossips and into a proper solution of her predicament.

Other plays to consider: *The Affair at Kirklees*; *All on a Summer's Day*; *Breakfast at Eight*; *Compromise*; *Grannie's a Hundred*; *Henry*; *Higgins the Highwayman of Cranford*; *The King's Warrant*; *The Lawyer of Springfield*; *The Marrying Sort*; *Robin Goes to Sea*; *The Sausage*; *The Sheriff's Kitchen*
Publishers: Deane; Gowans and Gray

Wilfrid Grantham English dramatist

Grantham was a specialist in the religious short play but often invented beyond the Biblical text to bring life and colour to the stories he told. In his play about the events surrounding the crucifixion of Christ, *The Sixth Hour* (1938) (frequently anthologised in collections of one-act plays in the 1930s and 1940s) he introduces a character Leah, who as daughter of the High Priest Caiaphas is presented as the temptress of Judas and the cause of that disciple's betrayal of his Master.

Another popular Grantham play is *Jepthah's Daughter* (1939) which dramatises effectively an already vivid Old Testament story. *Unto This End* is set outside Jerusalem, in 33 AD, and highlights different reactions to the news of Jesus's Crucifixion. In *The Garden*, a collection of female characters, including the Virgin Mary, respond to the news of the empty tomb.

In 1947 he collaborated with Seton Pollock to write a series of 12 half-hour scripts for BBC radio on individual Old Testament prophets and these were later published by Gollancz under the collective title *Men of God*. These would present an interesting challenge today to a company interested in stage adaptation of robust radio plays on religious themes.

Publishers: Evans; Samuel French; Nelson; Gollancz

George MacEwan Green (1931–) Scottish dramatist

Born in Nairn, George MacEwan Green is mostly known for his short plays. *Ritual for Dolls* (1970), written in the late '60s, remains one of the most frequently seen plays on the one-act festival circuit. With its themes of lust, forbidden desire, incest and murder, the ritual is re-enacted by four Victorian toys as they portray the intense events in the lives of the children who had owned them. A well-constructed play, it gives good opportunities for a highly theatrical presentation.

Another of the author's popular plays is *One Season's King* (1972). Set at a graveside during a funeral, the three men in the lives of charismatic Evelyn retell their personal involvement with her since childhood. This play, too, presents interesting challenges for imaginative direction. The themes of *Sequence of Events* (1974) are isolation, parental domination, and sexual frustration which leads, through a sequence of events, to murder and a hanging – all related by the genial Edwardian hangman.

In most of George MacEwan Green's plays there is element of looking back over past events to discover the reasons for subsequent happenings. Other plays include *No Panic* (1985) set in Germany in 1938, *Stop The Nightmare* (1984) set in the Far East, and *Goodbye Iphigenia* (1998) which has a basis of classical Greek legend.

GM Green has said, 'In my plays I am mainly pre-occupied with attempting to explore certain moments when ritualised structure breaks down and there is an escape of pent-up humanity, resulting sometime in enlightenment, sometimes in tragedy'.

Other plays to consider: *Terrace Talk*
Publishers: Samuel French; Evans

Lily Anne Green Canadian dramatist

Canadian writer Lily Anne Green is best known for her short play, *Forward to the Right*. This atmospheric two-hander focuses on the last days of Joan of Arc whose only companion is her rough prison guard. With her fervently-held beliefs she exercises a profound influence over him during those days and the shift in their relationship is revealed with warmth and subtlety. Since its first production in Oakville, Ontario in 1981 this play has proved a popular festival play far beyond the playwright's home country.

Publisher: Samuel French

Michael Green (1926–) British dramatist

Back in 1964 Michael Green wrote a very amusing book entitled, *The Art of Coarse Acting* in which he highlighted woeful ham-acted performances and appalling theatrical productions. Following the book's great success, he went on to write a whole series of short 'Coarse Acting' plays (1977–2000) which parody various dramatic genres whilst evoking great humour from the hapless company of players desperately struggling in painfully inept productions.

The play styles being sent up can easily be detected from the titles of some of his most frequently staged scripts: *All's Well That Ends As You Like It*; *Streuth*; *The Cherry Sisters*; *Present Slaughter*; *Stalag 69*; *Pride at Southanger Park*; and *A Collier's Tuesday Tea*. In all there are over a dozen of these plays, several of them first premiered in Festivals of Coarse Acting at the Questors Theatre in London where Green has been a member.

Michael Green has said that the plays 'are simply spoofs on bad amateur – or professional – dramatics. But like all send-ups, they rely heavily on a basis of truth'. The ever-earnest actors should be trying to put on a successful production in spite of all the many disasters which befall them. It should be remembered that to play incompetence and to make it genuinely funny demands highly competent and very serious performances. When Coarse Acting plays are well shaped and take flight, they can be great fun.

Other Coarse Acting plays to consider: *Cinderella*; *A Fish in her Kettle*; *Henry the Tenth (Part Seven)*; *Il Fornicazione*; *Julius and Cleopatra*; *Last Call For Breakfast*; *Moby Dick*; *Oedocles King of Thebes*; *Vagabond Prince*
Publishers: Samuel French

Paul Eliot Green (1894–1981) American dramatist

Once called the 'dean of American dramatists' by *The Denver Post*, Green taught for many years at the University of North Carolina and was involved with the productions of the noted Carolina Playmakers. Greatly involved in the writing, development and production of 'symphonic drama' outdoors, he was also interested in the one-act form.

He was a great champion of civil rights, and was against capital punishment, and these themes often emerged in his playwriting. His outstanding one-act play is *Hymn to the Rising Sun*, which movingly portrays the iniquities of prison life and the chain gangs, and was based on a report of prisoner abuse in the Carolina prison system. There are several published collections of his plays and he also wrote many shorter pieces which remain unpublished.

Other plays to consider: *The Critical Tear; Fixin's; The Goodbye; In Aunt Mahaly's Garden; The Last of the Lowries; The Lord's Will; The Man who Died at Twelve o'clock; The No 'Count Boy; Quare Medicine; The Southern Cross; This Declaration; White Dresses*
Publishers: Samuel French

Stephen Gregg American dramatist

One of the most-performed authors of plays for high schools in the 1990s, Gregg has written mostly comedies in the one-act form. *Sex Lives of Superheroes*, a wistful comedy about the fantasies of those who live humdrum lives was the hit of the Manhattan Punchline Festival and quickly proved itself as a popular piece elsewhere.

Other plays to consider: *Postponing the Heat Death of the Universe; A Private Moment; This is a Test; Why do we Laugh?*
Publishers: Dramatists Play Service

Lady Gregory (1852–1932) Irish writer and dramatist

Isabella Gregory was one of the founders of the Abbey Theatre in Dublin and had a life-time interest in Irish history, heritage and legend, which she encouraged on to the stage. Attracted to the theatre, more or less by chance, at the age of 46, she, along with WB Yeats (qv), became one of the mainstays of the Abbey Theatre and provided nearly 40 plays for the theatre in the years around the turn of the century.

The best-known of her one-act plays is *Rising of the Moon* (1907), centred around events on a quayside at an Irish seaport and reckoned by some to be one of the earliest 'agit-prop' plays, written in the service of the movement for Irish independence. A sergeant is deflected from his duty by the eloquence of a nationalist on the run. Another short play which illuminated aspects of Irish politics was *The Wrens*, about the single-vote which turned the Bill to pass the Union of Great Britain and Ireland in 1799.

On the other hand her plays in which Hyacinth Hervey is a leading character – a man in spite of the feminine-sounding name – (*Hyacinth Hervey*, 1906; *Full Moon*, 1923) show a generous and warm-hearted approach to country life. In the former, the hero tries desperately to rid himself of a virtuous reputation. *Spreading the News* (1904) is another rollicking rural piece in which the exaggerations of gossip form the focus of the comedy.

Other plays to consider: *The Gaol Gate*; *The Jackdaw*; *On the Racecourse*; *The Travelling Man*; *The Workhouse Ward*
Publishers: Samuel French; Maunsel

John Guare (1938–) American dramatist

New York-born John Guare is probably best known for his award-winning full-length play *Six Degrees of Separation*, but he first came to the attention of the theatre-going public with his one-act play, *Muzeeka* (1967), which won an Obie award in 1968. Described by *The New York Times* as 'a play that was at times beautifully poetic and always meaningful', the script combines humour, lyricism and a passionate point of view.

Following this success John Guare went on to write several more one-act plays. Four of these appear in a collection under the title, *The General of Hot Desire and Other Plays* (1998). In addition to the eponymous play, which has been described as 'a droll miracle play in miniature and a little masterpiece', the volume includes the two hander *Greenwich Mean*, the theatre-based *New York Actor* and *Talking Dogs* (1985).

The comedy *Day of Surprises* (1970) is written in a zany, absurdist style while the wild humour in *Kissing Sweet* (1971) has a more stringent point as the theme of the play is pollution and conservation. *Cop-Out* (1968) and *Home Fires* (1969), two of his dark – if not black – farces appear in one volume.

Other plays to consider: *In Fireworks Lie Secret Codes*; *The Loveliest Afternoon of the Year*; *Something I'll Tell You Tuesday*
Publishers: Dramatists Play Service; Samuel French

AR Gurney Jnr (1930–) American dramatist

'I write about the people and the society I know', says Gurney, a major contributor of well-worked plays to the American drama scene, both professional and amateur. As a former Professor of Literature at the Massachusetts Institute of Technology, it is not surprising that some of his one-acters centre around the experiences of the academic community.

Two of his best-known three-handers are *The Old One-Two* (1976), a strong drama about a love affair between two academics, and *The Love Course*, a bold and imaginative piece set in a university class (and with the audience as imagined participants in the class). A woman professor teaching a course about love in literature reveals her own strong feelings for her departing male colleague through the material they are teaching, and also gives sound romantic advice to two of the students in the class who become mixed up in the highly-charged exchanges.

Gurney moved from writing in the one-act form to fuller-length pieces in the late 1970s, but one of his recent longer plays *Sylvia* (a brilliantly conceived and executed comedy about the manifold effects of bringing a dog into a middle-class professional household) has a first act that is self-contained and it has been a very entertaining and successful choice for entry into one-act drama festivals.

Other plays to consider: *Another Antigone*; *The Comeback*; *The David Show*; *The Golden Fleece*; *The Open Meeting*; *The Problem*; *The Rape of Bunny Stuntz*; *Three People*; *Turn of the Century*; *Who Killed Richard Cory?*
Publishers: Dramatists Play Service; Samuel French

Alexander Guyan (1933–1991) New Zealand dramatist

Back in the early 1960s New Zealander Alexander Guyan wrote a short psychological human drama which has since been frequently presented in numerous countries world-wide and still compels and intrigues audiences.

The play is *Conversations with a Golliwog* (1963), which on the surface traces the mental decline of a once bright, imaginative girl. But various questions are posed: what, initially, triggered her breakdown; what is really going on beneath the surface of her relationships with her mother, her boyfriend and, especially her brother? And what of the giant awesome, masculine, golliwog, who features so largely in her life and mind? The fact that it is a very distinctive and strangely disturbing piece of theatre may be the reason for its universal appeal.

Publishers: Samuel French

Nick Hall American dramatist

Although an American playwright, Nick Hall sets his best-known short comedy, *Pastiche* (1978), in a quintessential English upper-class home. With a cast of stock characters, the play (as the title suggests) is a send-up of typical Noël Coward plays, but here, the rising tide of chaos develops into pure farce.

Publishers: Samuel French

Willis Hall (1929–2005) and Keith Waterhouse (1929–) British dramatists, scriptwriters, and journalists

Both these Yorkshire writers have enjoyed considerable success writing separately but especially together. Their writing talents have extended over screenplays, television scripts, musicals, adaptations of classic novels, children's plays and journalism. But at heart both are true men of the theatre; however their output of short plays has been comparatively small.

The Wedding and *The Funeral* were presented together under the overall title *Celebration* (1961). The plays focus on the same north country family initially preparing for a wedding breakfast and six months later assembling again following the burial of one of the many likeable characters who feature in the plays. With a cast of 14 these plays provide a rich gallery of humorous and sharply-drawn roles for the actors whilst any company staging the plays must create a sense the late '50s/early '60s. These scripts are now very much period pieces, but that is part of their appeal, as present-day audiences view with nostalgic interest how social attitudes have changed in the intervening years

Two of their other short plays which have often been presented together, are *The Sponge Room* (1962) and *Squat Betty* (1962). In the former, set in the Natural History Museum, three dreamers never take the opportunity to fulfil their fantasies – a recurring theme in much of Hall and Waterhouse's work, beginning with their best known full-length play *Billy Liar*. *Squat Betty* is a parody of the absurdist theatre of the '60s with the hallmark of seriously inconclusive dialogue.

Among the short plays written by Willis Hall alone are *The Railwaymen's New Clothes* (1974) which takes place in the shop of a self important tailor and the Easter play *The Day's Beginning* (1963). *They Don't All Open Boutiques* (1976) and *Final at Furnell* might appeal particularly to young actors and audiences.

Publishers: Samuel French; Hutchinson; Heinemann

Richard Harris (1934–) English dramatist

Though one of the most commercially successful playwrights in the professional theatre of the late 20th century (as *Outside Edge, Local Affairs,* and *Stepping Out* demonstrate) Harris has not neglected the one-act form. His *Albert* (1972) was an early significant contribution: a hilarious and original piece about the arrival of a Finnish au pair to a London flat and her encounters with an Italian visitor and an English suitor of the previous au pair. All three characters supposedly speak in their own language and do not understand each other. (The neat theatrical device to enhance the comedy was to have them all speak in English for the benefit of the audience.) *Is it something I said?* is another clever one-act comedy which starts with a suicide attempt in a hotel and ends with a helper driven by the suicidal candidate to contemplating the same fate.

More recently Harris wrote *Visiting Hour*, a suite of six one-act plays, mostly comedies, centred around a hospital ward and designed to make a whole evening's entertainment. Several of these make excellent stand-alone pieces – for instance, *Magic* in which a husband unsuccessfully tries to cheer up his sick wife with conjuring tricks; *Going Home*, a patient confrontation; and *Showbusiness* in which a TV crew create havoc as they invade the ward to film a quadruple bypass operation. Other plays in *Visiting Hour* are *Keeping Mum, Plaster* and *Waiting*.

Publishers: Samuel French

Vaclav Havel (1936–) Czech dramatist and politician

One time leading Czech dissident and, after the fall of the communist government, its first president, Vaclav Havel has written numerous plays which includes the trio of Vanek plays, named after the character who appears in each of them. *Audience, Private View* and *Protest* (1978) are gently ironic plays of character, integrity and personal relationships with underlying themes of loyalty and power. They were widely performed outside the writer's home land, even before the political changes which gave artistic freedom to the Czech people.

Publishers: Samuel French

Don Haworth (1924–) English dramatist, and radio and TV producer

Because all his short pieces have started as radio scripts, it is more than usually difficult to locate the work of Don Haworth in published form, but some are to be found offering an original and unusual element in modern one-act play anthologies. They have been regular features in the *Best Radio Plays of...* series – *Episode on a Thursday Evening* (1978), *Talk of Love and War* (1981), *Daybreak* (1984) – and one anthology consisting entirely of his work (*We All Come to it in the End and Other Plays*) has been published by the BBC.

Featured in a recent one-act collection, *On a Day in Summer in a Garden*, features the cultured musings of three dock plants who are fearful of the effects of a nearby insecticide-sprayer. The intriguing and complex *School Play* was included in the *Playbill* series in the 1960s. Here the performers and the stage roles and the stage instructions become incurably mixed up.

Amongst those pieces which have successfully been performed in the theatre, *There's no Point in Arguing the Toss* features two lads who deal with the unexpected problem of getting their suddenly-dead father on to a bus, because that is how he would like to have travelled home. In *Mr Bruin Who Used to Drive the Bus* a headmaster struggles in several hilarious episodes to restrain the generosity of a school-bus driver who insists on diverting down side-roads to help others whilst carrying his cargo to school.

The Manchester-based Howarth has a shrewd but charitable eye for the foibles and eccentricities of colourful characters in working-class life, as might be deduced from the fact that he was producer of the steam-loving steeplejack Fred Dibnah's TV excursions around Britain. Most of his radio plays (he has had over 50 broadcast), if adapted with imagination for the stage are certain to bring a smile to the face of both performers and audience.

Other plays to consider: *The Enlightenment of the Strawberry Gardener; The Illumination of Mr Shannon; The Prisoner; We All Come to It In the End; Where is This-here Building?*

Publishers: Heinemann; Hutchinson; BBC Publications

Ian Hay (1876–1952) Scottish dramatist, novelist and writer

Ian Hay was the nom-de-plume of John Hay Beith, a high-ranking Government civil servant whose recreational writing included light novels, short stories, war histories and full-length plays (with several distinguished collaborators such as PG Wodehouse and Stephen King-Hall) as well as one-acters. His one-act writing was almost invariably in the light romantic comedy vein (such as *Find the Lady*; *A Flat and a Sharp*, 1944) as well as excursions into farce (*A Blank Cartridge*) and fantasy (*Treasure Trove*).

His dozen or so neatly-crafted one-act plays exemplify the gossamer trifles which dominated the 1920s and '30s, though his writing spread into decades either side of those years. He deserves a place in the top echelon of one-act writers at least on the strength of an archetypal short 'absurdity', *The Crimson Coconut*, which was written in 1913, but is still in print today. This is an easy-to-play comedy on which many young performers have cut their teeth and contains many of the best-loved music-hall 'sight gags' and jokes in the business. Its story of terrorists clandestinely plotting in a down-market London café whilst harassed by an incompetent waiter (a theme pursued in relentlessly comic fashion) gives it an eccentric and ironic modern relevance.

Other plays to consider: Burglar Alarms; The Fourpenny Box; It's Quicker to Telephone; Personally or by Letter; Right of Search
Publisher: Samuel French

Catherine Hayes (1949–) English dramatist and TV script-writer

Now more likely to be noted as a writer of episodes of TV soap-operas, Hayes began her writing career with a significant one-act stage play. Her all-women three-hander *Skirmishes* (1982) was a very popular one-act festival piece in the 1980s, and still retains its bleak, uncompromising force. Two sisters confront each other over the bed of their dying mother – one has spent much of her life as a carer, while the other has made a life with the married lover of whom her mother disapproved.

In *Not Waving*, a female comedian's anxiety about the anxieties and uncertainties of her life are inter-mixed with her stage act, in which she finds it increasingly difficult to get good audience reaction.

Publishers: Faber and Faber

Jack Heifner (1946–) American dramatist

Heifner is an American writer from Texas who is the author of *Vanities*, the straight play with the longest-ever off-Broadway run: 1785 performances over four years. LW Heniford, an American scholar of the one-act form, suggests that the first act of *Vanities* (three young women setting forth hopefully into the world at their high school graduation) is an excellent one-act piece in itself.

Heifner has produced two significant double-bills of one-act plays which illustrate his view that 'my concern is with the world of the ordinary person – and I mean ordinary as a compliment – and those who are trying to figure out how to get through this life'. *Porch* and *Patio* are an exquisitely observed pair of two-handers which explore with wry humour the attitudes and longings involved in Texan small-town life. In *Porch* the wheel-chair bound Dot observes the empty world go by with wry humour, but incidentally traps her sister Lucille to a doleful existence in doing so; in *Patio*, Jewel is preparing to throw a farewell summer party for her friend, Pearl, who dreams of being a hairdresser to the stars in Hollywood, but the unrealistic dreams of both sisters are revealed as the afternoon wears on. *Twister* and *Tornado* (also known as *Tropical Depression* in a later form) are a second double-bill of similar style and quality.

Other plays to consider: *Bargains*; *Boys Play*; *Clara Period*
Publishers: Dramatists Play Service

Beth Henley (1952–) American dramatist, actress

Whilst still at Southern Methodist University, Beth Henley wrote her first successful one-act play *Am I Blue* (1973), an off-beat comedy which ranges from hilarity to pathos as it details the chance meeting of a college freshman and a precocious teenager. One critic described a later revival of this bitter-sweet comedy as 'stamped with the trademark of the fine and vital writer'.

Winner of the Pulitzer Prize for her full-length play *Crimes of the Heart*. Beth Henley went on to write several more highly theatrical plays, three of which are collected in one volume. *Control Freaks* (1992) mixes murder, mayhem and memories with a sense of Southern gothic humour. Written in 12 scenes each with a different theme beginning with the letter L, *L-Plays* (1996) is a fascinating study of style, character and rhythm. Completing the trio is *Sisters of the Winter Madrigal* (2001) is a trenchant black comedy under the guise of a medieval-style fairy tale.

Publishers: Dramatists Play Service

AP Herbert (1890–1971) English writer, poet and dramatist

Herbert was a man of many parts: a wit, controversialist, and reformer, as well as a writer of plays, libretti, and song lyrics. He was also an Independent Member of the British Parliament for some years. In the theatre he is best known for his collaboration with Vivian Ellis in a series of musicals presented in London immediately following World War II. *Bless the Bride* competed successfully with *Oklahoma* for public acclaim in 1946.

However, a one-act play of his, written early in his career (1929), has survived as a curiosity and was regarded by one critic as 'having the best Shakespearean couplets that Shakespeare never wrote'. This was *Two Gentlemen of Soho*, 500 lines of Elizabethan pastiche and parody which is still played on stage by adventurous amateur companies occasionally and can bring laughs if given skilful playing.

Herbert also wrote and published a jury-oriented one-act farce called *Double Demon* as well as a one-act comic opera.

Publishers: Samuel French

Don Hill English dramatist

Don Hill's one-act plays have won several playwriting awards in recent years and they often go beyond the naturalistic conventions of theatre. *Goodbye Casey Burnside* is a tragi-comic variation on the 'hereafter' theme: Casey returns to earth after sudden death to say goodbye to his nearest and dearest but gets a shock from his girl-friend. *Below the Belt* is a witty extended metaphor (the set is in the form of a boxing ring) of a marriage breakdown, with a sympathetic but inept marriage counsellor and a mother-in-law on opposite sides.

Other plays to consider: *Dead Man Talking*; *One and One is Two*; *Would You Adam 'n Eve It?*
Publishers: Garnet Miller

Barry Hillman English dramatist and actor

Hillman is an ex-professional actor turned playwright who has published a number of historical dramas which weave fictional stories around documented incidents. A good example of his work is found in the all-women play, *The Establishment at Arles*, which centres round the arrival at a French brothel of the prim English girl Candice in 1888. She is determined to rescue her friend, Yvette, with whom she has previously worked. But when a young destitute artist sends Yvette his ear, the Van Gogh resonances in the title of the play are confirmed. In the end Candice, fascinated by this passion, seeks a job as a wine-waitress in 'the establishment'.

Roly-Poly (1972) is based on a bitter-sweet Guy de Maupassant short-story in which a respectable woman takes advantage of a prostitute's services to secure her release from the Prussian army and then scorns her after using her help. *Beyond Necessity* is also based on a domestic de Maupassant tale,

Other plays to consider: *The Dispossessed*; *Face the Music*; *Partly Furnished*; *Six for the Charleston*; *Two Can Play at That Game*
Publishers: Samuel French

Norman Holland (1910–2000) English dramatist

Though working as a high-ranking British Government civil servant for most of his life, Norman Holland was also a prolific writer of both full and one-act stage plays for many years in the middle part of the 20th century. He operated effectively in a variety of styles. He won over a score of playwriting awards and was included in anthologies on both sides of the Atlantic. He had several of his short plays performed on radio and TV, and three were made into films. Among his one-act plays, the simple *Happiness My Goal* (1962), a beautifully crafted bio-graphical reflection, is outstanding, but possibly his most popular play has been *Liberation* (1953), a taut thriller set in occupied France during World War II.

Holland's plays always have credible character and motivation and range widely in content from historical pieces (*Clonagh the King*, set in Gaelic Ireland, *The Defeated*, a play about the Franco-Prussian War of the 1870s, *The Prattling Prentice*, a Chaucerian comedy) to thrillers (*Headline*, *Runaway* (1975), *Yellow Water*) and backstage comedies (*Enter Comedy* (1948), *They All Come Back*).

Some of his all-women one-act plays are amongst the best of their kind in their depth of character and deft plotting. These include *Second Easter*, in which Pilate's wife, now converted to Christianity, meets the two Marys and Salome, *One Hour Alone* (1954), about the young Queen Victoria, and *Women Against the World*, which chronicles an episode in the life of the Women's Suffrage movement immediately before World War I.

Other plays to consider: *Affair of Honour*; *At Scutari*; *Before the Coronation*; *Big Moment*; *Clouded Crystal*; *Crisis in Wimpole Street*; *Day of Reckoning*; *Diamond Jubilee*; *Farewell my Princess*; *Fond Farewell*; *Fool of Creation*; *Friar Matthew*; *The Golden Key*; *Green Bottle*; *High-Backed Chair*; *In All His Glory*; *Judgement Here*; *The Leopard's Spots*; *Miss Nightingale's Mission*; *My Name is Oscar Wilde*; *On the Frontier*; *Pavel the Fox*; *The Remedy*; *The Small Private World of Michael Marston*; *Smoke Screen*; *Tea with a Legend*; *Twilight*; *Widow of Charles Dickens*; *Will and Testament*; *The Young Queen*
Publishers: Samuel French; Deane; Hanbury Plays

Robert Holman (1952–) British dramatist

A playwright of great sensitivity and perception, Yorkshire-born Robert Holman writes gentle, complex, probing dramas which have never quite reached mainstream acclaim. However, in 1986 he wrote a successful triple bill of short plays which has enjoyed several revivals. In addition to the sensitive play which gave the evening its overall title, *Making Noises Quietly*, the triptych is com-pleted with *Lost* and *Being Friends*, all involving chance meetings overshadowed by class, gender and war.

Publishers: Methuen; Nick Hern Books

Evelyn Hood Scottish dramatist and novelist

A former journalist, Scottish writer Evelyn Hood has written over 30 novels, the popularity of those books having rather over-shadowed her writing for the theatre.

However, several of her scripts frequently appear in drama festivals, notably *Epitaph for a Hard Man* (1988) and *Curses Foiled Again!* (1986). In the former a widower converses with the tangible presence of his dead wife which brings about some dramatic revelations and skeletons tumbling from the family cupboard. In contrast to the touching quality of that play, *Curses, Foiled Again!* is a light-hearted look at the problems and internal strife to be found at a frenetic dress rehearsal for a Victorian tragedy.

There is a magical element in *Genteel* (1984) where a strange potion has the ability to make the disagreeable drinker shed 30 years to reveal his former charming self, while the surprise in *I Never Thought it Would be Like This* (1982) is the appearance of a mother and as yet unborn child to a couple stranded on a desert island.

Evelyn Hood has written two plays which have a particular appeal to her fellow Scots, partly because their setting is their homeland. The comedy *Yin for the Council* (1986) is a parochial comedy based on the 1700 rivalry between Paisley and neighbouring Renfrew, while the drama *A Wake for Donald* (1983) is set in the following century and has the infamous Edinburgh grave-robbers Burke and Hare disturbed by the widow of the corpse as they are carrying out their nefarious business.

Publishers: Samuel French; Brown Son & Ferguson

Nina Warner Hooke English dramatist

Nina Warner Hooke had early success with a published volume of short revue sketches and when she turned to writing longer pieces in the 1950s it was comedy which prevailed in her approach. She had particular success with a pair of one-act plays which were extended in-jokes about drama festivals.

In *Festival Nightmare* (1959), her most well-known piece, a drama adjudicator wrestles with her conscience at night, after having judged a festival. In her dreams she is confronted by actors who have been subject to her scrutiny. She in turn is judged (and condemned) and goes to the scaffold bravely quoting Sydney Carton: as she does, the actors pass scathing judgement on her performance. Hooke points out in an extensive preliminary note that the play is a satirical comedy, not a farce, and that characters needed to be rooted in reality not burlesque. It is an accomplished and effective non-naturalistic play which gets close to the heart of the angst of performers and which has won many drama festival awards. It remains in print nearly 50 years after it was first premiered by an amateur company close to her South Dorset home.

Rock Bottom (1956) is another lively and amusing play which purports to reveal what really happens backstage in a dressing-room when a team is entering a drama festival. Her light-hearted style is also seen to advantage in *The Godsend* (1959), which explores goings-on in the pavilion of an Arabian Sultan with several wives and *No Man's Land* (1959) in which a shipwrecked mariner finds seven women eagerly awaiting him on a desert island.

Other plays to consider: *Not in the Contract*; *The Picnic on the Hill*
Publishers: Samuel French

Israel Horovitz (1939–) American dramatist

Born in New England and later a drama student in Britain, Israel Horovitz has written more than 50 plays, the majority of which are in the one-act form.

He first made an impact on the theatrical world in the '60s with the remarkable *The Indian Wants the Bronx* (1968). Set in a New York back-street this powerful urban play combines sensitivity, humanity and searing violence. Less well known outside his own country is the strangely effective *Line* (1967), an allegorical play highlighting the American dream for success. Five disparate characters use guile, deviousness and force to outwit the others to come first in an unspecified queue thus highlighting the many petty battles we undertake in our daily lives

Often paired with *The Indian Wants the Bronx* is the funny, perceptive *It's Called the Sugar Plum* (1967), in which a young girl develops an increasingly warm relationship with the car-driver who had accidentally killed her boyfriend. Another strong two-hander where the truth beneath the surface of an enigmatic relationship is gradually revealed is *Hopscotch* (1974), which appears along with *The 75th* (1977), *Stage Directions* (1976) and *Spared* (1974) in a collection entitled *The Quannapowitt Quartet*.

The New York Times described the urban parable *Rats* (1968), as 'tough, rough, funny and moving', while *Acrobats* (1968) is in lighter mood. Here the two eponymous characters valiantly run through the complexities of their routine while beneath the smiling veneer they mouth the true feelings about their marital state.

Others plays to consider: *Faith*; *The Former One-on-One Basketball Champion*; *Free Gift*; *The Great Labor Day Classic*; *Leader*; *Play for Germs*; *Shooting Gallery*; *Speed*; *Trees*; *Uncle Snake*
Publishers: Dramatists Play Service; Samuel French.

Stanley Houghton (1881–1913) English dramatist

Stanley Houghton was one of the 'Manchester School' of playwrights who developed plays about Northern working-class life in the Edwardian period.

His life was sadly cut short at the age of 32, but not before he had left behind two significant full-length plays of radical social concern, *The Younger Generation* and *Hindle Wakes*, and one now seemingly immortal one-act comedy, *The Dear Departed* (1908). In the latter, a family are caught deciding with undue haste how to apportion the possessions of their grandfather when the supposed corpse reveals that he has merely been asleep and not dead as they supposed.

Other plays to consider: *Fancy Free*; *Master of the House*; *Phipps*
Publishers: Samuel French

Laurence Housman (1865–1959) English dramatist

Younger brother of the author of *A Shropshire Lad*, Laurence Housman's reputation in the one-act field rests securely and remarkably on a collection of no fewer than 50 one-act plays all of which centred around the life of the 13th century St Francis of Assisi and his companions. Housman researched a great cache of historical incidents and legends surrounding the gentle saint.

The Little Plays of St Francis (each lasting 25–30 minutes) were first published in a group of 18 in 1922, and rapidly achieved popularity and performance amongst church drama groups, but not only in this context. Each play dealt with an episode in the life of St Francis, and was the vehicle for aphorisms and homespun philosophy as well as humour. Housman's characterisation not only of the gentle Brother Francis but also of the other Brothers was vivid, especially the devoted, but somewhat foolish Brother Juniper, whose inability to work out God's teachings was frequently the centre of the action.

As an example, *The Order of Release* (chosen by Harley Granville Barker as his favourite of the 18 in the second collection) opens with Brother Juniper speaking to a lay-sister at the convent of the Poor Clares. The dying St Francis is being kept in the Bishop's palace and not allowed to return to the community which he founded. Juniper recounts bedside stories and the nuns console him and give him gifts of lavender to take back Then Brother Jerome arrives to say that Francis will be allowed to return to Portiuncula after all and has asked for Juniper to go with him ; as Juniper capers off, the nuns cheer his departure and are reproved by Jerome ('The Lord does not rejoice in any man's legs, Sister') 'and the excited motion of their hands is like the fluttering of doves in a cage.'

Volumes of plays under the same generic title and devoted to this single saintly life followed at regular intervals until 1935 , and there was also a set of *Four Plays of St Clare* (1934), on the same theme, designed to provide some major parts for women.

Other plays to consider: *The Christmas Tree*; *A Fool and His Money*; *The House-Fairy*; *Moonshine*; *The Torch of Time*; *The Village Conjurer*
Publishers: Sidgwick and Jackson

William Inge (1913–1973) American dramatist

A sequence of big New York play and film hits including *Picnic*, *Come Back Little Sheba* and *Bus Stop* brought Inge to prominence in the theatre of the 1950s. His own style has links in themes and style to that of his friend Tennessee Williams, and, like Williams, he wrote several one-act plays of distinction.

In *Glory of the Flower*, a bitter-sweet but beautifully-judged evocation of small-town life in America, a once-successful boxer returns to his home-town but is given a sharp lesson in values (and the need to grow into maturity) by his former-sweetheart piano-teacher. In *The Call*, Joe, dressed in the extravagant costume of a small-town parade marshal, calls on his brother Terry in New York. Nothing that Terry can do dispels Joe's unease about big city life, even the offer of hospitality, and in the end he leaves carrying his own heavy suitcase (an obvious metaphor) to find a hotel room somewhere.

Other plays to consider: *The Boy in the Basement; The Disposal; An Incident at the Standish Arms; Margaret's Bed; Memory of Summer; A Murder; The Rainy Afternoon; A Social Event; The Tiny Closet*
Publishers: Dramatists Play Service

Eugene Ionesco (1909–1994) French writer and dramatist

Ionesco, born of a Romanian father and French mother, and educated in both the countries of his parents, was one of the principal dramatists to experiment with the 'Theatre of the Absurd' in the 1950s and 1960s whilst living in Paris. He believed that French theatre needed to be jolted from its comfortable preoccupation with boulevard comedies.

He intended the audience to be so irked by *The Bald Prima-donna*, one of his first one-act plays written in 1949, that they would be provoked to boo and jeer at the final curtain. The play presents an ordinary French family at home but speaking in the phraseology of a textbook primer, resulting in a kind of stilted gobbledegook which seems to show the inconsequentiality and meaningless of some domestic relationships, as well as the quirks of language.

Two later small-cast plays, *The Chairs* (called 'a tragic farce') and *The Lesson*, pursue the theme of the absurdity and inadequacy of language; both are about an hour in length and involve fantasies seen only by the characters, who are wrapped up in their own private worlds. They are exciting and perplexing pieces, but with a great capacity to provoke audience reaction and discussion.

Other plays to consider: *The Future is in Eggs; The Hardboiled Egg; Jacques*
Publishers: Samuel French

WW Jacobs (1863–1943) English dramatist and writer

Born in Wapping, in East London, Jacobs first worked as a post-office official before becoming a full-time short-story writer who mainly chronicled the thriving late-Victorian life of London's river and told the stories of the bargees and watermen who inhabited the dockland districts around the Thames.

He is best remembered, however, for a short-story which turned into a one-act play in 1904 and which became one of the most famous curtain-raisers in the London theatre of its time. This was *The Monkey's Paw*, a piece with a strong sense of the supernatural, in which taking possession of a supposed 'lucky charm' brings grief and tragedy to a London household. It still has the capacity to make audiences uneasy today and has been reworked by several later adaptors.

Other plays to consider: *Admiral Peters*; *A Distant Relative*; *Establishing Relations*; *Keeping up Appearances*; *Master Mariners*; *Matrimonial Openings*; *The Warming Pan*
Publishers: Samuel French

Gertrude Jennings (1877–1958) English dramatist

A professional actress with Ben Greet's company at the start of her career in the theatre, Gertrude Jennings produced a stream of competent one-act comedies and farces, mixed with the occasional full-length piece, from the start of the 20th century until her death. Many of these featured all-women casts and some had West End runs, though she also wrote extensively with the non-professional theatre in mind. Over 30 of her plays were listed in the French's play catalogue of 1951, though all had been removed by the 1980s.

Many of her short plays centred around the conversational exchanges of everyday incidents or situations (cf. *At the Ribbon Counter* (1920), *Waiting for the Bus* (1920), *Allotments* (1918), *The Christening* (1937), *In the Black-Out* (1942)) but they have inevitably lost some of their sting and/or humour as times have passed on. One of her most performed one-act plays was the comedy, *The Rest Cure* (1919) in which a writer desperately seeking solitude is eventually persuaded to leave his typewriter to the nurse who is looking after him.

Jennings drew working-class and middle-class characters skilfully and her plays provide a wry observation of the social history of the times. As examples of the life of their period, they retain a certain charm and might well be revived successfully as unpretentious representations of the manners of an age.

Other plays to consider: *Acid Drops*; *The Bathroom Door*; *Between the Soup and the Savoury*; *The Bride*; *Calais to Dover*; *Cat's Claws*; *Elegant Edward*; *Fireworks*; *Five Birds in a Cage*; *Good Neighbours*; *Happy as a King*; *Have you Anything to Declare?*; *The Helping Hands*; *How Now Brown Cow*; *I'll Pay Your Fare*; *I'm Sorry It's Out*; *In the Cellar*; *In the Fog*; *Knit One Purl One*; *Me and my Diary*; *Mother of Pearl*; *The New Poor*; *No Servants*; *The Pearly Gates*; *Poached Eggs and Pearls*; *Puss in the Corner*; *Scraps*; *Secrets of the Castle*; *Spot*; *These Pretty Things*; *Too Much Bluebeard*
Publishers: Samuel French

Pamela Hansford Johnson (1912–81) and CP Snow (1905–80)
English writers and dramatists

As populariser, if not originator, of the idea of 'The Two Cultures', intellectual pundit, philosopher and author of a seminal sequence of novels about university life, CP Snow is perhaps a surprising figure to find amongst the one-act play writing fraternity. But writing in collaboration with his wife, Pamela Hansford Johnson, herself a distinguished novelist, he had half a dozen published in the 1960s and 1970s.

These are workmanlike pieces, though not deeply profound or at the cutting edge of experiment in dramatic form. The most interesting of them is *The Pigeon with the Silver Foot*, a charming story, based on legend, and set in Venice in a pavement cafe.

Other plays to consider: *Family Party*; *Her Best Foot Forward*; *Spare the Rod*; *The Supper Dance*; *To Murder My Mother*
Publishers: Evans

Philip Johnson English dramatist

Over 50 of Philip Johnson's one-act plays appeared in the Samuel French catalogue of published plays of 1951 – more than any other author. In the comparable catalogue of 2005, his plays had disappeared without trace. Such is the fate of an author writing (mostly) domestic comedies and dramas set in their own times and designed consciously to meet the needs of the amateur market. Yet it would be unwise to dismiss Johnson on this basis alone.

As early as 1928 he won the prize for the best new play of the year (*Legend*) in the National Festival of Community Drama run by the British Drama League and he had a full-length West End success, *Lovers Leap*, anthologised in *Famous Plays of 1935*. His comedies usually dealt with family situations – a reluctant bride (*Orange Blossom*, 1943), the reading of a will (*The Late Miss Cordell*, 1944), a carnival queen (*Today of all Days*, 1933). Most of his dramas also worked on a domestic canvas – a family discovering that their father is the public hangman (*Dark Brown*, 1946), the poignancy of a fading professional actor (*It's Autumn Now*, 1938), ill-fated love leading to a tragic death (*Master Dudley*, 1947).

Alongside these were are some period 'downstairs' comedies mostly set in the house of one Kensington family (*Charade*, 1944, *Green Grow the Cabbages*, 1949, *Hullabaloo*, 1941, *Novelette*, 1941, *Matrimonial*, 1942) and the occasional excursion into adapting literature (*Blood and Thunder*, 1949) – about the Crummles family in Nicholas Nickleby; social history (*The Spinsters of Lushe*, 1929) – set in Napoleonic times and maritime themes (*The Good and the Bad*, 1929).

Johnson had the art of writing actable parts and providing clear structures and climaxes for his plays, even if, in his later years, he did not attempt grand themes. A revival of almost any 1930s/'40s Johnson play in the 21st century would not only be an entertaining period curiosity but also provide good opportunities for performers learning their trade.

Other plays to consider: *Afternoon*; *April Shower*; *The Cage*; *The Charwoman's Daughter*; *Derelict*; *The Distant Drum*; *Enclosed Premises*; *Everlasting Flowers*; *Far Far Away*; *From Five to Five-thirty*; *Heaven on Earth*; *Her and Her George*; *Hope Springs Eternal*; *An Immortelle*; *In Waltz Time*; *The Inconstant Moon*; *Its a Small World*; *Life without Music*; *Love in a Suburb*; *The Lovely Miracle*;

Lovers' Meeting; Memoirs; Mr Twemlow is Not Himself; Mrs Methuselah; Nobody Knows; Off with the Motley; One of the Family; Only the Brave; Out Goes She; A Present for a Lady; Red Sky at Night; Respectable Façade; Romance in Grey; Russian Salad; Sad About Europe; Saturday Night; Send Her Victorious; Shame the Devil; The Sister who Walked in Silence; Sorcery in a Suburb; The Startled Saint; Storm in a Loving Cup; The Stunt; The Tinsel Duchess; Where Every Prospect Pleases; The Witching Hour; World Without End
Publishers: Samuel French

Gwenyth Jones Welsh dramatist

During a comparatively short published-writing career in the 1950s Gwenyth Jones has added a couple of classic one-act plays to the canon. *The Ass and the Philosophers* (1957) is a delightful comedy set in ancient Greece. The play opens with two philosophers arguing whether the Will is self-determined; a young man seeks their advice in helping him to decide on which girl he should marry. The philosophers in turn enlist the help of an ass; whichever bundle of hay the ass chooses will signify the right choice for the young man. But the ass is dilatory and the girls decide not to wait. The ass stampedes, the philosophers argue and the young man is left to eat the hay.

   The Mayor of Torontal (1953) amusingly chronicles the effect of a mysterious but fascinating female visitor on a late 19th-century East European town. The mayor's advice is sought by a selection of townspeople who have been variously, transfixed, duped or 'hypnotised' by the charismatic visitor. The Mayor determines to act on their behalf but when Madame Baranya calls he too falls under her spell and rapidly accepts her suggestion of marriage.

Other plays to consider: *The Finger on the Heart; Julia; Missing; Mrs Murphy; The Practical Approach; There's No Problem*
Publishers: Samuel French; Deane

Barrie Keeffe (1945–) British dramatist

An East Londoner, Barrie Keeffe has said that he writes plays for 'people who wouldn't be seen dead in the theatre', and his scripts are uncompromisingly gritty. *Gimme Shelter*, his 1977 trilogy of one-acters includes *Gotcha* (1976), previously banned by the BBC because of its storyline about a boy threatening to blow up his teachers. The other plays in this group are *Gem* (1975) and *Getaway*. In 1976 he wrote a further trilogy, *Barbarians*, which includes *Abide With Me*, *In the City* and the best known, *Killing Time*. All three focus on inarticulate, angry young Londoners whose voice combines abuse with tenderness.

Publishers: Methuen

*Tim Kelly (1935–1998) American dramatist and TV script-writer

The stage adaptor of the popular TV comedy series *M*A*S*H* in both full-length and one-act form (1973), Yale-educated Kelly was a prolific American writer who produced literally hundreds of scripts and often reworked novels and films for the stage. Many of these were in the one-act form since he enjoyed writing for what he called 'cross-overs – plays that can be performed by any level of theatre group from high school pupils to Equity members'. Horror stories, Westerns (as befitted an author of episodes of *Bonanza* and *High Chaparral*), gay nineties melodramas, children's classics, all came alike to his versatile pen. Unusually for an American writer he even ventured into short versions of the English pantomime form with *Aladdin, Jack and the Magic Beans* and *Raggedy Dick and Puss*.

He often poked fun at the classics of literature in spirited ways. He adapted and updated stories from Oscar Wilde, Chekhov, Cervantes, Conan Doyle, HG Wells and Dickens amongst others. His *Oliver Twisted* (1982) is a good example, written in the style of film noir of the 1940s. Private eye 'Chuck' Dickens is commissioned by the wealthy widow Mrs Lowe to find the missing boy Oliver. Dickens's assistants are the dumb but amorous Nancy and Mrs Bumble, who is masquerading as the cleaner. When the slinky and gorgeous Fay Gunn visits Dickens's office, it becomes clear that she is implicated but the denouement sees tough-guy Bill Sikes unexpectedly unmasked as an under-cover cop working for the Los Angeles Police Department. In similar vein *The Omelet Murder Case* re-hashes Hamlet as if it were written by a pulp-fiction author.

Some of his one-act titles indicate his jokey, energetic style – *Toga!, Toga! Toga!, Tap Dancing in Molasses, Lost in Space and the Mortgage Due, Help! I'm Trapped in a High School!* Relatively unknown in Europe, Kelly's large collection of one-act work is a rich treasure-chest for those looking for high-spirited and literate entertainment

Other plays to consider: *The Adventure of the Clouded Crystal; Always Marry a Bachelor; The Cave; Cinderella Meets the Wolfman; The Clods of Hopper; Creeps by Night; Dog Eat Dog; Fog on the Mountain; The Gift and the Giving; How to Get Rid of a Housemother; If Sherlock Holmes were a Woman...; I Want My Mummy; Ladies of the Tower; Lantern in the Wind; The Last of Sherlock Holmes; Lucky Lucky Hudson and the 12th Street Gang; The Marvelous Playbill; The Natives are Restless; Nicholas Nickleby; Not Far From the Gioconda Tree; The Remarkable Susan; Reunion on Gallows Hill; Second Best Bed; Seven Wives for Dracula; Sherlock Meets the Phantom; The Silk Shirt; Two Fools Who Gained a Measure of Wisdom; Up The Rent; Victor Hugo – in Rehearsal; While Shakespeare Slept*
Publishers: Bakers Plays; Dramatists Play Service; Samuel French; Hanbury Plays; Pioneer Drama Service

Arthur Kopit (1937–) American dramatist

Kopit, a leading American dramatist of the second half of the 20th century has often experimented with radical forms. He is best known for his full-length dramas, but wrote several one-acters which are well off the beaten-track in terms of themes and styles. Among the better-known are the comedy *Good Help is Hard to Find* (1982) in which the servant who comes to help an elderly couple turns out to be the angel of death and *Sing to Me Through Open Windows* (1959), an intriguing piece in which a boy unpacks memories from five years previously.

One of his most unusual one-act plays is *Chamber Music* (1963) in which a motley band of women dressed in extraordinary clothes (and with strange personas) discuss how to attack the patients in the male ward of a mental hospital. In *The Questioning of Nick* (1957) two detectives question a rough and hostile student and gradually play on his pride in order to eventually trap him and extract an admission.

Other plays to consider: *The Conquest of Everest*; *The Day the Whores Came Out to Play Tennis*; *Success*
Publishers: Samuel French

Neil LaBute (1963–) American dramatist and filmmaker

In an introduction to his triple-bill of plays *Bash* (2000), American filmmaker and dramatist Neil LaBute has said that 'Atrocity is "the new black"'. Certainly the plays have a dark centre as they explore the brutality, violence and evil at the heart of certain aspects of modern society. The two-hander *A Gaggle of Saints* begins with superficial banter between two college sweethearts but later reveals their repulsive prejudice. The challenging monologues *Iphegenia in Orem* and *Medea Redux* complete this absorbing, provocative and disturbing trio.

In 2005, his long one-acter (running for 100 minutes) *Some Girl(s)* played for a time in a major London theatre.

Publisher: Samuel French

* Bob Larbey (1934–) English dramatist and TV script-writer

Best known for his many successful TV series, some written with John Esmonde, such as *Please Sir*, *Ever Decreasing Circles* and *The Good Life*, and some written solo, such as the Judi Dench vehicles *As Time Goes By* and *A Fine Romance*, Bob Larbey has lately ventured into writing for the stage in both full-length and one-act form.

The story of the links he has forged between professional and amateur theatre, and between TV and stage writing is an interesting one. He grew up in south London and met his first writing partner, John Esmonde, while at grammar school in Clapham. They began their partnership providing sketch material for radio and for *The Dick Emery Show* on TV. They eventually split in 1995 on Esmonde's move to Spain.

Larbey and his wife had moved to the village of Ockley, Surrey in 1979, where they became attenders at the shows of the local drama society. His wife offered support by doing a stint as the Ockley DS Secretary, and Larbey then wrote a couple of one-act plays for them to perform, his first venture into theatre work.

Both these comedies, *Half an Idea*, about a writer whose play comes to life in unexpected ways, and *A Small Affair*, about the perils of TV rehearsal rooms, have since been published and are sometimes seen as a double-bill as well as individually in drama festivals. Larbey has gone on to write some full-length stage plays which have also proved popular. With a rich back catalogue of TV successes at his command, is it possible that, in the future, he may put other well-tested and actable short pieces into stage form?

Publishers: Samuel French

Hugh Leonard (1926–) Irish dramatist, scriptwriter, critic and journalist

Hugh Leonard – the pseudonym of John Keyes Byrne – is one of Ireland's most highly regarded contemporary writers with an output which encompasses television, cinema, memoir, criticism and journalism. However his greatest achievement has been through his successful theatre work. He was aged 28 when his first play was directed but he has said that he was middle-aged when he discovered a true sense of identity. His full-length plays have won plaudits on both side of the Atlantic, but he has also written interesting collections of short plays which have often been overlooked.

The first of these collections was presented in Dublin in 1975 under the title *Suburb of Babylon* (1983) each with a domestic setting. *A Time of Wolves and Tigers* (1975) is virtually a monologue where a desperate middle aged man faces problems at work and loneliness in his personal life. Although *Nothing Personal* (1975) begins in a light-hearted mood it takes on a sinister slant when later the troubles in Northern Ireland impinge on the characters. Completing the trio and proving most popular of the three is *The Last of the Last of the Mohicans* (1975), a hilarious comedy concerning a would-be philandering husband.

Betrayal is a recurring theme in Leonard's work and that is a strong feature in the gentle conversation piece *Roman Fever* set in 1930 and based on a short story by Edith Wharton. Basically a two-hander for women of a certain age, it appeared in another triptych of plays under the umbrella title *Scorpions* (1983). The other plays are the intriguing *Pizzazz*, a Chinese box where all is not as it seems and *A View from an Obelisk*, a theatrical adaptation of one of the writer's earlier successful television scripts. *Senna for Sonny* and *The Lily Lally Show* were presented as a double bill under the title *Chamber Music* at Dublin's Abbey Theatre in 1994.

Other plays to consider: *The Late Arrival of the Incoming Aircraft*
Publishers: Samuel French

Romulus Linney (1930–) American dramatist and novelist

Although not widely known beyond his native country, Romulus Linney has been described as 'a writer of substance and range, creating plays that crackle with challenging issues and theatricality'. He has said, 'My plays and novels are drawn from either historical subjects or memories of my childhood or direct personal experience'.

Sand Mountain Matchmaking and *Why the Lord Came to Sand Mountain*, two of his interrelated short plays, which appear in a volume entitled *Sand Mountain* (1986), are rollicking amusing studies of life on the Tennessee frontier. *Pops* (1986) comprises six short plays unified by the theme of aspects of love but also related by their 'musical' titles which underscore the themes and mood of this suite of plays. So the course of love can be tracked through the titles, *Can Can, Clair de Lune, Ave Maria, Gold and Silver Waltz, Yankee Doodle* and *Songs of Love*.

Another notable collection of imaginative one-act plays includes *April Snow* (1983), a deeply-felt study of love and loneliness, and *Yancey* (1988), which explores themes of cruelty and personal courage as a painfully shy country boy confronts two brittle urban actors. Completing the trio, which all can be played separately, is *Juliet* (1988) which focuses on the fiery discussion between a theatrical director and his temperamental leading lady.

The elegant, evocative folk play *Tennessee* won an Obie Award in 1979 and is often coupled with the powerfully effective *El Hermano* (1979), set in a seedy San Francisco bar in 1954. Played together they make a well-contrasted double-bill. In completely different mood is *The Death of King Philip* (1979), which takes the audience back to a dark time in colonial American history.

Other plays to consider: *Akhmatova; F.M.; Goodbye Howard; Goodbye Oscar; Hrosvitha; Komachi; The Love Suicide at Schofield Barracks; Stars*
Publishers: Dramatists Play Service

Henry Livings (1929–) English dramatist

'I go mostly for laughter', said Henry Livings once in an interview, and the doubts about whether or not he is a 'major' playwright are perhaps founded on reactions to that premise. A North of England playwright, Livings has usually concentrated on working-class preoccupations and predicaments in his full-length plays such as *Stop It Whoever You Are, Eh!*, and *Nil Carborundum*.

His occasional one-act plays and radio pieces echo the same style, though they have never attracted the same attention or performance levels. *Brainscrew* appeared in a collection for schools in 1973, and other short pieces of his were collected in *Good Grief* and *Pongo Plays 1–6*, and *Six More Pongo Plays*.

Publishers: Methuen

Federico Garcia Lorca (1898–1936) Spanish dramatist, poet and artist

In addition to being Spain's most celebrated dramatist, Lorca was a poet and artist. His fame rests mainly with his three great full-length plays – *Blood Wedding*, *Yerma*, and *The House of Bernarda Alba* – but some of his minor works continue to create interest.

He considered two of these plays 'unproduceable', yet bold, progressive companies have attempted to give the lie to that claim. In *The Public* (1931) Lorca asks the question, would the passion be the less true had Romeo been a man of 30 and Juliet a boy of 15? In this colourful script, which has elements of surrealism, folk theatre, poetry, and humour, he was able to give vent to his strong homosexual emotions which were clearly taboo in his day. Lorca's other 'unproduceable' play was *As Five Years Pass* (1931), a longer piece but sometimes played without an interval.

Avant garde when first written, **Play Without Words** (1936) broke with theatrical conventions to reflect the violence of its time. Fate decreed that within a few months of writing the play Lorca would be shot by paramilitary fascists and buried in an unmarked grave.

Early in his career, he wrote several short puppet plays, several of which are still in print and sometimes revived, notably **Don Christobel** (1931).

Publishers: Methuen; Samuel French

Arthur Lovegrove English dramatist and actor

Lovegrove was a London-born and educated professional actor (seen on screen in TV dramas ranging from *Dixon of Dock Green* to *The Avengers*) who also pursued a career as a playwright. He wrote a number of successful light full-length pieces for professional theatre production in the 1960s and 1970s, most notably *Goodnight Mrs Puffin*, a successful comedy vehicle for Irene Handl.

His one-act plays have the same light approach and are tailored to the resources of small amateur groups. *There's Always Spring* (1972) is a charming piece in which a young couple, not sure of whether or not to buy a new house, are visited both by an older resident and, in passing, by a benign shadow of the past, to help them make up their mind. *Clara's on the Curtains* (1973) lives up to its title in focussing on the comic preliminaries to a village play, and there is a similar location and atmosphere for the all-women *Her Grace will be Here* (1965). *Nasty Things, Murders* (1974) is another of Lovegrove's shorter plays with an all-female cast and is set in a retired home for gentlewomen. *Just Another Day* (1966) amusingly chronicles the trials and pitfalls of an 'ordinary' wedding-day.

Publishers: Samuel French

Miles Malleson (1888–1969) English actor and dramatist

Malleson had a long career in the theatre as both writer and actor, as well, for a time, as the administrator of the Arts Guild of the then-powerful Independent Labour Party in the 1920s. Malleson wrote several one-act plays for the Guild but his desire to encourage Arts Guild branches to explore the theatre classics led him into conflict with those who wanted to concentrate on political propaganda. Malleson has contributed several widely-used one-act translations and adaptations of European writers (*The Bet* based on Chekhov, *A Provincial Lady* from Turgenev, *Sganarelle* by Molière, and *Michael* from a story by Tolstoy – the latter pair being his most frequently-performed adaptations).

Malleson's ILP-period plays featured middle-class women who had either suffered loss through war or were seeking to break free from the shackles of unhappy marriage. His two one-act plays born from his World War I experiences (*The Black 'Ell* and *D Company*, 1916) had questions asked about them in Parliament at the time of first performance ('a calumny on the British soldier', said one MP) and were given a 21st century professional revival in London. One of his most frequently played pieces is quite a-political; *The Last Appearance* (1959) is a melodramatic piece which can be played by a mixed or all-woman cast and which deals with a dead woman apparently continuing to play her 'last part' in the theatre through hypnosis.

Other plays to consider: *The Great Boko; A Man of Ideas; Paddly Pools; Maurice's Own Idea*
Publishers: Samuel French

David Mamet (1947–) American dramatist

David Mamet burst on to American theatrical scene in 1974 with *Sexual Perversity in Chicago*, a free-form 90-minute play where the language is sharp-edged and jazzy as befits the theme of the piece – the sexual exploits of youth and attitudes to women, set in the playwright's home city. Critics discerned a new theatrical voice and were soon seeking out one of his earlier scripts: *Duck Variations* (1972), another fairly long one-act play where two old men meet on a park bench to philosophise and speculate – in 14 variations – on life in the 20th century. *A Life in the Theatre* (1977), which runs for 75 minutes, traces the relationship between an older experienced actor and a talented new recruit to the acting profession.

Over succeeding years David Mamet has written a wide variety of work including film scripts, plays for children and adaptations of classics of Russian theatre. Along side such notable full-length scripts as *Oleanna*, he has written numerous short plays and monologues. One of his most popular pieces is *The Shawl* (1985), a carefully constructed series of duologues building to a séance which profoundly affects all those taking part. The author has described this play as 'my twilight zone episode'.

The Reunion (1976) is a haunting piece where after 25 years a woman meets her ex-alcoholic father. Here one critic described Mamet as 'in near-Pinteresque mood, lightly touching our emotions and leaving an after-taste of solitude'. Thematically-linked and also featuring a father-daughter relationship, *The Dark Pony* (1977) was written as a ten-minute curtain-raiser to *The Reunion*. Another play where the central relationship is explored in depth is *The Woods* (1977) in which a city couple escape for an isolated romance, only for arguments and violence to erupt before they come to close understanding of their needs.

More than 25 of Mamet's short pieces appear in three collections: *No One Will be Immune* and *Other Plays and Pieces* (1994), *Short Plays and Monologues* (1981), *Dramatic Sketches and Monologues* (1985).

Publishers: Dramatists Play Service; Samuel French

Charles Mander British dramatist

Charles Mander has written several popular comedies highlighting the problems facing a rather inept amateur drama society. In *World Premier* (1995) the focus is on the chaotic dress rehearsal where, with the non-appearance of the set, director and stage crew, things become increasingly frenetic. In his earlier *Cup Final* (1984) Mander takes a light-hearted look at the emotional recriminations among a company as they emerge into the dressing room following their performance of a well-known play at a drama festival.

In more serious mood, *Shop for Charity* (1984) poses the question as to whether charity workers are there to help the Third World or are just salving their middle-class consciences. Social morality is also questioned in *Sparrows* (1980) which is set close to a power station. *The River* (1979), located in the playwright's own Somerset, is a neat parable with themes covering the environment, pollution, and the pressures of modern human existence.

Other plays to consider: *The Deterrent; Fine Weather for Repentance; Getting Along; Monmouth*
Publishers: Samuel French

Wolf Mankowitz (1924–1998) British dramatist, novelist, and script-writer

Wolf Mankowitz said that he never considered himself to be a playwright, but a storyteller using whatever means the story seems to require. Thus his diversified output has included novels, short stories, screenplays, television plays and scripts for several musicals, including *Pickwick*, *Make me an Offer* and *Expresso Bongo*.

In the area of straight theatre drama, he enjoyed the greatest success with his one-act plays. These poignant, humorous and shrewd works are warm anecdotes of Jewish life. For instance the quintessential Mankowitz play, *The Bespoke Overcoat* (1953), a whimsical story of two old tailors, was written in the early '50s and has since been become a minor classic. *The Hebrew Lesson*

(1976) began life as a screenplay but later became a one-act play being staged in London and New York in the late '70s. The play is set in Ireland in 1921 during The Troubles where a young man seeks help from an ageing Jew to escape from the Black-and-Tans.

A book of five of his one-act plays has been published, the best known being *The Last of The Cheesecake* (1956), a bitter little marital comedy, *It Shouldn't Happen to a Dog* (1955), a re-working of the Old Testament story of Jonah and the Whale, and *The Baby* (1955), an adaptation of a work by Chekhov.

Other plays to consider: *The Mighty Hunter*
Publishers: Samuel French

Jean McConnell (1928–) British dramatist, script-writer, actress and journalist

A one-time professional actress, Jean McConnell started writing plays in the 1950s, since when she has produced numerous scripts for radio and television. However, her first love is for live theatre and, although she has enjoyed success with her full-length plays, she has carved out a particular niche with her popular short plays for women

Under the overall running title of *Deckchairs*, which now runs into three volumes (1995–2001) she has written 11 warm, appealing plays which are often seen on the drama festival circuit. Simple to stage (as the only essential demand is a couple of deckchairs) they afford excellent opportunities for characterisation. In tone and style they range from serious human drama such as *The Guilt Card* to the broad seaside-postcard humour of *Day Trippers*. The settings vary: in the comedy *Cruise Missile* the deckchairs are on an ocean liner, while the drama *The Last Post* is set in a country garden. With an end-of-the-pier background *Theatrical Digs* is a farcical battle of wills between two actresses.

There is often a strong sense of comedy running through much of her work – such as in *A Lovesome Thing* (1994) and *Blush Pink* (1968); however she has also written period dramas such as *The Red Cloak* (1955), set at the time of the French Revolution, and *Wine in a Venetian Goblet* (1968) in the era of the Borgias.

Although all the plays mentioned above have female casts, Jean McConnell has written several scripts for mixed companies, a good example being *Ripe For Conversion* (1975), a drama set against the French Resistance movement. Having debuted most of her scripts with a company in festivals in Kent and Surrey, she says that drama festivals are an important life-blood for new short plays.

Other plays to consider: *Haul for the Shore; Look out for the Catch; A Memory of Frank Danby; Millie's Tale*
Publishers: Samuel French; Kenyon-Deane; English Theatre Guild

Frank McGuinness (1953–) Irish dramatist

Donegal-born Frank McGuinness has won considerable praise for his sensitive full-length plays, particularly the hostage-drama *Someone Who'll Watch Over Me*, and the success of these has overshadowed the merit of his one-act scripts. Three of these shorter plays – *Bride of the Bag Lady, Flesh and Blood* and *Feed the Money and Keep Them Coming* (1998) – were collected under the umbrella title *Times In It*. He has also written several adaptations of short European plays, notably Strindberg's *The Stronger* (2002) and Pirandello's *The Man with a Flower in his Mouth*.

Publishers: Samuel French

James McLure (1953–) American dramatist

One time actor, James McLure made his mark as a playwright in the late '70s with several one-act plays set in his native deep south of America.

Lone Star (1979) refers not just to Texas, the Lone Star state, or the beer of that name which features heavily in the script, but most importantly to Roy, the Vietnam veteran who feels he has come back home as a star. While the text contains much ribald comedy, it is always rooted in truth, with touching moments of emotion which has made this script the writer's best-known short play. The cast of *Lone Star* comprises Roy, his brother Ray, and an old school friend. In his next play, *Laundry and Bourbon* (1980), McLure focuses on the three women in their lives. Once again, on the surface light-hearted banter prevails but underneath there is a strong undercurrent of disappointment and yearning. In both plays, which have proved hugely popular on both sides of the Atlantic, a sense of place and mood are essential.

In *PVT Wars* (1979) the characters are, once again, three Vietnam veterans. Confined to hospital, each facing his own private war, they tease, torment, entertain, exasperate and, on occasions console each other. Told in a series of brief scenes these make up a satisfying mosaic which is funny, compassionate and honest – the qualities which epitomise McLure's writing.

Other plays to consider: *Ghost World*
Publishers: Weinberger; Dramatists Play Service

Terrence McNally (1939–) American dramatist

Terrence McNally hit the New York stage in 1964 with *And Things Go Bump in the Night*, a bold, outspoken script that had audience members leaping onstage and denouncing the author and his work as immoral. Since then he has emerged as one of the most respected contemporary playwrights, having written an eclectic list of plays which have ranged from searing mordant social comment to the book for such successful musicals as *The Rink* and *The Full Monty*.

His acclaimed output in full-length work has been equalled by his notable short plays which number well over 30. He has said that as he has aged he has become prolific and many of his scripts reflect an inner urgency. Fifteen of these plays have been collected in one volume which illustrate perfectly the range of his work. Sensitive, direct and, at times, funny, *Sweet Eros* (1968), one of his most provocative plays, explores the darkest recesses of the mind of a young man who enslaves a young girl. It was originally staged in a double bill with the satirical black comedy *Witness* (1968). Under the umbrella title *Apple Pie* (1969), he wrote three bitingly telling, yet amusing comments on American army life in the Vietnam period; *Tour, Next* and *Botticelli*.

Hope (1988), which was part of another trio of plays entitled *Faith, Hope and Charity* by different authors, concerns two young people who meet in Central Park to remember a friend who has killed himself after contracting HIV. As the title indicates this touching play ends with more than a touch of hope.

Several of McNally's plays such as *Andre's Mother* (1988) and *Street Talk* (1998) run for barely ten minutes, while some like *The Ritz* (1975) run for well over an hour. *Full Frontal Nudity* (2004) explores the power of perfection when set against the reality of human loss and yearning.

Other plays to consider: *Bringing It All Back Home; Cuba Si; Hidden Agendas; Last Gasps; Prelude and Liebestod; Street Talk; Whiskey; The Wibbly Wobbly Dance That Cleopatra Did*
Publishers: Dramatists Play Service; Smith & Kraus

Kathy Mead   British dramatist

For many years Kathy Mead has been writing plays for her own Essex-based company, culminating in her winning a national play-writing award in 2001 for *Reckoning*, an intriguing script which gradually reveals its theme of angst-ridden family dynamics: love, hate, unresolved feelings and retribution. The emotional whirlpool ends in a death but the author keeps the audience guessing as to where the blame lies.

Another award-winning play is *After the Child* (1995), a play concerned with the spiritual world as parents face up to the death of their daughter. In *The Common Bond*, a two-hander, a couple meet in a nursing home having both attempted suicide, but as their friendship grows their common bond gives them strength to face life afresh.

One of Kathy Mead's most popular works is *The Anderson* (1995) which is set in East End London where an unquenchable cockney spirit shines though a family trapped in their air-raid shelter following a blitz. By contrast *Line of Descent* is set in a German barn in 1944 where the atmosphere between two very different families builds in conflict, suspense and dramatic power.

There are several Kathy Mead plays suitable for young casts. *Arandoe's Room* may be set in a fairy-land of gnomes and pixies, but on a deeper level is an allegory about racial intolerance. With a gender-flexible cast, *Summer Vocation*

(2003) has global weather as its theme. Both these plays have opportunities for theatrical costuming.

Other plays to consider: *Any Other Tuesday; Consequences; Key to the Dark; The Other Other Woman; Standing Still*
Publishers: Garnet Miller; Kenyon-Deane

Leonard Melfi (1935–2001) American dramatist

Leonard Melfi said, 'My plays are about my fellow human beings in and out of trouble, like all of us at various times – in other words celebrating the miracle and mystery of human life'.

He first came to the attention of American theatregoers with his short plays for Café La Mama, a birthplace for the off-off Broadway fringe in the late '60s, *Encounters* (1967) includes six of these early plays about uptight people looking for fulfilling styles of love. Probably the one which has enjoyed the greatest number of productions is *Birdbath* (1965), an off-beat encounter between an obsessive young man and a murderous young woman. By contrast the surreal fantasy *Times Square* (1966) is peopled by childlike dreamers inhabiting the seedy side of New York. Other encounters in this volume include *Ferryboat* (1965), *Lunchtime* (1966), *Halloween* (1967) and *The Shirt* (1967).

In most of those plays there is an affecting juxtaposition or violence and romance whereas ten years later the seven short plays collected under the title *Later Encounters* (1980) have a darker edge and a softer centre. For instance, although *Lena and Louie* freeze to death in Central Park there is a sense of optimism running through the play.

Leonard Melfi contributed *Night* (1968) to *Morning, Noon and Night* and *Charity* (1988) to *Faith, Hope and Charity*, two successful trios of related short plays by respected playwrights.

Other plays to consider: *Mr Tucker's Taxi; Rusty and Rico; Taffy's Taxi*
Publishers: Samuel French; Dramatists Play Service

George Middleton (1880–1967) American dramatist

George Middleton was an American author of one-act plays, who had several collections of such plays published in the period just before World War I. He was a serious student of the one-act form, and anxious to secure its (and his own) reputation with scholars and professional theatre managers.

He wrote in the days when curtain-raisers were still being performed on Broadway and his *Tradition* (about a daughter freeing herself from the cloying affection of her family and setting out on her own) was presented at the Berkeley Theater in New York in 1913. It was a small-cast piece, (three-handed, like many of his plays) with pretensions to literary merit, though at this distance in time, there is a stilted air of unreal formality about some of the language in the play.

Middleton's plays were mostly solemn studies 'of contemporary life' at the turn of the 19th and 20th centuries and set in a mix of American small-town and city domestic situations. *Waiting* was a sentimental piece in which a spinster schoolmarm and an orphan gradually move into a closer relationship; *Embers* was a skilful interpretation of American middle-age; *Madonna* was described by a critic of the time as 'an exquisite brief study of delicate maidenly modesty on the brink of marriage'.

Professor William Lyle Phelps (of Yale University, later to be on the Board of Judges for the Pulitzer Prize for Drama in the 1920s) was impressed by Middleton's plays and told him, 'The little dramas are full of cerebration, and I shall recommend them in my public lectures'.

Other plays to consider: *The Cheat of Pity*; *The Failures*; *The Gargoyle*; *In His House*; *The Man Masterful*; *Mothers*; *On Bail*; *Their Wife*
Publishers: Bell; Henry Holt

Arthur Miller (1915–2005) American dramatist

Arthur Miller was the dominant American playwright of the late 20th century, largely as a result of such monumental major works as *The Crucible* and *Death of A Salesman*. However, he began by writing short plays, several specifically for radio. *That They May Win* was published in *The Best One Act Plays of 1944* and 11 years later a double-bill of his plays opened on Broadway. Coupled with an interesting early one-act version of *A View from the Bridge* was *A Memory of Two Mondays* (1955), a reminiscence of his youth and his desire to break out of his mundane work life

He returned to the one-act form in the 1980s with two double bills. The cleverly titled *Two Way Mirror* (1982) includes the atmospheric *Elegy for a Lady*, which the author describes in his autobiography as 'a play of shadows under the tree of death; a play with multiple points of view.' It was originally produced with another two-hander *Some Kind of Love Story* an intriguing cat-and-mouse game between a detective and his old girl-friend.

His next double bill was entitled *Danger: Memory* (1987) which affords some fine roles for older actors. *I Can't Remember Anything* is a poignant study of enduring friendship and the loss of memory while *Clara* concerns a father who gradually opens up disturbing events which have been locked away in the deep recesses of his mind to hide the pain.

Emotional pressure is also a theme of *The Last Yankee* (1991) which explores the relationship of two couples and their attitude to mental breakdown. This sad, yet heart-warming play is often presented without an interval when it runs for just over an hour. Another 'short' full-length play which runs without a break is *Mr Peter's Connections* (1998), a lyrical script in which the ageing central character, in a state of semi-consciousness, looks back over his life with images and characters mingling in a strangely affecting way. Some commentators feel that this is a highly personal play from a playwright who wrote the reflective script when he was well into his 80s.

Publishers: Methuen; Dramatists Play Service; Weinberger

Jason Milligan (1961–) American dramatist and script-writer

American author Jason Milligan has written many one-act plays and numerous monologues as well as scripts for musicals, television and films. Five of his short plays have been collected under the title *New York Stories* (1991) which can be played independently or as a complete evening on various aspects of life in the Big Apple. The wild farce *The Best Warm Beer in Brooklyn* concerns two old friends reunited in a late-night bar while *John's Ring* has three young women fighting over the ring given to them by John Lennon. *Shoes* develops into a searing, yet touching, conflict between two brothers over how to help an enigmatic shoeless stranger. The other plays in this quintet are *Next Tuesday*, a duologue between a prisoner and a church visitor and *Nights in Hohokus*, a funny and poignant look at what happens to friendship when one party grows up and moves on.

The Prettiest Girl in Lafayette (1987), which has proved popular with college groups, is a light comedy in contrast to the tense drama *Instincts* (1990), another two-hander set in a prison cell. *Can't Buy Me Love*, a play for three teenage girls, is part of a collection of five of Milligan's scripts entitled *Southern Exposure* (1990) which includes *Lullaby*, *Spit in Yazoo City* and *Willy Wallace Chats With The Kids*.

Other plays to consider: *Clara and the Gambler*; *Class of '77*; *The Genuine Article*; *Getting Even*; *Juris Prudence*; *Less Said the Better*; *Life After Elvis*; *Lullaby*; *Money Talks*; *Next*; *The Quality of Boiled Water*; *Rivals*; *Road Trip*; *Shore Leave*; *Strange As It Might Seem*; *Waiting for Ringo*
Publishers: Samuel French

AA Milne (1882–1956) English dramatist

The writer of the Winnie the Pooh stories was also an accomplished dramatist and produced a considerable number of full-length pieces as well as some shorter plays. Most of Milne's one-acters were in light vein, but they include a gentle large-cast fantasy about Noah (and notably) Mrs Noah and the Ark (*Before the Flood*, 1951). *Wurzel Flummery* (1922), in which two self-important MPs are challenged to change their name to win a legacy, had a vogue with amateur societies in the 1930s and 1940s though, like some other of Milne's pieces, its humour now looks insubstantial.

Perhaps his most interesting one-act play, however, is *The Man in the Bowler Hat* (1923), which appears to be a light domestic comedy apart from the mysterious presence of a man reading a newspaper in the corner of the room throughout the action. There are shades of the Monty Python comedic style here 50 years before it was seen on television.

The light humour and satire of *The Ugly Ducking* (1941) is typical of Milne's frequent excursions into fairy-tale worlds in his stories and plays. The supposedly unlovely Princess Camilla is quite secure in her own radiance and successfully negotiates a true-love marriage to the surprise of her scheming parents.

Other plays to consider: *The Boy Comes Home*; *The Camberley Triangle*; *Miss Marlow at Play*; *Stepmother*

Publishers: Samuel French

Anthony Minghella (1954–) English dramatist and film director

Though best known nowadays as a distinguished film writer and director (*Truly, Madly, Deeply* and *The English Patient*) Minghella lectured in Drama at Hull University for a time and wrote several full-length stage plays.

Some of his earlier work for TV and radio also adapts well to the stage in short-play form. Notably, *Cigarettes and Chocolate* (originally a radio play which won the Giles Cooper Award in 1989), provides demanding acting opportunities for a large cast, as well as being sprinkled with comedy. Gemma, a young 20-something, decides that she will give up speaking for Lent (last year it was cigarettes, the year before chocolate) and play the St Matthew Passion on her CD player in her London flat instead. This is to the consternation and bewilderment of her friends and relations, who, in seeking to solve her apparent 'problem' reveal their own insecurities and agonies. The play proceeds largely in telephone calls to Gemma, unanswered by her, and ends with three revealing long monologues. Gemma, musing on the Tower of Babel, decides, 'It's words that are the punishment'.

Other plays to consider: *Days Like These*; *Hang Up*; *Mosaic*

Publishers: Faber and Faber

* Yukio Mishima (1925–1970) Japanese dramatist, novelist and poet

Yukio Mishima's iconic fame has spread far beyond his native Japan; in the '50s and '60s he enjoyed an almost cult following both in Europe and America. He was nominated for the Nobel Prize for Literature on three occasions. In 1970 his notoriety was heightened by his spectacular public suicide by ritual disembowelment.

He had produced a fascinating collection of short modern Noh plays. The traditional Japanese Noh and Kabuki plays afford a rich source of highly theatrical and stylised drama. Various collections of these remarkable plays are in print and are worth seeking out by those adventurous societies looking for striking, colourful and unusual theatre. The most popular of Mishima's is *Lady Aoi* (1963). There is a naturalistic opening to this enigmatic script, but the piece develops simmering undercurrents and presents some strong opportunities for theatrical imagery.

The short plays *The Damask Drum* and *Sotoba Komachi* played in a double-bill in London in 2004

Publisher: Samuel French; Penguin

Ferenc Molnar (1878–1952) Hungarian dramatist, novelist and director

Probably best known for his full-length play, *Liliom*, which provided the basis for the American musical *Carousel*, Molnar was even better known in his native Hungary as a novelist. However, he wrote more than 40 dramatic works including one-act pieces – often with a theatre backdrop.

Theatre (1921) is a trio of sardonic comedies portraying adulterous thespians and deals with the conflicts between illusion and reality; the individual titles are *The Violet, Marshall* and *A Prologue to King Lear.*

Shortly before the Second World War Molnar emigrated to New York, later becoming an American citizen. In *The President* (1952) he satirises the speed of American business as a humble taxi-driver is transformed by a desperate banker into a high-powered executive and a nobleman. The play later appeared in a film version directed by Billy Wilder entitled *One Two Three. Anniversary Dinner* is a comedy with a culinary theme.

Other plays to consider: *Actor from Vienna*; *Still Life*; *The Witch*
Publisher: Vanguard Press (NY); Weinberger

Allan Monkhouse (1858–1936) English dramatist

One of the 'Manchester School' of playwrights along with Houghton and Brighouse (q.v) , Allan Monkhouse was amongst those who brought new realism to sketches of Northern English working-class life at the start of the twentieth-century. He left the cotton-business to become a member of the staff of *The Manchester Guardian* in 1902 and for thirty years wrote drama and literary criticism for them, as well as producing a stream of novels and plays. He mixed the writing of full-length and one-act plays.

His first one-acter *Reaping the Whirlwind* (1908) was one of the first productions at Annie Horniman's Gaiety Theatre in Manchester. One of his most famous one-acts is *Night Watches* which is a comedy set in a hospital ward. *Mary Broome*, a more serious play, deals with a forced marriage of a housemaid to the son of the household and trenchantly raises issues about class and the status of women in the years before World War I.

Other plays to consider: *The Choice*; *The Grand Cham's Diamond*; *The King of Barvender*; *Nothing Like Leather*; *O Death Where is thy Sting*
Publishers: Samuel French

Leonard Morley Welsh dramatist

Several of Morley's short plays have won awards from the Drama Association of Wales. *The Harpy and the Slob* has an original take on a rugby club party (the girl Richard takes to the bedroom is in the process at work of obstructing his insurance claim) and won the 1978 HTV Award for High Comedy.

Hell and High Water also has a highly original premise; the Manor is gradually being flooded and Lord Charles and his family and retainers are sloshing about in Wellington boots and waders as they eat dinner, though the audience have to imagine the rising water-level. *Hell and Damnation*, the sequel, sees Lord Charles in a battle with the tax inspectors. *Looking for Rosy* is a zany piece about a dysfunctional household in which forgers, rent officials, and a disparate family collide.

Other plays to consider: *Sit Vac; The Suitor; Uncle Jasper*
Publishers: Cressrelles; New Playwrights Network

TB Morris (1905–1986) English dramatist and novelist (see also under Yves Cabrol)

Thomas Baden Morris vies with Philip Johnson and David Campton as being the most prolific one-act playwright published in the twentieth century. He had over one hundred one-act plays published between the 1930s and the 1970s. They ranged from an ambitious large-cast play written in verse and performed in the ruins of the old Coventry Cathedral in 1944 (*I will arise*) to a series of 'shorter' plays published with schools and youth groups in mind and books of monologues and sketches.

Morris's main audience was the amateur theatre group and he showed an extraordinary versatility in varying theme and content. One of his early successes (*Everybody Comes to Mabel*) was a light-weight amusing domestic trifle, but he also wrote many vivid historical pieces (*Carnival of Steel*, 1942 – set in 1572; *Oranges and Lemons*, 1939 – about King Charles II's secret love for Frances Stewart, Duchess of Richmond; *Tutankamun, Son of Ra*, 1953; *Isabella – Friend of Columbus*, 1952; *Rain in Majorca*, 1948 – about Chopin and George Sand and plays with religious themes (*The Fields of Bethlehem; Man in a Street*, 1940; *Night on the Hill*, 1943; *The Light is Darkness*, 1952).

Most of Morris's pieces are distinguished by their excellent craftsmanship and varied characterisation. He wrote a considerable number of meaty plays for all-women casts including, *Mirror to Elizabeth; Check to the Queen; Elizabeth in Love* (all about Elizabeth I); *Not as a Gift*, 1958 (a comedy about art); *Mountain Paths are Stony* (set in 19th century Italy); *Ophelia*, 1948 (an imagined extra scene to *Hamlet*); *Progress to Fotheringay*, 1941 and the thriller *When the Leaves Drift*. Many of his plays proved to be of winning potential in the hey-day of the amateur festival and though they have drifted out of print in the later years of the twentieth century, some are certainly worth recovery and revival.

Other plays to consider: *Adventure at Midnight; Aurora Smith; Background for Tragedy; Battered Halo; Cassandra; The Cats of Egypt; Cloud Over the Morning; The Crooked Tree; Dark Betrothal; Deserted Knight; Druid's Ring; Even this Evening; Gossip's Glory; Island of Sirens; The Little Nut-Tree; Mademoiselle Departs; Mine Enemy my Friend; Nine Days; No Coffee for One;*

Pawn to Move; Petticoats Preferred; Prison Across the Street; The Red Cap; The Red Herrings; Renaissance Night; The Scarlet Pest; Shall we Leave the Gentlemen?; The Spanish Lady; Spanish Rhapsody; Squaring the Circle; Stratford Boy; Swan Song; The Tail of Fire; They Made her Wild; This State of Life; The Trial of Helen; Tudor Thorns; Turn Right for Ponte Vecchia; Two Aunts and a Grandmother; The Two Turtles; Unto Which it Shall Please God; The Vagabond; Very New Order; The Voice of the People; Waiting for Margot; When Queens were Pawns; White Queen Red Queen; Wild for to Hold; The Woman; Women are Wonderful; Women on the Warpath
Publishers: Samuel French; Deane

John Mortimer (1923–) British dramatist and novelist

Dramatist, novelist, barrister and journalist, John Mortimer has said, 'Comedy is the only thing worth writing in this despairing age, providing the comedy is on the side of the lonely, the neglected, the unsuccessful'. So he writes from a liberal standpoint and always defends the vulnerable against the inhuman establishment.

Most of his short plays were written in the '60s and '70s and often have themes related to marriage, infidelity or the law, reflecting the author's background as a barrister. His first success was *The Dock Brief* (1957), a play which has often been revived decades after its first production. Some plays such as *Lunch Hour* (1960) and *I Spy* (1959) probably need to be played as period pieces simply because attitudes to sexual relationships have changed so dramatically since the plays were first written. Law and marriage are again intertwined in *Edwin* (1984) which, like several of his short plays, was first broadcast and subsequently adapted for the stage.

In 1970 John Mortimer wrote a series of short plays under the umbrella title *Come As You Are* – each named after a London district. Of these *Marble Arch*, *Knightsbridge* and *Bermondsey* are still often performed.

Other plays to consider: *Collect Your Hand Baggage; Desmond; Gloucester Road; Mill Hill; What Shall We Tell Caroline?*
Publishers: Samuel French

JM Morton English dramatist

Morton's place in the history of the one-act play rests almost entirely on the writing of one early farce *Box and Cox*, which many regard as the first 'theatre' one-act play in Britain. First produced in 1847 it portrayed the amorous adventures of two lodgers who unknowingly share the same lodgings (one is on night-shift work), fall in love with the same girl and then want to escape the entanglement. They are relived when the word comes that she has eloped with a Mr Knox. The plays is occasionally revived as a historical curiosity on both sides of the Atlantic and on most occasions the comedy of classic situational farce still works.

Publishers: Bakers Plays; Samuel French

Ros Moruzzi English dramatist

Accompanying her success with a collection of short monologues and sketches about life from cradle to grave, Ros Moruzzi has produced a number of plays (both full-length and one-act) which deal with twenty-first century issues and preoccupations.

Our James is a black comedy about a woman who discovers she is a test-tube baby. As she sets out to find her father's identity, the possibilities become more and more alarming. In the all-women *Park Hotel* two elderly bag ladies are met by a couple of socialites; a funny and moral tale about ambition and attitudes towards the less fortunate. *Skin* delves into the world of cosmetic surgery with a darkly comic plot involving a doctor, his scheming receptionist, his cleaner, and some of their strange customers.

Publishers: Deane

Cedric Mount English dramatist

Cedric Mount's short plays were often produced by amateur companies in the 1930s, and in particular his *Twentieth Century Lullaby* was often quoted as an example of 'experimental form'. It opens with a mother cooing over a cradle, daydreaming of a great future for her son. Representative figures – schoolmaster, clergyman, bride, businessman and politician – appear to show what might (or will?) happen to the boy. Then the Virgin Mary appears in a final reassuring vision to trump and question these earlier projections of the future and give hope to the mother's dreams.

Dirge without Dole (1937) is also 'experimental' in three scenes: first a group of players are seen presenting a play, then an adjudicator picks it apart and then the cast are seen picking both play and judgement apart in the dressing-room. *Jonah* is a delightful satire on the Biblical tale, with Jonah escaping from the whale only to decide to return to Nineveh in the face of his wife's repeated hectoring. By contrast, *Such Sweet Sorrow* is a strong drama about a woman in a totalitarian state sacrificing her chance of escape so that the man she loves can escape with his wife

Publishers: Samuel French

Edward Murch (1920–) English dramatist

Murch has lived in Devon, England for most of his life and published many of his own plays from there. His outstanding one-act success has been *No Name in the Street*, a play first presented in 1966, but given literally thousands of stage performances since then. It has been featured on radio and television in both Britain and USA. The play is set in and around Jerusalem during the events surrounding the crucifixion of Jesus Christ, and combines rhythmic poetic passages with sharp, taut and emotionally-charged dialogue. A major female character whom one might suppose to be Mary, the mother of Jesus, turns out in the end to be the mother of Judas Iscariot, and concludes the play with a dramatic and direct appeal to the audience which includes the chilling line, 'All you who are gathered here: is there not some of Judas in your hearts?' It can be played in a simple setting in church or hall, allows a cast of single or mixed-sex and can vary between eight and 14 players.

Murch has written other one-act plays on religious and Biblical topics, including several which explore Christmas or Easter themes sensitively. One of the strengths of Murch's work is that most of his plays can be flexibly cast (in gender and number) and simply staged, and many of have won high praise from drama festival adjudicators. He has written 'an improbable history' about Shakespeare, *The Relapse*, and a number of comedies (mostly historical), some based around the figure of Captain Savage, a figure from Napoleonic times.

Other plays to consider: *The Beggars of Bordeaux*; *Bethlehem Boy*; *Caroline*; *The Dipper*; *Five Minutes from the Sea*; *The Journey of the Star*; *The Last Blue Mountain*; *Morning Noon and Night*; *On the Hill*; *The Parting Shot*; *The Poet of Goosey Fair*; *The Revival*; *Saint Germaine*; *Spring Flowers for Marguerite*; *Tell it to the Wind*; *The Thin Red Line*; *Things that Go Bump*; *Wits End*
Publishers: Kenyon-Deane; Samuel French; Yennadon

John H Newmeir English dramatist

Able to test out the viability of his material by performance with his own drama group based in the eastern suburbs of London, John H Newmeir has written a number of one-act plays which have proved popular on the festival circuit in recent years.

Babysitting Calvin has a clever twist, with an adult actor playing the baby Calvin and doing his best to thwart the unwelcome attentions of the babysitter's over-amorous admirer. The piece won the New Play Award of the National Drama Festivals Association in 1998. *Semblance of Truth* is an intriguing piece in which we are never sure till near the end if the nurses in a mental hospital are the real thing or inmates cleverly impersonating their carers in order to extract a confession from a fellow-patient.

Other plays to consider: *At Last the Day*; *Contrary to Beliefs*; *Festival Rites*; *Simply the Best*
Publishers: Samuel French; New Playwrights Network

Josephina Niggli (1910–83) Mexican-American dramatist and novelist

Niggli was a Mexican-born American playwright some of whose plays were based on Mexican folk tales, written in 1936 whilst still studying for her Masters Degree at the University of North Carolina under Paul Eliot Green (q.v.). Some of this work was premiered by the Carolina Playmakers. These plays were derived from folk-tales and presented in what Niggli called 'saenetes', a form of play from the Spanish theatre in which the lives of the 'lower' and rural classes are depicted with affection and humour.

The plays were later published in collected form and two were taken up and republished by Samuel French. These have proved very durable and performable pieces in the amateur theatre over many years. *Sunday Costs Five Pesos* is a sharp and witty comedy in which the eager young wood-carver Fidel is strung along by his girl friend Bertha and her companions. *The Red Velvet Goat* features the experience of Esteban as he tries to present a play in the market-place. Later one-act plays of hers featured episodes of Mexican history stretching between the period before the Spanish conquistadors came (*Azteca*) and the revolution of 1910 (*Soladadera, This is Villa*).

Niggli went on to become a member of the staff of UNC's Drama Department as well as a highly-regarded novelist who portrayed Mexican life in her books. She had a period as Visiting Professor at Bristol University, England, to teach playwriting in 1955–56. She published a number of books about the craft of writing plays and was a polished and effective exponent of the one-act form.

Other plays to consider: *The Cry of Dolores; The Fair God; Miracle at Blaise; The Ring of General Macias; This Bull Ate Nutmeg; Tooth or Shave*
Publishers: Samuel French; Arnold

Don Nigro American dramatist

Don Nigro is considered the most published contemporary American playwright with more than 200 scripts to his credit. These range from major historical plays to popular collections of telling monologues, but also include numerous one-act plays in a variety of mood and themes.

He was born in the country in Ohio where he grew up, later teaching the art of playwriting at Ohio State University. One of his best known short plays is *Scarecrow* (1979), a compelling erotic gothic tale set on a remote farm where a young girl discovers lust and sexuality in the form of a stranger out in the cornfield. It appears in a volume of the writer's short plays which also includes a couple of two-handers *Something in the Basement* (1979) and *Lurker* (1979).

In *Spectre* a man crashes his car in an attempt to avoid hitting a woman. Their subsequent conversation veers from love to hatred as they play out a riveting series of malicious mind and power games. *Wonders of the Invisible World Revealed*, which has a nod to HG Wells, is a dark, fascinating, heartbreaking love story exploring the many meanings of invisibility.

Different views of desire are explored in many of his plays. *Fair Rosamund and her Murderer* is set in medieval England and paints a ghostly and lyrical portrait of tragic love in the court of Henry II. The setting for *Necropolis* is a Middle Eastern war-torn country where an American has a one-night stand with a female sniper. Eventually their affair becomes a plaintive plea for human connection. *The Sin Eater* has a Welsh location and combines passion with humour while *Palestrina*, another two-hander, is set on the porch of a house back in the writer's home state.

Other plays to consider: *The Ballerinas*; *Bible*; *The Bohemian Girl*; *Crossing the Bar*; *Deflores*; *Demonology*; *The Devil*; *The Daughter of Edward D Bolt*; *Gogol*; *The Green Man*; *Heironymus Bosch*; *Malefactor's Bloody Register*; *McNaughton's Dowry*; *Netherlands*; *Ragnorak*
Publishers: Samuel French

Eugene O'Neill (1888–1953) American dramatist

O'Neill is widely regarded as one of the major American playwrights of the 20th century, though for the most part he stood, as one critic put it, 'stonily unreconciled to society in a land of plenty and promise'. His major full-length plays are often of epic proportions, dealing seriously with metaphysical themes, but his early work was almost exclusively in the one-act sphere and he wrote a score of short plays between 1912 and 1920. He had the benefit of having his writing tried out in performance by the Provincetown Players, who began in a small converted shed on a Cape Cod wharf, before moving to New York to play successful seasons there.

O'Neill's own experiences as a young seaman led to a series of plays set on board ship or in dockside locations and the British tramp steamer *Glencairn* frequently appears as a context for his plays. Of these *Bound East for Cardiff* (1913), *Ile* (1916), and *Moon of the Caribbees* (1916) are among the most actable, powerfully dealing with the drama and emotions of sea-going life. The plays have mostly male characters but not exclusively so. In 1924, O'Neill adapted Coleridge's poem *The Ancient Mariner* for the stage, with performers acting in total or partial silhouette.

Other plays to consider: *Abortion*; *Before Breakfast*; *The Dreamy Kid*; *The Emperor Jones*; *Fog*; *Exorcism*; *Hughie*; *In The Zone*; *The Long Voyage Home*; *The Movie Man*; *Recklessness*; *The Rope*; *Shellshock*; *The Sniper*; *Thirst*; *Warnings*; *The Web*; *A Wife for a Life*; *Where the Cross is Made*
Publishers: Samuel French

Rene de Obaldia (1918–) French dramatist, novelist and poet

A light-hearted surrealism characterises many of de Obaldia's plays. He is often considered a playwright in the tradition of the 'Theatre of the Absurd', but his plays usually avoid pessimism and are laced with an imaginative wit even if situations become far-fetched. De Obaldia was born in Hong Kong, but educated in Paris, where he has continued to live for most of his life, producing a stream of plays, novels and poems.

Donald Watson translated most of his theatre work into English and these include *Seven Impromptus for Leisure* (short plays) in Volume 1 of *Plays*. These include *Cayenne Pepper, Edward and Agrippina, The Grand Vizier, The Hangman's Sacrifice, The Late, Nitrogen, The Twinkling Twins*.

The Babysitter, written in 1971, might be considered a fair example of his one-act work. A couple are anxiously waiting for their babysitter to arrive so that they can go out to dinner. An enthusiastic young female Salvation Army member arrives on the doorstep, is inveigled in as a deputy, but then begins a fervent evangelistic campaign on the couple. As a result the couple never get to their dinner, the Salvationist appears to pull a gun on them and there is a wild, improbable apocalyptic climax to the evening.

Other plays to consider: *The Jellyfish's Banquet*; *The Unknown General*; *Wide Open Spaces*; *Two for One Ghost*
Publishers: Calder and Boyars

Clifford Odets (1906–1963) American dramatist

Born in Philadelphia to a poor working-class Jewish family, Clifford Odets later moved to New York where he became a founder member of the radical Group Theater. Here, in 1935, he shot to fame with the short play *Waiting for Lefty*. Told in eight episodes, the play is set against the background of the city taxi strike and that gritty first production spoke in a new urban voice and took the critics by storm. Suddenly this writer seemed to have found the quintessential language of America in the thirties, and a succession of full-length plays followed, notably *The Golden Boy* and *Awake and Sing*. Fame meant Odets was later lured, against his better wishes, to Hollywood where he wrote screenplays (e.g. *The Sweet Smell of Success*) and became a film director (*None But the Lonely Heart*).

However, he is still best remembered for his plays from the '30s and notably for the still-relevant, instantly successful, left-wing, hard-hitting, drama *Waiting for Lefty*. In the original production the play was paired with another of his short scripts, *Till the Day I Die* (1935), an anti-Nazi play set in Germany with themes of betrayal, torture and suicide.

Publishers: Dramatists Play Service

* Michael Olsen (1966–) Australian dramatist

Michael Olsen has won awards and considerable acclaim for his one-act plays, both those written for adults and those for young audiences. Undoubtedly his most popular short play is the dark comedy, *Two Women and a Chair* (2001), which has been presented in many countries. In 2004 it appeared at the Edinburgh Festival. Simple to stage – the only essential item being a impressive chair – this intriguing play has themes of image and personality change as the two women face up to what lies behind an unseen mirror. The very black comedy *Double Tap* (2000) takes a journey through the darker side of human nature veering from grimness to hilarity.

Other plays to consider: *Floating*
Publishers: Maverick Musicals

For other references to Australian short plays see the entry under Michael Gow

Joe Orton (1933 – 1967) British dramatist

Like a flamboyant firecracker, Joe Orton hit the London stage in the mid-'60s, making audiences laugh at such hitherto taboo subjects as sodomy, casual murder, nymphomania, sexual licence, religion, and the police. And all this was carried out in his own unique elegant style; indeed, he was once famously described as 'the Oscar Wilde of the Welfare State'. His special anarchic mix of comedy, sex and violence was mirrored in his own life which was tragically brought to an early end when he was bludgeoned to death by his lover in 1967.

Although it was thought that Orton wrote no short plays for the theatre all four of his radio and television plays have been adapted for the stage and run for less than hour. His first play *Ruffian on the Stair* (1966), written for radio and showing a distant echo of Pinter, is the easiest to stage. But *The Erpingham Camp* (1967) and *The Good and Faithful Servant* (1971) – both originally televised – are more substantial pieces demanding a larger cast, an imaginative director and an inventive stage designer. Both quintessentially Orton they are very challenging pieces but well worth answering those heavy demands. Completing the quartet of Orton short plays is *Funeral Games* (1970), an intermittently witty, stylish satire allowing the playwright to throw wickedly pointed barbs at one of his major targets – religion.

In the late '90s two very early one-act plays were discovered: *Fred and Madge* and *The Visitors* show flashes of that special style which later became widely known as 'Ortonesque'. Of course the impact of his acerbic assault on the society of the mid-'60s has lessened over the intervening decades, but Orton remains a unique and important theatrical voice.

Publishers: Methuen; Samuel French; Nick Hern Books

Mary Pakington (1878–1956) English dramatist

Within a long career of writing for the amateur theatre, the Honourable Mary Pakington covered the ground from published sketches for Scout and Guide entertainments (she was a life-long supporter of the Baden-Powell movements) to several dramatic one-act plays.

Her best-known (and most frequently performed) one-act play is *The House with Twisty Windows* (1926), which deals with events surrounding the Bolshevik Revolution. It tells the story of the travails and eventual escape of British subjects held in a gloomy cellar, during the 'Red Terror'. She wrote several other historical pieces, including *The Black Horseman* (1929; set in 1785 and about a mysterious visitor to a Quaker household who is at first taken for the Devil). *The King's Servant* (1938; set in the Stuart Period and featuring the clash between Charles I and the Scottish kirk) and *All Camouflage* (1931; a Great War episode).

Experiment (1932), reproduced in the BDL Prize Plays volume of that year, was a rare venture away from her usual naturalistic style, and in World War II she wrote several light comedies: *The First Shift* (1941) about an ARP post, *Knitters of the Deep* (1941) about life on the Home Front.

Other plays to consider: *Blow, Bugle, Blow!*; *Cats and Kittens*; *A Doctor's Engagements*; *The Little Schoolmaster*; *Nil Medium*; *Nowell*; *Poet's Corner*; *The Polar Post*; *Ready!*; *The Queen of Hearts*; *The Scarlet Mantle*; *Tear up the Joker*; *Time and Mrs Podbury*; *The Valley of a Dream*
Publishers: Samuel French

* Dorothy Parker (1893–1967) American dramatist and writer

Though better known in the theatre for her acidic and epigrammatic reviews for *Vanity Fair* and *The New Yorker* Dorothy Parker occasionally ventured into the writing of plays such as *Ladies of the Corridor* and *The Coast of Illyria*.

The style and structure of some of her published short-stories also represent likely material for adaptation to the stage as one-act plays or sketches. They are often extended conversations or vignettes of a particular scene. In *Here We Are*, already adapted and published as a one-act play script, a young couple nervously exchange conversation about everything except the forthcoming consummation of their marriage, as the train takes them on to their honeymoon hotel.
Publishers: Viking Press

John Patrick (1905–1995) American dramatist, scriptwriter

Prolific writer of radio, film and play scripts, John Patrick found that the highlight of his writing career was his 1954 Pulitzer Prize-winning, *The Teahouse of the August Moon* but he also wrote numerous one-act scripts. These were often loosely linked into triple bills: *The Gift*, *The Divorce*, and *Co-incidence*, three canine comedies, were presented under the title *It's a Dog's Life* (1984). Another trio revealing amorous events in New York apartments include *Strategy*, *Decision*, and *Progression* which were presented under the title *Love Nest For Three* (1974). *People* (1976) includes the comedies *Christmas Spirit*, *Boredom* and *Aptitude*.

Other plays to consider: *Fettucini*; *Masquerade*; *Raconteur*: three plays presented under the title *That's not my Father*
Publishers: Samuel French

Robert Patrick (1937–) American dramatist, director

It has been claimed that Robert Patrick was New York's most performed playwright of the '60s; whether this is true is open to doubt, but what is certain is that his remarkable play *Kennedy's Children* (1973) captured brilliantly the mood and essence of that great decade. Told through five monologues the play is often played without an interval.

The range and style of Robert Patrick's work is extremely varied. Popular for many years in high schools, *Camera Obscura* (1977) is a piece of science fiction while *The Arnold Bliss Show* (1969) is a slick New York farce. *One Man, One Woman* (1978) comprises six playlets on human relationships, one of which – *Something Else* – was nominated for a special Obie Award. *Light, Camera, Action* (1966) is a triptych of mini-plays which can be presented separately or as a complete evening's entertainment. A two-hander for women, *My Cup Ranneth Over* (1978), a perceptive and ironically humorous play, has been very widely performed.

Other plays to consider: *Cornered*; *Help I Am*
Publishers: Samuel French

L du Garde Peach (1890–1976) English dramatist

L du Garde Peach's one-act plays were a mainstay of the fare offered by small drama groups in England in the 1930s and '40s. They were well-crafted pieces, often based on historical documentary evidence, and always within the acting compass of inexperienced players. They were frequently developed from radio scripts and thus usually relatively brief.

Peach learnt his trade as a short-play writer through many years of providing scripts for schools broadcasts in the 1930s and 1940s, and some of these were later published as volumes of short plays. Later, he bought a house in the Peak District and turned the adjoining barn into a theatre. For some years, the Great Hucklow Playhouse was a mecca for drama enthusiasts and Peach enjoyed presenting high-quality amateur entertainment there.

Amongst his best-known plays are those with historical contexts such as *The Six Wives of Calais* (1945), *Four Queens Wait for Henry*, *The Queen's Ring* (1947) (set in the Palace Apartments in 1601), *An Improbable Episode* (1947; about King Alfred burning the cakes) and *The Saxon Wives of Ellandune*. *It Won't be a Stylish Marriage* (1946) amusingly brings the *Daisy, Daisy* lyric to life as a late Victorian comedy.

Peach also knew the interests and background of his likely customers and wrote several comedies set in village halls or committee-rooms (e.g. *Christmas and Mrs Hooper*, 1961; *All in Favour*, 1948) and about light-hearted domestic episodes (*Loser Takes All, Stung*).

The Last of Corporal Micklass (1945) was one of his best one-act plays, a foray into the starkly dramatic, set in a cottage in an occupied country, and with high drama and tension as 'freedom fighters' cleverly turn the tables on a pair of soldiers from the occupying power.

Other plays to consider: *African Angle; An Arrest is Expected; At the Golden Ram; The Cohort Marches; Criminal Introduction; Cross Calling; Cross Roads; The Liar; Light and Shade; A Matter of Course; A Night of Horror; The Parting; The Perfect Alibi; Princess Parker; Reggie Makes a Complaint; Seventy-Three North; Shells; Smugglers Cove; The Story of Ruth; Stranger; 3C; The Tribulations of Wing Lu; Underground; Wave Lengths; While Shepherds Watch; Win or Lose*
Publishers: Samuel French

Jimmy Perry (1924–) English dramatist and writer

Perry was the originator of one of the greatest British TV series of all-time, the much-loved *Dad's Army*, which chronicles the exploits of a motley group of volunteers who make up the Walmington-on-Sea Home Guard, called on to man the defences of the South Coast against the threat of invasion in the early years of World War II. Besides being turned into a full-length play, the original 30-minute episodes of *Dad's Army* (written with David Croft) are available in script form and may prove attractive to a company who wants the challenge of adapting them to the stage in order to have their audiences joyously recognise favourite jokes and situations.

Three of the episodes – *The Deadly Attachment, The Godiva Affair, Mum's Army* – have already been specifically rewritten for the stage, with the latter having a generous number of female parts to supplement the male stalwarts known to millions.
Publishers: Samuel French; Methuen

Arthur Wing Pinero (1855–1934) British dramatist

Highly regarded by late-Victorian England theatregoers – notably for his farces such as *Dandy Dick* and *The Magistrate*; and dramas such as *The Second Mrs Tanqueray* – Pinero had begun his career as a dramatist by writing short light-hearted curtain-raisers, but these were never published.

After his main works began to lose some of their appeal, he returned to the one-act form, most successfully, in 1913, with *Playgoers*, a comedy set in the upstairs/downstairs world of an Edwardian household. With a gallery of contrasting character cameo roles for actresses this amusing piece remains popular.
Publishers: Samuel French

Harold Pinter (1930–) British dramatist, director, actor

In 1957, at the suggestion of a university friend, Harold Pinter wrote his first play, *The Room*. Even in this initial short play there can be detected themes and echoes which were to reverberate through his subsequent work. There is a sense of confinement, a sense of territory in danger of being violated by unseen outside forces, a sense of menace. This is further heightened by Pinter's powerful use of the loaded pause – indeed one of his later plays is entitled *Silence* (1969). His plays, often enigmatic and elliptical in style, somehow seem to touch something deep inside the human psyche. They are constantly being revived and re-examined.

When *The Room* was staged in London it was presented with *The Dumb Waiter* (1960), a play in which elements of comedy were added to the menace. Although written for radio or television, many of his early short plays were quickly adapted for the stage. *A Slight Ache* (1961), *The Collection* (1962), *The Lover* (1963) and *A Night Out* (1961) are still regularly seen in their stage versions. Another popular script with a strong central acting role is *A Kind of Alaska* (1982) which centres on a woman waking from sleeping sickness after 29 years.

In recent years Pinter has portrayed his strongly-held political views in such powerfully disturbing plays as *One for the Road* (1984) and *Mountain Language* (1988). At the other end of the genre spectrum is a series of amusing revue sketches such as *The Last to Go* and *Request Stop* (1959) which could be linked together as part of an entertainment.

In 1999 in a fascinating double bill the Almeida Theatre staged Pinter's first play *The Room* along with his then most recent work *Celebration* (2000). This unique writer has declined to explain the meaning of his plays, although he once said enigmatically, 'I write about the weasel beneath the cocktail cabinet.' In 2005 Harold Pinter won the Nobel Prize for literature.

Other plays to consider: *Applicant*; *Ashes to Ashes*; *The Basement*; *The Black and White*; *The Dwarfs*; *Family Voices*; *Landscape*; *Moonlight*; *The New World Order*; *Night*; *Night School*; *Party Time*; *Precisely*; *Press Conference*; *Tea Party*; *Victoria Station*
Publishers: Samuel French; Faber and Faber; Methuen

Luigi Pirandello (1867–1936) Italian dramatist, poet and writer

'A serious theatre, mine ... it is certainly not a comfortable theatre. A difficult theatre. A dangerous theatre'. Luigi Pirandello's *Six Characters in Search of an Author* is often quoted as a key, early (1921) example of Expressionist, even Absurdist theatre. It is part of a wider oeuvre which included 43 plays, eight volumes of verse and over 300 short stories.

His 13 one-act plays have been translated into English by William Murray and published in a collected volume. They encompass 'realistic melodrama, ironic comedy, philosophical discourse, the play of illusion and reality involving the participation of the audience, the use of fantasy and dream to reveal the truth behind a seemingly simple, even humdrum, surface situation'.

They include the well-known *The Man with a Flower in His Mouth* set in a Paris sidewalk café, in which the eponymous character pours out his mysterious life-history to a commuter; *Chee-Chee*, in which a generous and courteous clown comes up against a one-eyed commander; and *The Imbecile*, which has, as its focus, a bullying provincial newspaper editor who is eventually made to make an admission of his cowardice. His last one-act play *I'm Dreaming, But Am I?* (1931) both in title and content (the hope-filled fantasies of a young woman) is a fair representation of his output. Pirandello, born in Sicily and educated at Rome and Bonn, completed most of his major plays after his jealous and deranged wife was confined to a mental home in 1919.

Other plays to consider: *As You Desire Me; At the Exit; Bellavita; The Doctor's Duty; The Festival of Our Lord of the Ship; The Jar; The Licence; The Other Son; Sicilian Limes; The Vise*
Publishers: Samuel French

Gillian Plowman (1941–) British dramatist

For many years Gillian Plowman held a senior post in a hospice near her home in Sussex. All her plays are shot through with a deep concern for humanity which may have stemmed from her experience of being close to people in a heightened emotional condition.

Many of her characters are on the edge of mainstream society, some with learning disabilities (*David's Birthday*, 1986), some with physical disabilities (*Cecily*, 1991, and *There's None so Blind*, 1998). Some face poverty (*Tippers*, 1990), some face unemployment (*A Kind Vesuvius*, 1994) and some face death (*Philip and Rowena*, 1996). One of her more recent scripts, *The Allotment* (2005) is a telling all-female play concerning themes of justice, fantasy, reality, truth, guilt and redemption.

Although the problems being faced are hard and genuine, most of the scripts are peppered with a warm-hearted humour, but the comedy is never at the expense of the characters. Her most frequently performed work is *Me and My Friend* (1990), now a full-length script which veers from hilarious farce to deeply harrowing moments. Act one was originally a stand-alone short play and a stand-alone second act followed later. Both acts often appear in festivals as separate plays.

Plowman wrote most of her well-honed plays for her own group, The Flat Four Players, who appeared with notable success throughout the '80s and '90s. Her dialogue is crisp, the plotting interesting and above all the plays are full of sensitive compassion illuminating the human condition.

Other plays to consider: *Amy on a Tuesday; Beata Beatrix; Close to Croydon; The Improper Appointment; The Janna Years; The Primrose Path; Two Fat Men; Two Summers; Umjana Land; Touching Tomorrow; The Wooden Pear*
Publishers: Samuel French; New Plays Network

* Dennis Potter (1935–1994) English dramatist and script-writer for radio, film and TV

Potter, a major British playwright of the later 20th century, originally wrote almost exclusively for television, but some of his work has been adapted and presented on stage. One of his early TV plays about his Forest of Dean childhood, *Blue Remembered Hills*, in which adult actors play the roles of children, is sometimes presented with effect in one-act drama festivals, though a cut in the text needs to be negotiated in order to fulfil the usual time demands.

Many of his other TV plays (which were usually designed to last 50–60 minutes length), can bring rich theatrical fare to the stage if adapted with imagination by the innovative director.

Publishers: Samuel French

James Prideaux (1935–) American dramatist and scriptwriter

American dramatist and scriptwriter James Prideaux made his off-Broadway debut with two one-act plays: *The Autograph Hunter*, which takes a humorous but scathing look at the obsessive celebrity-chaser; and *Lemonade*, an equally funny and perceptive play concerning the frustrations and loneliness of middle-age. Among the several short plays which followed, the poignant *Laughter in the Shadow of the Trees* (1995) is one of his best known.

Other plays to consider: *Abraham Lincoln Dies at Versailles*; *An American Sunset*; *Elephants*; *The Librarian*; *Postcards*; *Requiem for Us*; *Stuffings*
Publishers: Dramatists Play Service

JB Priestley (1894–1984) British dramatist and writer

Priestley's short plays have been overshadowed by his successful solid well-made major plays, but there are recurring themes in both; for instance in *The Rose and Crown* (1947) there is the arrival of a stranger who affects deeply the customers in a bar, which echoes the unsettling arrival of the police officer in *An Inspector Calls*. The newcomer in *Try it Again* (1953) is a film director who plays with time, as the playwright does in the full-length plays *Dangerous Corner*, *I Have Been Here Before* and *Time and the Conways*. There is a touch of the supernatural in *Mother's Day* (1953), a domestic drama; another domestic piece is *A Glass of Bitter* (1954) where, once again, a police inspector calls to shake up the lives of a devoted couple.

Publishers: Samuel French

Terence Rattigan (1911–1977) British dramatist

Often dubbed 'the master of the well-made play', Terence Rattigan enjoyed enormous success throughout the mid-20th century. Maybe because of his half-hidden sexuality he was a master of illuminating the repressed emotions of the English middle-class and that emerges from four of his well-known short plays.

In different decades Rattigan wrote three double bills, the first in 1948 under the overall title *Playbill*. The more substantial of these pieces, *The Browning Version*, is quintessentially Rattigan as it beautifully explores the deep emotions of an apparently arid public schoolmaster on the brink of an unhappy and lonely retirement. To accompany and counterpoint this moving human drama, he wrote *Harlequinade*, a farce satirising the struggles of a theatrical touring company in the forties.

The '50s saw the highly acclaimed *Separate Tables* (1954), two plays linked both by the setting of a small Bournemouth hotel and the theme of sexual longing for fulfilment. The two plays, *Table by the Window* and the more widely staged *Table Number Seven* were later given a glossy Hollywood film version.

In the '70s Rattigan wrote *In Praise of Love* (1974) comprising *Before Dawn*, a lightweight farcical curtain-raiser, using the opera *Tosca* as its tenuous storyline, and *After Lydia*, another of his moving plays of hidden feelings. As the second piece proved the more popular, he developed and lengthened that script under the title *In Praise of Love* and *Before Dawn* was dropped.

Frequently revived, the plays of Terence Rattigan continue to be admired for their craftsmanship and their exploration of personal emotion.

Publishers: Samuel French; Methuen

Stuart Ready English dramatist

In the mid-20th century the one-act plays of Stuart Ready were frequently performed in drama festivals. In particular, his firm grasp of the thriller genre often made his plays gripping; *The Legend of Raikes Cross* was a typical example, conjuring up eerie happenings in a taut atmosphere that, with tight production, could have pre-TV audiences on the edge of their seats if played with the right conviction. Another typical example of his work is *Mr Hunter* (1945), a thriller set on a railway station platform, for an all-women cast.

Other plays to consider: *An Apron for my Lady*; *And This Our Life*; *Back Stage*; *The Bonny Earl of Moray*; *Captain Cook and the Widow*; *Cherry Brandy*; *The Dogsbody*; *Down to the Seas*; *Escape Route*; *Five at the George*; *Five Freaks a' Fiddling*; *Jackie*; *The Last Word*; *Members of the Jury*; *Mrs Tyler's Rival*; *A Nice Cup of Tea*; *No Time for Tears*; *The Old Man of the Sea*; *Pest at the Post Office*; *Poor Mr Pembleton*; *Six Maids a'Mopping*; *Summer Vacation*; *Tomorrow's Vengeance*; *Top of the Bill*; *Vassals Departing*
Publishers: Deane; Garnet Miller; Samuel French

Paul Reakes English dramatist

Reakes has come to the fore in recent years as a writer of modern pantomimes and also of skilful one-act comedies and thrillers. The most frequently-seen is *Bang You're Dead!*, a piece which combines both aspects. A murder is first 'rehearsed' on stage and then takes place with an intriguing variant on the original plan. In *False Pretences* a film star is inveigled to a house by a star-struck daughter on the unlikely pretext that she will become his biographer.

Other plays to consider: *Act of Murder*; *Catspaw*; *Mantrap*; *Night Intruder*
Publishers: Samuel French; New Playwrights Network

John Reason English dramatist

With strong dramas and thrillers, John Reason often won the New Play Award
at drama festivals in the 1950s and 1960s, and his plays still have considerable
impact today. Reason often stepped outside the conventional forms of setting
and story, as in *Cat*, an unusual play featuring a mysterious girl who appears in
a dark city alleyway. Similarly, *Romance* is an interesting experiment in
dramatic form in which three manifestations of the same woman (as a young girl
contemplating marriage, as a middle-aged disillusioned wife, and as a
grandmother) together look back over life and reflect on its vicissitudes.

In lighter mode *Heroines and Heroes* reveals members of a film club acting
out their fantasies as they impersonate those whom they see on the screen; *The
Triplets* is a rather bizarre all-women comedy about a trio who have reached
their century in age and are awaiting civil approval in a town hall waiting room.

Other plays to consider: *The Adulterers*; *The Choristers*; *Comedienne*; *Death of
a Dummy*; *Last of the Vamps*; *A Short Intermission*; *Wives Play*
Publishers: Evans; Samuel French; New Playwrights Network

Phoebe Rees Anglo-Welsh dramatist

Based at Watchet in Somerset, Phoebe Rees, was for many years a member of
the British Drama League's governing body. From the 1930s to the 1960s she
was also an expert provider of one-act material which was within the compass
of quite inexperienced groups. She had the accolade of having some of her work
translated into both Welsh and Gaelic by her play publisher. Some of her short-
plays, such as *The Last Straw*, *Mix-up-amatosis* and *Rats* chronicle the amusing
trivialities of country life.

She also dramatised a number of historical episodes from the time of the
French Revolution – *The Incorruptible* (about Robespierre's home life) and
Sanctuary (about a plot to kill Napoleon) – and from Biblical times: *The New
Jerusalem*, an appropriate play to mark the Golden Jubilee of the Somerset
Women's Institutes since it was about the Glastonbury legends, *The Trumpet
Shall Sound* (1963) about Saul of Tarsus, and *The Answer* (1963).

Other plays to consider: *Blinds Up*; *The Dream*; *Hide and Seek*; *Idols*;
Marriages are Made in Heaven; *Second Wedding*; *That There Dog*; *TV Thriller*
Publishers: Nelson; Deane; Garnet Miller

Alan Richardson (1949–) Scottish dramatist

Still living in Edinburgh, the city of his birth, Alan Richardson has been very
active in the amateur stage movement both as an actor and a director, but it his
playwriting skills that have taken his name far beyond his native city.

His most frequently-produced play, and winner of a national playwriting competition in 1991, is the sparky comedy *Perfect Partners*, set in a dating agency run by a couple facing both their impending divorce and a visit from a highly critical investigative journalist. A taut two-hander *When a Man Knows* (2003) is a dark, disturbing well-structured drama, a strong contrast to the madcap spy spoof *The Spy Who Came In for the Phone*, which is set in London in the swinging '60s.

Alan Richardson has written numerous dialect plays which have proved extremely popular in his native Scotland. The comedies include *A Tale of Twa Undertakers* (1979), *Farewell Ploy* (1977), and *The Bailie's Stratagem* while the dramas include *Liddersdale* (1980), *The Black Ring* and *The Broken Band* (1990). Several of the dialect plays have been adapted for production beyond Scotland.

Other plays to consider: *The Burglar Confesses; A Fine Gentleman; Mr Perfect; Platform Party; Out of Sight; Tell Tale*
Publishers: Samuel French; New Theatre Publications; Brown Son & Ferguson

Jack Richardson (1935–) American dramatist and writer

At the outset of the 1960s, four young playwrights held the attention of the American theatre, as they were simultaneously active at The Actors Studio in New York – Edward Albee, Arthur Kopit, Jack Gelber and Jack Richardson.

Richardson's subsequent disappointingly small amount of published work for the theatre has shown a detatched air about the human condition. He writes with a formulaic purity – everything drawn to match its opposite, with a neo-classical emphasis on verbal precision. Some critics suggest that his plays are 'intentionally intellectual in the French tradition'.

Richardson's first play *The Prodigal*, a re-telling of the Orestes story, was highly praised and he followed this up with a notable double-bill of one-act plays, written with Shavian exhuberance. In *Gallows Humour* (1961) the first of the pair of one-act plays published under this overall title features Walter, a condemned murderer, who has a fatalistic passion for order and conformity, but is seduced back to a celebration of life, chaos and, ultimately, illusion by Lucy, the prison prostitute. In the second play the reverse situation is presented – Philip, the Executioner, wants to 'dress up' but Martha, his wife, brings him back towards conformity and order.

Publishers: Penguin

Cyril Roberts English dramatist

Cyril Roberts wrote many one-act plays that proved attractive to amateur groups in the 1930s. With plays performed by the Bristol-based Clifton Arts Club, he won the new play award at the Welwyn Drama Festival three times in four years in that period. He continued to write short plays until the 1950s.

Roll of the Drum (1939), a romantic story with a circus background, is probably his best-known piece and has been frequently anthologised. In quite different style, *The Last Rib* (1933) starts apparently inconsequentially with two typists in desultory conversation, but takes a more serious turn when some businessmen arrive. It delves into a discussion about the dangers of modern science and has a strong moral message as its conclusion.

Other plays to consider: *Do not Disturb*; *Exit*; *Genuine Antique*; *Mr Effingham*; *Mr Gaylord Remembers*; *Progress on the Whole Satisfactory*; *Tails Up*; *The Second Best Bed*; *So Good*; *Village Industries*; *Young Love*
Publishers: Samuel French; Nelson; Lovat Dickson

HF Rubinstein (1896–1970) English dramatist

Rubinstein wrote a popular history of English Drama for Benn's Sixpenny Library in 1928, and was one of the most prolific English one-act playwrights of the inter-war period. The critic John Hampden noted his 'mastery of dialogue and characterisation' and his 'experiments in technique to good purpose'.

Rubinstein pursued a wide range of historical and literary themes, as a selection of his titles indicates: *Johnson was No Gentleman* (1938), *Blake's Comforter* (1950), *Whitehall 1656*, *Bernard Shaw in Heaven*, *Words by Mr Gilbert* (1950). *On the Portsmouth Road* (1931) dealt with the birth of Dickens, *Poets and Peasants* (1950), with the Wat Tyler Rebellion, and *They Went Forth* with the plight of the Russian Jews under Czar Nicholas II.

Rubinstein also wrote one-act plays with Vera Arlett (who herself wrote some 20 one-acters, mostly on Biblical themes). Jewish by birth, Rubinstein was also deeply interested in philosophical and religious issues and wrote several sets of probing plays about characters from both the Old and New Testaments. He said, 'sensing deeply the basis of an ultimate reunion between Jew and Christian, I shall go on asking my questions ... while I remain on earth'.

One particular lighter piece of his, *The Theatre* (1914), though dated in context, still provides an excellent acting exercise for companies who might wish to give a large number of members the chance to show their paces. The scene is set in the auditorium of a theatre, and various types of theatre-goer are caricatured as the harassed author anxiously watches (and interacts with) them and the fate of his material from the back of the circle. Though Rubinstein was copiously represented in play catalogues of the 1950s, none of his one-act plays remain in print today, an ill-deserved twist of fate.

Other plays to consider: *Afterglow*; *Arms and the Drama*; *The Deacon and the Jewess*; *The Dickens of Grays Inn*; *Dramatic Endeavour*; *Grand Guignol*; *Insomnia*; *Jew Dyte*; *London Stone*; *Nights of Errors*; *Old Boyhood*; *Posterity*; *Postwar*; *Repertory*; *Revanche*; *A Specimen*; *To the Poets of Australia*
Publishers: Samuel French; Nelson

Willy Russell (1947–) English dramatist

Russell is well-known for his powerful musical *Blood Brothers* and for his full-length plays concerning the contemporary struggle of Northern women to find their own niche in society (*Educating Rita, Shirley Valentine*) but he wrote some short plays before he moved to the full-length form.

His story about a school outing (***Our Day Out***, 1983) was originally a television play, but he has adapted it successfully for the stage and it is frequently performed by youth theatre companies and schools who enjoy meeting its large-cast demands. The day coach trip to Conway Castle made by the euphemistically named 'progress' class of a Liverpool secondary school raises plenty of laughs but also touches some deeper educational issues. *I Read the News Today* was first written for schools radio in 1977, but has since been adapted for the stage and is a dramatic piece about a gunman loose in a radio station.

Publisher: Samuel French

William Saroyan (1908–1981) American dramatist, short-story writer and poet

Californian born and bred, Saroyan was a prolific and gifted writer about the American scene but struggled to win acceptance from critics and audiences throughout his life. 'Is Saroyan crazy?' asked George Jean Nathan in a 13-page 1942 article reviewing his work, though not answering in the affirmative. Eric Bentley, an influential mid-20th century drama critic, has put Saroyan alongside JB Priestley as 'the two prime instances in the dramatic world of highbrows trying to be lowbrow without losing caste. Hence their exaggerated home-iness, their forced simplicity, their patriotism and insistent local colour, their chronic fear of the esoteric'.

Saroyan wrote most of his dramatic work in the 1940s (including his one great full-length success, *The Time of Your Life*) and he wrote numerous one-act plays in this period. Of these ***Hello Out There*** (1941) is perhaps the best-known, an apparently naive but curiously magnetic piece about a young woman coming to visit a bewildered prisoner in a small-town jail. The young man is then shot by a wrongly jealous husband and the young woman echoes the victim's questing cry which gives the play its title as the curtain falls. It was played as a curtain-raiser to Shaw's *The Devil's Disciple* at Santa Barbara in 1941.

Many of his earlier shorter pieces were included in a collection published in 1942 and called *Razzle Dazzle*. They include 'a ballet poem', the text of 'an Armenian opera in English', and several radio plays. Most of them mix idiosyncrasy and profundity in about equal measure. A second collection of 20 short pieces titled *Making Money* was published in 1960

Other plays to consider: *The Agony of Little Nations; Assassinations; Bad Men in the West; Coming Through the Rye; Dentist and Patient; Elmer and Lily;*

The Great American Goof; The Hungerers; Husband and Wife; Jim Sam and Anna; The New Play; Once Around the Block; Opera Opera; The Ping-Pong Game; Radio Play; Talking to You; There's Something I Got to Tell You
Publishers: Faber and Faber; Samuel French

Jean-Paul Sartre (1905–1980) French dramatist and philosopher

The existentialist French philosopher Sartre has left behind several powerful one-act pieces in which he represented his views through drama. Ionesco said that Sartre's plays were best thought of as 'political melodramas' and they feature profound discussion rather than action.

The best-known of these is *In Camera (Huis Clos)* (1945) in which three characters consider their plight in an elegant Second Empire drawing-room which turns out to be Hell. *Crime Passionel* (1948) is another piece frequently revived. The lesser-known *Bariona* uses the events of the Nativity of Christ to present an anti-colonialist stance. *The Respectable Prostitute* (1948) is set in the deep South of the USA and thoughtfully and provocatively raises issues of morality and racism, as a black man pleads to be sheltered from a potential lynch mob.

Other plays to consider: *The Flies*
Publishers: Samuel French

James Saunders (1925–2004) English dramatist

Saunders began his writing career by providing material for the amateur Questors Theatre in West London in the late 1950s. The quirky humour of his *Barnstable* (1959) provided him with an early success, in a style reminiscent of Ionesco. The play is a very English comedy with undefined menace, presenting a middle-class family blithely unaware of the world collapsing around them. *A Slight Accident* (1961; in which a wife seeks to explain her accidental shooting of her husband) also had absurdist overtones whereas *Double Double* (1963; an inventive comedy set in a bus garage canteen and originally written for RADA students) was much more mainstream in style. Though originally designed with actors doubling roles (hence the title) the roles can be played individually without injury to the humour of the play.

Saunders went on to write several significant full-length plays (*Next Time I'll Sing to You*, *A Scent of Flowers*, *Bodies*) but never entirely forsook the one-act form, though his later style became more conservative compared with his early experimental pieces. More recently, the reflective nostalgia of *Random Moments in a May Garden* has provided sensitive directors with good opportunities to explore both textual and visual aspects of theatre. The strangely titled *After Liverpool* (1971) is a series of short pieces which can be selected and played in any order and with varying numbers of performers; it gives scope for virtuoso playing and direction. A recent collection of his short plays in print is called *Savoury Meringue*, an equally mysterious but appealing appellation.

Other plays to consider: *Alas Poor Fred*; *Birdsong*; *Bye Bye Blues*; *Games*; *The Island*; *Neighbours*; *Over the Wall*; *Play of Yesterday*; *Return to the City*; *Who was Hilary Maconachie?*
Publishers: Amber Lane; Samuel French

Murray Schisgal (1926–) American dramatist and film-script writer

In spite of occasional writing forays in the cinema – notable for the award-winning *Tootsie* – Murray Schisgal remains a man of the theatre, for which he has written many short plays. A native of Brooklyn he was a musician, teacher, and an attorney before turning his hand to writing, with his first plays being presented in London at the British Drama League in 1960. These were two short plays entitled *The Typists* and *The Tiger*; the former, an ironic piece showing the futility of the lives of a couple who share an office over 50 years, is still popular today.

Success came later in his native country where eventually his zany world, teetering between lunacy and an odd comic sense, came to be appreciated. Set in New York, *The Pushcart Peddlers* (1979) is a comic fable about two new immigrants learning to survive in a new land as they barter and banter as banana salesmen. His wackiness and broad satire arc also features of *Twice Around the Park* (1982), a comic double bill for two actors – *A Need for Brussels Sprouts* and *A Need for Less Expertise*.

In deeper and more enigmatic mood is *Fragments* (1965) in which a social worker visits three young men in a claustrophobic room – or do they represent three aspects of just one man? In contrast song, dance and vaudeville patter intertwine in *Extensions* (1994), which highlights a show-biz couple's desperate isolation and need for each other.

Other plays to consider: *The Artist and the Model*; *The Basement*; *The Chinese*; *Closet Madness*; *The Consequences of Goosing*; *Dr Fish*; *Ducks and Lovers*; *Fifty Years Ago*; *The Flatulist*; *Jealousy*; *Man Dangling*; *Memorial Day*; *The Old Jew*; *74 Georgia Avenue*; *Sexaholics*; *A Simple Kind of Love Story*; *Walter*; *Windows*
Publishers: Dramatists Play Service; Samuel French

James Scotland (1917–1983) Scottish playwright

At one time the plays of James Scotland, former Principal of Aberdeen College of Education, were often seen in his native country. If they now appear less frequently, it is not because of lack of merit, but probably because his style of writing in dialect is currently not so popular. However, such plays as *Hogmanay*, *Hallowe'en*, *The Daurk Assize* (1975) and *The Girl of the Golden City* (1975) are still seen at drama festivals.

Several of his plays, including *A Surgeon for Lucinda* (1974), *Himself When Young* (1975) and *A Shilling for the Beadle* (1970) have won the final of the Scottish One-Act Play Festival.

Other plays to consider: *Highlander, Union Riots*
Publisher: Brown Son & Ferguson

Peter Shaffer (1926–) English dramatist

Best known for his major plays painted on a rich colourful canvas, Peter Shaffer also wrote four short plays, where the brushstrokes are less broad. These more intimate plays date from the mid-'60s around the time of his international theatrical success, *The Royal Hunt of the Sun*.

The Private Ear and *The Public Eye* formed a popular double bill, each demanding a cast of two men and one woman. The tragi-comedy of the former with its plot of the sexual rejection of a sensitive music buff is contrasted with the second, a high comedy concerning the effect that an apparently eccentric private detective has on a couple's marital problems.

When the Chichester Theatre wanted a one-act play to accompany their production of *Miss Julie* in 1965, Shaffer wrote **Black Comedy**. With a cast of eight clear-cut characters, this hilarious farce uses the age-old Chinese theatrical device of reversing light and dark, and has become a classic 60-minute piece.

Two years later **Black Comedy** was given its own Shaffer companion piece – **White Liars**. Linking the plays was not only the colour reversal in the titles, but the theme of deception. However, the second play had a much more serious and complex tone – and a plot that saw the author re-write the play several times each under a slightly different title.

New audiences may feel that one or two of these plays are dated and may be better presented as period pieces but all four are still worth revival.

Publisher: Samuel French

GB Shaw (1856–1950) Anglo-Irish dramatist and writer

Amidst his vast output of provocative and challenging material, Shaw experimented with the one-act form, though some of the pieces bear signs of being hastily written and may justly be considered 'trifles'. Most of his crafted one-act plays came from the 1900–1910 period, when he wrote curtain-raisers to some of his own longer plays.

How He Lied to Her Husband (1904) was originally written as a curtain-raiser to *Candida* and is a clever three-handed variation on the theme of the major play. It nevertheless stands up well on its own if given crisp performance. *Passion, Poison and Petrifaction* (1905) is a more fantastical piece with a larger cast, a melodramatic pastiche of romantic comedy, which can produce many laughs if played with brio. *Village Wooing* (1933) is an interesting but wordy two-hander which (like many of his plays) needs linguistic skill and resourceful performances to sustain its progress.

Plays such as *The Fascinating Foundling* (1909), *The Shewing-up of Blanco Posnet* (1909; a Wild West piece, once banned by the Lord Chamberlain for its 'blasphemy'), and *O'Flaherty VC* (1917) are pieces which have lost their impact as their topicality has waned. Other one-act plays (*The Inca of Perusalem* (1916) and *Annajanska, the Bolshevik Empress*) feature the supposed 'human side' of European royalty or rulers but are mainly vehicles for Shavian wit and opinions rather than deep explorations of differentiated characters. If producing Shaw nowadays, both choose and handle the play with care.

Other plays to consider: *Augustus Does His Bit*; *Arthur and the Acetone*; *Beauty's Duty*; *Cymbeline Re-finished*; *The Dark Lady of the Sonnets*; *The Glimpse of Reality*; *Great Catherine*; *The Music Cure*; *Overruled*; *Passion Play*; *Press Cuttings*; *Shakes versus Shaw* (a puppet-play)
Publishers: The Bodley Head

*Phillip Sheahan (1940–) English dramatist

Sheahan originally researched the history of laundries of the London suburb of Acton through the reminiscences of local residents. It was part of an 18-month project called Playback, which was organised by his local community theatre, the Questors Theatre of Ealing in the late 1990s. The resulting short play, *Soapsud Island*, proved to be a highly entertaining piece in which a large cast played laundry-girls, managers, drivers, and assorted customers in a melange of episodes portraying the rise and decline of the laundry industry from the 1880s to the 1950s. In one particularly effective section, the play presents a day trip to the seaside, creating coach, café and beach scenes with great verve, using songs of the period to enhance atmosphere.

The play turned out to be an audience-pleaser far beyond the confines of its own local area. The significance of Sheahan's work is that it demonstrates that local historical themes and episodes can provide distinctive and fruitful material as short plays, that the material gives attractive and accessible opportunities for new writers and that resulting plays may have appeal beyond their particular origins if dramatised skilfully.

Other plays to consider: *If Only*
Publishers: Samuel French

Sam Shepard (1943–) American dramatist and actor

Writing about his plays Sam Shepard has said that they represent 'a home where I bring the adventures of my life and sort them out, making sense or non-sense out of mysterious impressions. I feel that language is a veil hiding demons and angels which the characters are always out of touch with. Their quest in the play is the same as ours – to find those forces and meet them face to face and end the mystery'. That quest has resulted in some of the most interesting short plays in modern American theatre.

Typical of his work is the powerful *Fool for Love* (1983), a blistering play of extraordinary intensity set in a seedy motel room. The author asks that the play should be performed *relentlessly*. If the central relationship is played with the vital passionate fire and uncompromising physicality then this makes a blazing piece of theatre. *States of Shock* (1991) is a wild, surreal scathing anti-war play where the characters embody the conflict and violence in the state of the American mind.

His early more fantastical short plays are collected in *The Unseen Hand and Other Plays* (1971), the title play, *The Unseen Hand*, taking a surreal, Kafkaesque approach to illustrate the dehumanisation of modern society. With a similar theme *The Holy Ghostly* (1969) is a father/son confrontation showing the gradual death of human spirit while *Shaved Splits* (1970) shows brutal reality busting into a girl's dream world. The danger of ignorance and the power of superstition are themes of the powerful *Back Bog Beast Bait* (1971). Also in this volume are *Forensic and the Navigators* (1967), the intriguing *The 4-H Club* (1965), and the writer's first play to be produced, *The Cowboys*, which was staged with *The Rock Garden* in his first double-bill in 1964.

Shepard has always encompassed American pop and media culture as instanced in *Mad Dog Blues* (1971), a play for nine actors and musicians and *The Melodrama Play* (1967) with its central rock star caught up in a jungle of fantasy and deception. In 2005 *The God of Hell*, a 70-minute play, had a successful run at the Donmar Warehouse, London.

Born in Illinois, the author worked in a variety of temporary menial jobs before taking up acting and writing, a career which has been marked by many awards including a Pulitzer Prize.

Publishers: Samuel French; Dramatists Play Service; Faber and Faber; Methuen

Richard Brinsley Sheridan (1751–1816) Irish dramatist, theatre manager, and politician

Dublin-born Sheridan became the master dramatist of 18th-century comedy of manners with such major works as *The Rivals* and *The School for Scandal*. Two of his plays are often shortened and played without an interval: *The Critic: or a Tragedy Rehearsed* (1779) is a deliciously comic satire of the theatrical follies of his day and *St Patrick's Day: or The Scheming Lieutenant* (1775) is a rumbustious fast-paced farce. Both plays need a sense of period style – and a sense of fun.

Publishers: Collins

Martin Sherman (1938–) American dramatist

The characters in the plays of Philadelphia-born dramatist Martin Sherman are often outsiders on the fringe of society. In his best known double bill, the witty and poignant *A Madhouse in Goa* (1989), comprising *A Table for a King* and *Keeps Rainin' All the Time*, the central character is shy unworldly, gay and Jewish. *Things Went Badly in Westphalia* was published in *The Best Short Plays of 1970* while *Passing By* (1974) was given a lunch-time performance by a Gay Sweatshop cast which included a young Simon Callow.

Publishers: Amber Lane; Methuen

Rae Shirley Anglo-Welsh dramatist

Rae Shirley has produced a number of popular one-act plays in the later part of the 20th century, following on in the style and tradition of Gertrude Jennings, Patricia Brooks and Cherry Vooght. Some of her plays reflect her Welsh background (the hymn *Bread of Heaven* turns up more than once as part of the plot) and are concerned with domestic dramas.

Round and Round the Gooseberry Bush and *The Kitten* (1972) amusingly feature relatively trivial events in Edwardian drawing-rooms and are written for all-women casts. By contrast, *What Shall we Do With the Body?* is a neat country comedy in which a female detective writer gets caught up in one of her own plots.

Perhaps her most innovative piece is the mixed-cast *Merry Regiment of Women* (sub-titled *A fragment from the old Globe Theatre*) in which a group of Shakespearean female characters (Kate, Juliet, Lady Macbeth, Cleopatra) meet with Petruchio, Romeo, and Henry V and offer a light-hearted tribute to their originator, all in iambic pentameters. Another piece based on historic events is *Not Even a Wimple* in which the consequences of a Lady Godiva with short hair are posed.

Other plays to consider: *Bread of Heaven*; *Bus Stop*; *The Flesh Game*; *Jester of Stratford*; *Scarlet Ribbons*; *Sherry in the Trifle*; *Think the Beautiful Thoughts*; *Time the Sad Jester*

Publishers: Samuel French; Baker's Plays; Pioneer Play Company

Neil Simon (1927–) American dramatist

Neil Simon has proved the most popular American playwright of the late 20th century. His hallmark is the snappy comic one-liner; the style is brittle and witty; the characters are largely middle class Americans – just the sort of people who flock to his plays as audiences. Ever since *Come Blow Your Horn* in 1960, he has enjoyed a long line of success with his full-length comedies. His one-act plays appear in his three 'suites' where he uses hotel rooms to set eleven comedies.

The first of these, *Plaza Suite* (1968), set in Manhattan, includes one of his funniest short pieces – *Visitor From Forest Hills*, in which a bride locks herself in the bathroom on her wedding morning, much to the increasing consternation of her frenetic parents. The other plays in this group are *Visitor from Hollywood* and *Visitor from Mamaroneck*.

Rejecting the accusation that he was just a writer of New York plays he set in his next quartet in a Los Angeles hotel. The highlights of *California Suite* (1976) include *Visitor from Philadelphia*, in which a wife disturbs her husband in bed with an unknown drunken woman, and *Visitor from London*, in which an edgy actress has arrived for an Oscar ceremony. She and her husband reappear in *Diana and Sidney*, one of the quartet of plays which comprise *London Suite*.

Both *California Suite* and *Plaza Suite* were successfully filmed. *London Suite* (1994) has not so far enjoyed the same acclaim as its predecessors but all 11 sharply-written plays from the three suites are worth re-assessment.

Other plays to consider: *Going Home; The Man on the Floor; Settling Accounts; Visitor from Chicago; Visitor from New York*
Publishers: Samuel French

NF Simpson (1915–) English dramatist

Simpson, a South London adult education teacher, rose to swift prominence after his full-length play, **A Resounding Tinkle**, won third place in a 1956 playwriting competition organised by *The Observer* newspaper. It was then adapted into a one-act play, which has proved a durable and easily stageable piece for 50 years. The suburban life of Bro and Middie Paradock is full of absurdities (a caller comes to the door and Bro returns to complain, 'He wanted me to form a government but it's past six o'clock') and when Uncle Ted comes to visit he turns out to be a shapely young woman who is offered paragraphs to read, rather than cakes to munch. Later Simpson's full-length play *One Way Pendulum*, a piece with similar surrealistic situations, was a West End success.

Whilst retaining the same style, Simpson wrote several other one-acters. He revealed a deeper philosophical strain in **The Hole** (1959) which explores the different 'visions' of life people see whilst regarding the same scene. Telling social criticism surfaces amidst the whimsy in the large-cast **Was He Anyone?** (1973) in which the combined apparatus of bureaucracy, grinding on in excrutiating pedantry, fails to organise itself to save a drowning man. Simpson is an acquired taste, but his peculiarly English brand of 'Theatre of the Absurd' can delight audiences and prove rewarding for performers and directors.

Other plays to consider: *The Form; We're Due in Eastbourne in Ten Minutes*
Publishers: Samuel French; Dramatic Publishing Company

Frank Sladen-Smith (?1880–1955) English director and dramatist

Following his early days as an art-critic in London and Manchester, Sladen-Smith became identified with the work of the Little Theatre in Manchester, which belonged to a drama group called The Unnamed Society. He was artistic director and producer for many years, as well as frequently providing the theatre with material for performance. He became known as one of the foremost exponents of the one-act play during the 1920s and 1930s, writing over 50 examples of the form, and his **St Simeon Stylites** (in which, from the top of his pillar, the Saint routs the Devil) was the first play sent by the British Drama League to represent Britain at the New York Little Theatre Tournament. His plays twice won the BDL National Festival in the early 1930s, a period when he was much in demand as tutor, adjudicator, lecturer and reviewer.

In those days, his work was seen as 'experimentalist' since he often eschewed naturalistic story-telling in favour of more adventurous styles. Of all his short plays, *The Man Who Wouldn't Go to Heaven* (1929; in which a richly diverse collection of characters react to finding themselves at the Pearly Gates) is best known and still receives production today. *An Assyrian Afternoon* (1933; in which some world-weary onlookers observe the Ark being made ready without having any idea why) demonstrates his gentle humour and is frequently anthologised. But he wrote in other styles as *The Poison Party* (1933; historical burlesque) and *The Invisible Duke* (a Gothic farce) well demonstrate.

Other plays to consider: *The Affliction of St Thomas*; *Bazhouka Meets the Gods*; *The Confutation of Wisdom*; *The Crown of St Felice*; *The Destiny of Paulo*; *Edward About to Marry*; *A Guilty Passion*; *The Harlequin Bridge*; *Henbury*; *The Herald*; *The Insuperable Obstacle*; *Love in the Ape House*; *Polonaise*; *Pongo*; *The Resurrection of Joseph*; *Stephen*; *Sweet Master William*; *The Waters of Lethe*

Publishers: Samuel French; Gowans and Gray; Garnet Miller

Stephen Smith English dramatist

Audiences who revel in the repartee of the witty one-liner get plenty of enjoyment from the plays of Stephen Smith, a Cambridge-based writer who has been producing clever contemporary pieces since the mid-1980s. *Departure* is about casual encounters in an airport lounge, *Parentcraft* about encounters in an ante-natal clinic, *Background Artiste* about encounters whilst waiting to get a job as an 'extra'. *On Location* makes a suitable partner piece to the latter, taking the characters on to the church-hall set of a tacky sci-fi film.

But Smith also constructs neat plots, as in *One-Sided Triangle* (about drug-smuggling in the Far East) and *Penalty*, a play with a clever and unexpected final twist, which shows the perils facing an English soccer referee left alone in a foreign country. His interest in football is also evident in another play *Mismatch* (1988), a comedy in which the referee has the complication of being in love with the chairman of the home team's daughter.

Publishers: Samuel French; Cambridge Publishing Services

Michael Snelgrove English dramatist

Whilst working as a college lecturer, Michael Snelgrove wrote a number of short plays which achieved considerable festival success for his local Berkshire theatre society. The most enduring is the comedy *Hidden Meanings* (1980), a highly original mix of Sherlock Holmes, murder, farce, suicide and *The Pirates of Penzance*! Based on the playwright's first-hand observations, *Maurice (Dancing)*

(1983), tells of the hectic problems which can occur just before an official royal visit. With a cast of fourteen character roles – plus extras – this amusing script offers a rare vehicle for a large society.

Other plays to consider: *Definitely Eric Geddis*; *Sleep Tight Tonight*; *Urban Cycles*
Publishers: Samuel French

CP Snow and Pamela Hansford Johnson British dramatists

See under Pamela Hansford Johnson and CP Snow

Shelagh Stephenson (1955–) British dramatist

Best known for her 'Three Sisters' play *The Memory of Water*, Shelagh Stephenson adapted her award-winning radio play *Five Kinds of Silence* (1997) into a one-act play for the stage. It is a harrowing, devastatingly disturbing story about an abusive father and the effect his extreme control has on his wife and two daughters.

Publishers: Samuel French

Hal D Stewart (1899–?1990) Anglo-Scottish dramatist

After a career as an Army officer, Stewart combined work in West End stage-management with the writing of a number of light-hearted short pieces which were played frequently in the 1930s and 1940s. Some he called 'historical impertinences'. Best-known and most-played of these was *Henry Hereafter* (1958), in which the six wives of Henry VIII fail to make a case against their king, who, after cross-examination by a celestial court, is deemed worthy of heaven – unlike the wives.

Stewart was Scottish-born but spent most of his life in England. He was general manager of the Players Theatre, Villiers Street, the home of traditional Victorian music-hall, from 1954 until his retirement.

Other plays to consider: *The Blind Eye*; *The Causeway*; *The Crime in the Club House*; *Fire Policy*; *The Home Front*; *John Brown's Body*; *Ladies Only*; *More Things*; *Mrs Watson's Window*; *The Nineteenth Hole*; *Rizzio's Boots*; *Robbers Rendezvous*; *Southward Ho!*; *Tommy Turnbull's Trousers*; *Trade Union*; *Window Pains*
Publishers: Brown Son and Ferguson; Gowans and Gray; Nelson; Samuel French

Tom Stoppard (1937–) English dramatist

Stoppard, one of the major playwrights of the 20th century, is Czech in family origin but brilliantly felicitous in the English language, and a fount of intellectual explorations in his writing. Characteristically, he has adventured into the one-act form in many innovative ways.

Some of his early short comedies for radio (*Albert's Bridge* (1969) about a painter who becomes fixated on his work; *If You're Glad I'll be Frank* (1966) about the supposed human story behind the speaking clock) have successfully transferred to the theatre. Later pieces written for TV (such as *Teeth*, 1966), exploiting the comic possibilities of a dentist having his wife's lover as a patient, and *A Separate Peace* (1969), about a man who is not ill but who prefers to live in a hospital), have also proved effective and enjoyable pieces of stage drama.

Stoppard created a very successful double-bill with *The Real Inspector Hound* (a spoof of murder-mysteries) and *After Magritte* (1970) the shorter of the two plays, a beautifully constructed comedy that shows that things are not always what they seem – an arresting and remarkable opening stage picture is fully explained by the end of the play, thanks to the indefatigable investigations of Inspector Foot of the Yard.

Dogg's Hamlet and *Cahoot's Macbeth* (1980) are inter-linked short-plays, as are *Dirty Linen* and *Newfoundland* (1976); the latter pair had a successful professional West End production. Several collections of his short plays are in print and they may provide a fruitful cache of stimulating material for imaginative companies.

Other plays to consider: *Another Moon called Earth*; *Artist Descending a Staircase*; *The Dissolution of Dominic Boot*; *The Dog it Was That Died*; *M is for Moon Among Other Things*; *Where Are They Now?*
Publishers: Samuel French; Faber and Faber

August Strindberg (1849–1912) Swedish dramatist, novelist, poet, and painter

Sweden's greatest and most prolific playwright, Strindberg was also a writer of autobiography, criticism and philosophy. He wrote about 70 plays ranging through histories, folk drama, naturalistic pieces, and eventually to symbolism and surrealism.

Within this prodigious output very few one-act plays emerged; however one which is still seen frequently is *Playing with Fire* (1892). It is said that the play is a reminiscence of his early association with his first wife and any production needs to create a fiery hothouse atmosphere where the main characters are indeed playing with emotional fire.

Also autobiographical is *Creditors* (1889), a psychological thriller and *The Storm* (1907) which he wrote later in his life following the divorce from his third wife, the passing storm representing a man's re-awakened painful passion.

His greatest play *Miss Julie* (1888) runs for well over an hour but is often played without an interval, which adds further to the intensity of the seductive passion between a manservant and his master's daughter. It is a play about class, power, fulfilment, sensuality and sex – all themes which continue to appeal to modern audiences.

In a similar way *The Ghost Sonata* (1907) is sometimes played in a shortened version. One of Strindberg's late chamber plays, its strange mix of macabre naturalism and expressionistic fantasy, continues to wield a powerful grip over audiences. Suitable for an accomplished actress, *The Stronger* (1890) is a dramatic monologue set in a café on Christmas Eve.

Publishers: Samuel French; Methuen; Nick Hern Books; Dramatists Play Service

Graham Swannell (1950–) British dramatist

A quartet of one-act plays under the overall title *A State of Affairs* (1985), presented in London in the mid '80s, first brought Graham Swannell to the attention of theatre-goers. Commitment and betrayal lie at the heart of these plays with the author making some frank and perceptive comments on human frailty and foibles. Two of the four have proved the more popular: *The Day of the Dog*, which concerns a brief moment of marital infidelity, and *Stuttgart*, in which a couple find a way to revive their ailing sex life. The other plays in the quartet are *Commitment and Consequences.*

All Swannell's plays are about the subtleties of human relationships, for example, *The Border* (1990) is an intriguing exploration into the roles people play after a long period spent together, while the main character in *Marrakech* (1989) if facing a male mid-life crisis which brings about a comedy of deception and role reversal. One of the author's later plays, *Hyde Park* (1992), is a moving, ironic exploration of love and friendship.

Publishers: Samuel French; Weinberger

JM Synge (1871–1909) Irish dramatist

Often said to be the first modern Irish playwright, John Millington Synge died at an early age with a legacy of just six plays, but those few plays created a springboard for a renaissance in Irish theatre. His masterpiece was his full-length *The Playboy of the Western World* but he also wrote a couple of notable short plays.

Hailed as one of the best one-act plays of its time, the intense *Riders to the Sea* (1904) focuses on the looming presence of death. This stark tragedy set on the west coast of Ireland is strongly influenced by the playwright's visit to the remote Aran Islands, a journey which deeply affected him and his writing. Although the mood is sombre there is an almost lyrical tone in the dialogue of the grief-stricken peasants.

Set on the other side of Ireland, in County Wicklow, *In the Shadow of the Glen* (1903) has been described as a sombre comedy of marital incompatibility. With its story of a young wife, a husband feigning death, and a knowing tramp, there is a robust folk tale quality to the writing which typifies Synge's interest in isolated peasant communities. His village comedy *The Tinker's Wedding* (1909) was originally written in one-act form, and that version is still often presented today.

The fact that Synge died so young makes the fact that death features so widely in his plays all the more poignant.

Publishers: Methuen; Samuel French

AJ Talbot English dramatist and critic

Alfred Julian Talbot wrote articles about drama for *The Daily Telegraph* and for the *New York Theatre Guild Magazine* in the 1930s and also produced a stream of light one-act comedies which entertained many audiences. Some, such as his satire on Euripides' *The Spartan Girl* (a winner of the British Drama League's Howard de Walden Cup in 1936), were in verse, but the majority were in witty and elegant prose, and were well-crafted pieces. Those which are light-hearted commentary on historical events, might well repay rediscovery today.

In *Lucretia's Borgia's Little Party* (1933) a love potion provided by Leonardo da Vinci gets mixed up with the intended poisons for the guests and provides a hilarious stage climax in which four couples are becoming enthusiastically amorous simultaneously as the curtain falls.

Talbot's early one-act play *Emily's Excuses* (1927) was toured by the Arts League Travelling Theatre for some years and a burlesque in rhyming couplets he subsequently wrote for them, *The Old Firm's Re-awakening* (1928; about a bookie recognising a 'higher calling') became a favourite with amateur groups.

He was able to work in a wide variety of comedy styles: *The Murder in the Foyer* (1933) was described as 'a burlesque Grand Guignol'; *The Duke of Cul-de-Sac* (1930) as 'a very modern melodrama'; *The Betrothal of the Princess* as 'a play in doggerel' and *All Fool's Eve* as 'a fantasia', set in Parliament Square.

Other plays to consider: *At a New Dawning; At the Pit Door; Bailey's Crowded Hour; The Burglar's Christmas Eve; The Cabinet Minister's Fireside; The Casket Scene Up-to-date; The Centurion's Billet at Swacking Bulphen; Chez Boguskovsky; Daniel in the Lionesses Den; The Devil's Deal with Mr Pincott; The Fur Coat; If Journey's End Had Been Written to Please Theatre-Managers...; In a Dentist's Waiting Room; Incorrigible; In the Outer Darkness; Marmaduke; A Night at the Borgias; November the Tenth; One Evening at Nero's. The Passing of Galatea; A Social Evening; Tarnish; T'Drama League Coop; White Jasmine; Will Shakespeare's Bespoke Supper*
Publishers: Gowans and Gray; Samuel French

Jean Tardieu (1903–1995) French dramatist and poet

Though sometimes bracketed with other French 'Theatre of the Absurd' dramatists who came to prominence in the 1960s, Jean Tardieu's work has an altogether sunnier and more optimistic aspect. Older than the other Absurdists, he was head of the Experimental Workshop of the French Radio and TV Service after World War II when already an established writer and translator of poetry.

Most of his theatre writing was in the short-play style, but its range is wide, extending from the fantastic to the lyrical, and from the plotted comedy to the abstract use of language merely as sound. Though his work is anthologised in French, little of it has been given published translation in English as yet. A collection of his poetry and three of his one-act plays were translated by David

Kelley in the 1990s. *The Enquiry Office*, subsequently played with success on the amateur drama festival circuit, reveals him to be a gentle and sophisticated writer in a play reminiscent of NF Simpson's style; a well-meaning client desperately tries to provide the answers that an officious official wants from him. Having eventually completed this task, the client walks out of the office and is immediately run over.

Other plays to consider: *The Contraption*; *The Keyhole*; *The Underground Lover*
Publishers (English versions): Black Apollo Press

Jules Tasca (1928–) American dramatist, lecturer

A complete man of the theatre American writer, Jules Tasca has taught playwriting skills in American and English universities and performed with a *commedia del'arte* group in central Italy. He has dramatised French short stories and adapted a CS Lewis novel into a musical. In addition he has written more than a hundred short plays. He has said, 'In my younger days I wrote comedy but as middle-age advanced I became drawn to tragedy. There is no sense in satirising an attitude if you turn off those who hold it. You should not appear superior to your audience. Greeks, Shakespeare, Molière were all very popular entertainment in their time'.

One of his best-known short plays on both sides of the Atlantic is the extremely funny and original comedy *The Spelling of Coynes* which was included in a collection *The Best Short American Plays of 1994*. He wrote six modern short plays in the theatrical *commedia del'arte* style under the title *Commedia Americana* in which the seven deadly sins come to lusty life. Peopled by the traditional characters, each of these plays stands up on its own. *The Necklace* and *Forbidden Fruit* (1984) are just two of several plays adapted from de Maupassant short stories. *The Tiger* and *Secret Sin* are two of eight *Tales by Saki*, and *Cannibalism in Cars* is an adaptation of a Mark Twain story.

Other plays to consider: *Angels on a Train*; *The Background*; *The Baker's Neighbour*; *Deus X*; *Extraction*; *Finding the Love of Your Life*; *Going to the Catacombs*; *Hardstuff*; *The Hen*; *Inflatable You*; *Make-Up*; *Outrageous*; *Passion Comedy*; *The Rape of Emma Bunche*; *Second Vows*; *Snocky*; *That Pig Morin*; *The Unrest Cure*
Publishers: Samuel French

CP Taylor (1929–1981) Anglo-Scottish dramatist

Of Glasgow-Jewish origin, Cecil Taylor spent much of his life in the North-east of England. He wrote in a variety of spheres, ranging from TV dramas to full-length West End pieces and plays for schools. Though socialist in outlook, he often explored the impracticality of idealism. This is well demonstrated in *Allergy* (1966), one of his best one-act plays. A Marxist journalist, Christopher, comes to realise that he is allergic to adultery (physically as well as mentally) despite his talent for seduction. He returns from the Scottish Highlands to suburban conventionality (and capitalism) and hands over his unconsummated affairs to his friend Jim, a fellow Marxist, who hopes that the magazine he edits and produces from a remote cottage (circulation 150) will bring world revolution.

Fable (1965) is a parable-play about a lion and a jackal discussing the morality of killing an antelope and ends with the lion being killed by a hunter. Taylor also wrote a number of short television plays.

Other plays to consider: *Apples*; *Castro*; *Charles and Cromwell*; *Lenin*; *Words*
Publishers: Hutchinson; Penguin

Megan Terry (1932–) American dramatist

'I design my plays to promote laughter – thought may follow', said Megan Terry, when once asked about her work. She has always worked outside mainstream commercial theatre in the USA but has been a prolific writer of plays in a variety of styles and at a variety of lengths. She has made a particular virtue of what she calls 'transformation' in plays, abruptly having actors shift characters, or changing locations and times in mid-scene, in order to emphasise a parallel or make a point.

Keep Tightly Closed in a Cool Dry Place (1967) is a one-act play set initially in a prison in which three inter-linked characters play out their own predicament, but also branch out into scenes culled from both history and the movies (Custer and the Indian risings, Queen Elizabeth and Walter Raleigh). *Comings and Goings* (1967) is sub-titled *A Theatre Game* and is a self-consciously 'transformational' piece about male–female relationships which has actors 'sent in' to replace other actors in the style of substitutes in a foot ball match. *The Gloaming, Oh My Darling* (1967) is a sunny piece in which two grandmotherly ladies review their past lives and enjoy their nostalgia.

Other plays to consider: *Calm Down Mother*; *Ex-Miss Copper Queen on a Set of Pills*; *The Magic Realists*; *One More Little Drinkie*; *The People versus Rauchman*; *The Pioneer*; *The Pro Game*; *Sanibel and Captiva*
Publishers: IE Clark; Dramatists Play Service; Samuel French; Simon and Schuster

TC Thomas Welsh dramatist

Creating the character of the lovable rural rogue, Davy Jones has assured TC Thomas of something approaching immortality in Wales. Davy Jones's countryside exploits, along with that of his companions, were televised in a popular 1960s' HTV series as well as made into a succession of amusing one-act plays (*Davy Jones's Dinner*, 1956) *Davy Jones's Locker*, 1957; *Davy Jones's Clock*, *Davy Jones Goes Hunting*, *They Simply Fade Away*) given widespread performance.

But Thomas could also write in dramatic style as two of his plays on New Testament themes show. *Mirage* (1954), a dramatic, large-cast play set on the

Road to Calvary, which reached the final of the BDL National Festival, and *Lonely Road* (1952) a play with strong atmosphere, as the Holy Family in flight from Bethlehem are given hospitality at a roadside cottage

Other plays to consider: *On with the Dance*; *Profile*; *There Comes a Time*
Publishers: Deane; Garnet Miller; Quekett

Mike Tibbetts (1947–) Scottish dramatist

Scottish playwright Mike Tibbetts won the 1997 Geoffrey Whitworth Award for new playwriting for *The Dancing Fusilier* which is based on his father's experiences in an artillery regiment during and after the Second World War. The cast list contains a whole gallery of characters but with doubling the play can be presented with ten actors. Seventeen years earlier the playwright won the same national award with the comedy *Funny, You Don't Laugh Jewish* (1980).

One of his most-performed plays is *Bottles with Baskets On* (1996), which takes place on the night before a wedding when, after the comic banter, feelings become emotional and events take a dramatic turn. Another popular script is *LittleBro Morning and BigSis Afternoon* (1999) which focuses on two children facing with fortitude a world without loving parents. What makes the play doubly interesting is the way the piece moves backwards and forwards in time so that we see the faces and attitudes of the social workers, the teacher and the father. Though the script is episodic in structure it needs an energised production of simple integrity. *A Talent for Giving* (1999) is a verse play based on an incident in the life of the painter, Albert Dürer.

Other plays to consider: *Murdering Mums; Tre Amici*
Publishers: Samuel French; Brown Son and Ferguson

Jean Lenox Toddie Canadian dramatist

Jean Lenox Toddie is best known for her apparently simple *Tell me Another Story, Sing me Another Song* (1978), which takes a warm and witty look at the mother/daughter relationship. Told in a light-hearted style, this short script explores the irritations and misunderstandings which often build walls between generations – and the love which can help destroy those walls. The script lasts barely 12 pages, in which the two actresses age 40 years.

The three women in *And Go To Innisfree* similarly cross the generations as the central character faces an important life decision while the choice is argued over by her sensible logical self and her carefree spirited younger self.

Other plays to consider: *A Bag of Green Apples; By the Name of Kensington; Is That the Bus to Kensington; The Juice of Wild Strawberries; Keeping Charlie Company; Late Sunday Afternoon – Early Sunday Evening; A Little Something for the Ducks; A Scent of Honeysuckle; White Room of my Remembering*
Publishers: Samuel French

Sue Townsend (1946–) English dramatist

Commenting on her own work Sue Townsend has said, 'I suppose I write about people who do not live in the mainstream of society. My characters are not educated; they do not earn high salaries – if they work at all. I look beneath the surface of their lives. My plays are about loneliness, struggle, survival and the possibility of change. Strangely they are all comedies. Comedy is the most tragic form of drama'.

Written before her comic diaries of the adolescent Adrian Mole made her famous, *Womberang* (1980) is a rumbustious comedy is set in the waiting room of a gynaecological clinic. Yet beneath the broad outrageous humour there are some serious personal heartaches as well as some telling swipes at officialdom, religious fanaticism, the silent majority and the state of the NHS. *Womberang* remains Sue Townsend's best-known short play although her longer script *Bazaar and Rummage* (1982), a genial but revealing comedy featuring a group of agoraphobics and their social workers at a jumble sale, is often played without an interval.

Publishers: Samuel French; Methuen

Michel Tremblay (1942–) French-Canadian dramatist and novelist

Probably the best-known French-Canadian contemporary playwright, Michel Tremblay is a prolific novelist as well as a dramatist. He wrote his first one-act play, *The Train*, in 1964, but his best known short play on both sides of the Atlantic is *Albertine in Five Times* (1984), in which five actresses portray the central character at different times in her life, with each conversing freely with the others. What emerges is the bleak life of a woman repressed by life yet still exhibiting great passion and vitality. Naturally, this affecting play has proved popular with all-female companies.

Publisher: Nick Hern Books

William Trevor (1928–) Irish dramatist, novelist and scriptwriter

Prolific writer of novels, short stories, radio and television scripts, Irish-born William Trevor has written comparatively few plays, and several of those he has produced have been adaptations of his prose works and radio scripts.

In the sensitive, touching *Going Home* (1970) a teenage boy finds himself in a railway carriage with an ageing spinster teacher. After initial antipathy they discover that what links these disparate souls is their loneliness and a feeling of being outcast by their families. It is a many-layered play where the façades of character are gradually stripped away.

The two–hander *Marriages* (1973) focuses on a newly-widowed middle-aged woman and her meeting with the 'other woman' in her husband's life. Adapted from his television script, one of William Trevor's early short plays, *The Girl*, was produced in 1968. Set in suburban London the piece has been described as Pinteresque in style and mood.

Publishers: Samuel French

David Tristram English dramatist

Energetically promoting his own work through a web-site and his own publishing company, David Tristram has rapidly advanced into the forefront of one-act comedy writers in the late 20th century. His first comedy, *Last Tango in Little Grimley*, was a hilarious spoof on the art v. audience appeal debate that goes on in many amateur drama companies, and the four characters who formed its backbone – Gordon, the energetic but harassed chairman; Bernard the dour stage-manager; Margaret the indomitable 'star' performer and Joyce, the meek secretary – are recognisable 'types' in many drama groups.

Last Tango was taken up with alacrity by amateur companies who could laugh at their own lifestyle and it clocked up over a thousand performances in the UK in three years. It was followed with a comparable success, *Last Panto in Little Grimley*, a spoof on pantomime rehearsals which proved to be a copper-bottomed guarantee for laughs for almost any audience. The play has won many festival awards. The trilogy of one-act plays which feature the hapless four has lately been completed by *The Fat Lady Sings in Little Grimley*, in which the spectre of a rival society looms.

Tristram's work has since widened to other contexts. *Brenton v. Brenton* is a spoof of American soaps and mini-series, set in a Chicago advertising agency. *A Jolly Sinister Jape* is a pastiche of the 1920s' thriller. *The Extraordinary Revelations of Orca the Goldfish* exists in both full-length and one-act form and is a two-hander which calls for virtuoso playing as the couch-potato Henry fantasises and recalls episodes in his former life.

These plays are fast-paced, laced with both one-liners and vigorous physical action and plotted deftly. Tristram's one-act plays rank amongst the most accessible and successful comedies of the present-day.

Other plays to consider: *Joining the Club*; *What's for Pudding?*
Publishers: Flying Duck Publications; Samuel French

Philip Turner (1925–) English dramatist and writer

Returning to become ordained as a priest in the Anglican church after service in the Army in World War II, Philip Turner unleashed a series of powerful short dramatic pieces designed for use mainly in churches, which had much vogue in the 1950s and 1960s. Their style was in modern blank verse, and they mixed Biblical stories and modern imagery, laced with contemporary language.

Of these *Christ in the Concrete City* has proved the most durable, and is still found (subsequently updated by Turner) in print and in frequent production 50 years after it was first performed in 1953. Written for a cast of six actors, who play many different roles (varying between contemporary cameos, Biblical characters and a chorus), in 60 minutes it tells the story of Christ's last days, interspersed with modern scenes which provide ironic contrast to the events of Holy Week. Its effectiveness comes from combining sparse poetic lyricism (Turner acknowledges the influence of Henri Gheon's meditative classic *The Way of the Cross* and the plays of RH Ward) with some flashes of strong social comment and knockabout comedy.

Cry Dawn in Dark Babylon (1959), intended as a sequel to Concrete City, is in the same style, and deals with how an ordinary family combat the grief of the loss of one of their children. *Madonna in Concrete*, (1971), took a similar approach to the story of the Nativity mixing Biblical and modern scenes.

Turner also wrote a series of short plays which were originally performed in the streets and pubs of his Leeds parish and later used by Pamela Keily's New Pilgrim Players for performance on the back of a truck in open-air spaces in the towns and cities of Northern England. These were necessarily punchy and terse, and reflected a kind of Christian agit-prop approach but they had deeply moving quieter moments (as, for instance, in the administration of the sacrament to a dying man in *Passion in Paradise Street*, 1959). This play, along with *Mann's End* and a piece performed on the shop-floor of factories (*Six-fifteen to Eternity*) was collected in a volume called *Tell it With Trumpets*.

When he turned to writing stories for children, Turner won the Carnegie Medal for the Best UK Childrens' Book of 1965.

Other plays to consider: *Cantata for Derelicts*; *Casey*; *How Many Miles to Bethlehem?*; *Men in Stone*; *So Long at the Fair*; *This is the Word*; *Watch at the World's End*; *Word Made Flesh*
Publishers: SPCK; Baker's Plays; Joint Board of Christian Education of Australia and New Zealand

* Richard Tydeman (1915–) English dramatist and writer

Tydeman has combined his life as an Anglican priest with writing many short pieces designed for amateur performance. He was prolific in writing 'mini-dramas' which proved to be a popular genre in their own right when first published in the 1960s and 1970s. These are 15–20 minute pieces designed to need little rehearsal, costume or props, and able to be played by mixed or all-women casts. There are a score of them which cover a wide range of topics (some of the best are *Ah! Cruel Fate!*; *Hip-Hip-Horatius*; *Hi-fi Spy*; *Puss in Slippers*; *Red Hot Cinders*; *Spacewoman*; *Way out West*) all written in a light-hearted revue sketch style, using neat rhyming couplets, and requiring only a minimum of line-learning by cast members. Many of them have remained in print for decades. Their style makes them ideal for use as a 'quick fix' when some entertainment is needed for a social occasion and for imitation by neophyte writers.

Tydeman also wrote a number of one-act plays on more serious themes. *Idea for a Play* (1957) tackles the weighty theme of 'what can save the world?' in amusing symbolism, and in *The Thistle in Donkey Field* (1956) the characters typify how mankind, like thistles, react to the 'donkey' which may destroy their world. *Ballista* (1960) is set in a small central Mediterranean island which hosts a Roman army and creates clever analogies to modern arguments about war and peace. *Dawn on our Darkness* is an effective, though relatively simple, presentation of the Nativity of Christ.

Other plays to consider: *Duet with Dowagers*; *Gilbert and Solomon*; *Hearts and Humours*; *Garden Meeting*; *High Tension*
Publishers: Evans; Samuel French

Jean-Claude van Itallie (1936–) American dramatist

Born in Brussels, Van Itallie exploded on to the off-Broadway theatrical scene in the mid-'60s. Those were exciting times where revolt and reformation were widely expressed in the world of the arts, and his plays were part of the new theatrical voice. He has said that he was intent on playing around with many forms and styles to express a clear 'theatre optic'.

One of his earlier successes was a trio of short scripts under the title of *America Hurrah* (1966), the most notable being *Interview*, a clever rhythmic interplay of words and eight characters set in an employment agency where all the applicants are called Smith. *TV* illustrates the dumbing down and trivialisation of much of the mass media while *Motel*, subtitled *A Masque for Three Dolls*, comments about the cheap superficiality of modern life.

His first play to be produced was *War* (1963), a strong three-hander which pits mere man against the 'winged chariot' of time. Over the succeeding years he has written dozens of short plays and monologues, many having being collected under such titles as *Seven Short and Very Short Plays* (1975) which include the biting satire on consumerism, *Eat Cake* and the disturbing *Take a Deep Breath*. In lighter mood are two pop-art Hollywood comedies *Almost Like Being* (1964) and *I'm Really Here* (1964) which have been referred to as the 'Doris Day plays', as they reflect the artifice of the show business world.

A further triptych of plays comprise *Bag Lady* (1979), a day in the life of the witty eponymous Clara, *Sunset Freeway* (1983) featuring prattling actress Judy lost in her fantasy world as she drives alone along a Californian highway, and *Final Orders* (1983) in which two astronauts are faced with an earth–shattering decision.

Other plays to consider: *The Girl and the Soldier*; *Harold*; *The Hunter and the Bird*; *Photographs: Mary and Howard*; *Rosary*; *Struck Dumb*; *Thoughts on the Instant of Greeting a Friend in the Street*; *Where is the Queen?*
Publishers: Dramatists Play Service

Frank Vickery (1951–) Welsh dramatist and actor

Once described as 'the Alan Ayckbourn of the Welsh Valleys', Frank Vickery has written many plays which have found considerable favour far beyond his native Wales. His subject is human relationships – often family relationships – where he finds warmth, understanding and considerable humour. As an actor too, he knows how to write good character roles which adds to the appeal of his work.

He now runs his own theatre company for which he writes mainly full-length plays but six of his earlier shorter pieces still appear frequently. Of these the most popular has proved *After I'm Gone* (1978) which won the British Final of One-Act Plays in 1978 and is typical of the writer's work.

Green Favours (1994) is a romantic comedy set in the unlikely location of an allotment shed while the humour in *A Night Out* (1986) comes from a daughter's desperate attempts to have a evening of passion with her boyfriend only to find she is forever thwarted by her parents. The parents in *The Drag Factor* (1994) have to come to terms with the fact that their son is gay, their attitudes suggesting that this might now need to be played as a period piece.

Other plays to consider: *Bedside Manner*; *See You Tomorrow*; *Split Ends*
Publishers: Samuel French; Drama Association of Wales; New Plays Network

Cherry Vooght English dramatist

Rooted in middle-class (and usually country-town or village) England, Cherry Vooght's work has been a popular choice for women's groups and some of her one-act plays still have vigorous life in them when played today. A set of five of her one-act plays is collected in a volume called *A Seat in the Park*.

One of the pieces in this is the frequently-played *See if I Care* (1972), in which two old ladies meet daily on a park bench to find refuge and mutual solace. The pathos of the fantasy world which they conjure up contrasts with the unsentimental real-life relationship which binds them closely. Another of Vooght's best-known one-act plays, *People Like Us* (1976), offers a similar situation and is a wry and sensitive piece in which three women on a caravan holiday site eventually reveal their insecurities and loneliness to each other.

Vooght often writes large, all-female one-act plays. *Bright Society* (1966) is an amusing and well-characterised piece about last-minute rehearsals for a drama festival and, in the same vein, *Let's Be Friends* (1963) features hectic preparations for a local radio programme.

Other plays to consider: *Barbecue*; *Be an Angel*; *Bright Interval*; *Come Live with Me*; *Dark Remedy*; *Everything in the Garden*; *Night Song*; *Nineteen the Beacon*; *Outrageous Fortune*; *The Pleasure of your Company*; *Repent at Leisure*; *Ring Out Wild Bells*; *Still Life*; *Wednesday's Child*; *A World of her Own*
Publishers: English Theatre Guild; Samuel French; Weinberger

Nick Warburton (1955–) English dramatist

Nick Warburton has specialised in the one-act form in his stage work since the 1980s and his plays generally have humour, compassion, imagination and are genuinely practical. Before publication, they have often been tested out by local drama groups in and around Cambridge, England, where he lives. A trilogy of some of his one-act comedies about aspects of Shakespeare (*Don't Blame it on the Boots*; *Distracted Globe* (1993); *Easy Stages*; *The Droitwich Discovery*) would make an entertaining 'themed' evening.

Warburton was a primary-school teacher before he became a full-time writer and he frequently writes with junior and youth cast performance in mind (see *Ghost Writer*; *Melons at the Parsonage*). *Zartan* is a brilliant pastiche on the Tarzan story and can be played with success by youth and adult casts alike. *Round the World with Class Six* has become a favourite play for companies with junior members, since it gives a plethora of opportunities to young performers as Drake's voyage around the world 'comes to life' in the middle of a boring classroom day. A company playing it reached the final of the All-England Theatre Festival in 2004.

Warburton is a frequent contributor of scripts to BBC television series (*Doctors*, *EastEnders*, *Holby City*) and also to radio drama and his *Conversations from the Engine Room* was joint-winner of the BBC/Radio Times Drama Award in 1985. He has adapted some of his shorter radio plays for the stage (*Waiting for Nesbit*; *The Loophole*; *Babushka*; *Music Lovers)* and remains strongly interested in amateur theatre and in writing new one-act plays. Recently some of these have been successfully premiered as lunchtime pieces at Alan Ayckbourn's Stephen Joseph Theatre at Scarborough

Other plays to consider: *Dickens' Children*; *Domby-Dom*; *Garlic and Lavender*; *Keeping Secrets*; *The Last Bread Pudding*; *The Nativity Letters*; *Not Bobby*; *Office Song*; *Receive this Light*; *Sour Grapes and Ashes*
Publishers: Samuel French

John Waterhouse (1928–) English dramatist

Waterhouse has produced a stream of clever one-act comedies in recent years, which have deservedly won frequent performance by amateur groups. *I Spy* is a spoof on Bond movies, with hero Cyril working from his Bradford council house and involved with the intelligence services and a beautiful Russian femme fatale. There is similar farcical mayhem in *In the Doghouse* in which a pair of brothers are bullied by debt-collectors who, in turn, are mistaken by the brothers' wives for pall-bearers. *Off the Rails* (1973) has echoes of the classic Will Hay film, *Oh! Mr Porter*.

Other plays to consider: *The Cardboard Cavaliers*; *Frank's Feathered Friend*; *Hazel's Nuts*; *Heaven to Betsy*; *Jump Off*; *Just the Ticket*; *Mayhem at Mudlark Manor*; *Miss Clithold's Class of '58*; *A Nest of Cuckoo*; *Pillar to Post*; *Ping-*

Pong; *The Siege of Sevastopol Terrace*; *Six of the Best*; *Strictly for the Birds*; *Talk of the Devil*
Publishers: Samuel French; New Playwrights Network

Keith Waterhouse and Willis Hall British dramatists

See under Willis Hall and Keith Waterhouse

Frank Wedekind (1864–1918) German dramatist

In his use of non-naturalistic devices, Wedekind clearly led the movement of Expressionist theatre in Europe in the early part of the 20th century. Though his well-known one-act play, *The Singer* (1898), amusingly chronicles the dressing-room histrionics of an opera star before a performance, most of his plays have a capacity to shock. *Death and Devil* is a drama set in a brothel.

Publishers: Calder and Boyars; Samuel French

Fay Weldon (1931–) English dramatist and novelist

Turning from writing novels to the theatre in mid-career, Fay Weldon has produced some interesting and thoughtful one-act plays which have rapidly proved themselves on the festival circuit. *The Reading Group*, as its name suggests, deals with the relationships of a disparate group who assemble on a regular basis. *Words of Advice* (1975) contains much thoughtful dialogue as friends try to advise a couple whose marriage is on the rocks. The recent *Flood Warning* (2003) explores the human side of a topical environmental theme and develops the tension between two sisters who in turn release a metaphorical flood of family secrets as the waters rise and their fragile relationship collapses.

Other plays to consider: *Friends*; *Permanence*
Publishers: Samuel French

John Whiting (1917–1963) English dramatist

Probably because of their allusive, elusive style, John Whiting's plays have never been hugely popular with audiences but have often found acclaim from critics, directors and actors. Typical of his work is his only one-act play, the intriguing *No Why* (1964) in which a child eventually commits suicide. This provocative play can be taken as a metaphor or parable and needs to create a languid decadent atmosphere of simmering emotion.

Publishers: Samuel French; Heinemann

Percival Wilde (1887–1968) American dramatist and critic

Wilde was pre-eminent amongst American exponents of the one-act form in the period between the First and Second World War. He began working as a banker, but became a book reviewer for the *New York Times* and then a full-time writer.

He wrote over a hundred one-act plays, displaying command of a wide range of styles, and many of them were placed in inter-war anthologies. He was also the author of *The Craftsmanship of the One-act Play*.

He could be sharply critical of the work of his colleagues in the one-act form, not fearing to call GB Shaw 'sloppy', Eugene O'Neill's one-acters 'overwritten' and Noël Coward's short plays as 'often marred by the introduction of songs and dances which have no place in the play and which were written in to please the actors'.

The Blood of the Martyrs (1937; set in a prison cell in an unnamed country) *Pawns* (about Russian mobilisation) and *The Traitor* (1923; set in the Boer War) represent some of his more frequently-performed serious plays, but he also wrote many comedies and burlesques. Of these, *Lot's Wife* (1931; in which some comic American stereotypes are thinly disguised as a Biblical family) is one of the best and *The Sportsmen* (1950; described as 'a war-time Lancashire one-act comedy') one of the more unusual.

Other plays to consider: *Catesby; Comrades in Arms; Confessional; Dawn; The Enchanted Christmas Tree; The Finger of God; The Lift that Never Failed; The Line of No Resistance; The Moving Finger; Ordeal by Battle; Playing with Fire; A Question of Morality; Refund; The Sequel; The Short Cut; The Thing; The Villain in the Piece*
Publishers: Samuel French

Thornton Wilder (1897–1945) American dramatist and novelist

Thornton Wilder is seen by many as a dramatist who epitomises the values and optimistic outlook of 20th-century 'middle America', where he was born and raised. Most of his plays are leavened with home-spun philosophy and with a sunny optimism about life and the human condition. He was an early user of Brechtian devices such as the creation of elaborate scenes with minimal props, and characters breaking out of role to address the audience with asides and commentary on the play. Though best known for major full-length plays such as *Our Town* and *The Skin of Our Teeth*, Thornton Wilder also wrote some significant one-act plays. His second published work for the theatre, in 1928, was a set of short-pieces under the title *The Angel That Troubled the Waters*, and none of them were longer than 17 pages long. Despite being known as 'three-minute plays' they were designed to be read rather than performed.

A more significant contribution to the one-act genre came in the volume called *The Long Christmas Dinner* (1931). The intriguing play which gave its title to the whole volume covers the life of a single family over a hundred years and requires considerable skill in playing and costuming. Wilder himself liked *The Happy Journey* (1931) the best of all his one-act plays. Here, with the aid of only a few chairs, he re-creates the atmosphere of a family outing with the portrait of a caring middle-class mother at its heart. *Pullman Car Hiawatha*

(1931) is a fascinating large-cast piece which portrays the inner-thoughts and feelings of a disparate group of travellers in various compartments of a sleeping-car on a train crossing the continent, whilst also locating them in the wider cosmic scheme of things. *Such Things Only Happen in Books*, on the other hand, is rooted in the life of a single-household where a novelist believes his domestic context is mundane and the irony is that he is blissfully unaware of all the family dramas unfolding around him. Wilder also wrote many novels and won the Pultizer Prize for Literature but said, 'I consider the theatre as the greatest of all art-forms'.

Other plays to consider: *Childhood; The Drunken Sisters; Love and How To Cure It; Queens of France*
Publishers: Samuel French

Tennessee Williams (1911–1983) American dramatist

One of the foremost American dramatists of the 20th century, Tennessee Williams is best known for his major full-length plays. However, their success may have overshadowed his rich output of more than 40 short plays written between 1934 and 1981. Whilst some of these scripts did not find favour and were not published, there are about 30 still in print. The length of these plays varies widely. *This Property is Condemned* (1942) lasts barely 15 minutes whilst *Suddenly Last Summer* (1958) runs just over the hour. Both these works were developed into film versions. An even more famous cinema version came in 1956 when *27 Wagons Full of Cotton* (1955) emerged as *Baby Doll*.

All the themes that have made his major works so popular are to be found in most of his minor works – a search for fulfilment, fragile delicate beauty facing a crude rawness, a seething undercurrent of sexual passion, lonely desperate souls seeking solace and brief pleasures, and lost dreams. They are plays of mood and atmosphere, usually the hothouse atmosphere of the American deep South. Two or three plays might be linked together to create a Tennessee Williams evening, for example, *This Property is Condemned, Talk to me Like the Rain* (1958) and *Hullo from Bertha* (1945) would trace Southern women at three stages of their lives.

The Purfication (1944) is unique in that it is the playwright's only verse play – a highly theatrical, almost operatic poem. Originally staged as a curtain raiser to *Suddenly Last Summer* under the title *Garden Suburb, Something Unspoken* (1955) affords splendid opportunities for two older actresses, while *The Case of the Crushed Petunias* (1973) is a delicate lyrical fantasy.

Other plays to consider: *Auto-Da-Fe; Confessional; The Dark Room; The Long Goodbye; The Frosted Glass Coffin; The Gnadiges Fraulein; I Can't Imagine Tomorrow; In the Bar of The Tokyo Hotel; I Rise in Flame Cried the Pheonix; The Lady of Larkspur Lotion; Lord Byron's Love Letters; Mooney's Don't Cry; The Mutilated; A Perfect Analysis Given by a Parrot; Portrait of a Madonna;*

The Strangest Kind of Love Letters; *Ten Blocks on the Camino Real*; *The Unsatisfactory Supper*
Publishers: Dramatists Play Service; New Directions

David Henry Wilson (1937–) British dramatist

Playwright, novelist, lecturer and writer of children's stories, David Henry Wilson has won critical acclaim for his short plays in Britain, the States, and in Europe, especially in Germany where he founded the university theatre at Konstanz.

Part of his wide appeal may arise from his serious universal themes which are often leavened with humour. Truth, loneliness and death feature largely in his work but his view is often taken from a perceptive philosophical stance. In *The Death Artist*, a miser receives the strange eponymous visitor who gradually undermines his confidence and former attitudes to life and death. Death lies beyond the prison cell door in the harrowing *The Fourth Prisoner* where, once again, a night visitor calls to give some hope and emotional strength to face a life beyond the cage. Freedom is one of the many themes in *The Escapologist* where other subjects raised are the existence of God and the fate of Man.

There is more than an undercurrent of religion in one of the author's more popular plays, *Are You Normal, Mr Norman?* (1984), in which an insane dentist meets a very sticky end. The play also points out the thin line between normality and lunacy. In completely different mood, the children's play, *All the World's a Stage* (1968) has a flexible cast and can be played on a bare stage.

Other plays to consider: *How to Make your Theatre Pay*; *If Yer Take a Short Cut*; *The Wall*; *Wendlebury Day*
Publishers: Samuel French

Lanford Wilson (1937–) American dramatist

One of several new young American playwrights who emerged on to the off-off Broadway scene in the '60s, Pulitzer Prize-winning Lanford Wilson's themes often concern loneliness, isolation, decay and loss, frequently set against a family or socially deprived background. His dialogue is sharp and realistic.

It was the short play *Home Free* (1964) which first brought the writer's name to the attention of New York audiences. This demanding script centres on an intense, incestuous brother–sister relationship in which the couple have withdrawn from reality to create their own safe fantasy world. Although the characters are fragile, the performances need to be strong to bring out the subtle sensitivity of the emotions. This popular play needs a production of integrity.

Another frequently performed two-hander is the highly inventive *The Great Nebula of Orion* (1970), in which two girlhood friends meet up after an absence of some years. While on the surface they have achieved success in marriage and career, it gradually becomes evident that under the façade there is an aching void in their lives.

In the clever *Wandering* (1966) rapid-fire dialogue is used to illustrate a man's life and human existence in a mere matter of minutes while *The Madness of Lady Bright* (1964) depicts the demise of an ageing lonely drag artist as his past comes to haunt him. Loneliness is also the underlying theme of *Brontosaurus* (1977) which explores the truth hidden behind the wise-cracking banter of a cynical female antiques dealer.

Another of Lanford Wilson's many successful off-Broadway plays is *The Sand Castle* (1965) which explores the passion, heartache, joy and pain of growing through adolescence. With seven characters this is one of the larger cast plays in this author's extensive collection of highly regarded one-act plays.

Other plays to consider: *Abstinence*; *Days Ahead*; *The Family Continues*; *Say de Kooning*; *Sextet (Yes)*; *Stoop*; *This is the Rill Speaking*; *Thymus Vulgaris*; *Your Everyday Ghost Story*

Publishers: Dramatists Play Service; Weinberger, Methuen

Snoo Wilson (1948–) English dramatist

From the outset of his career Wilson has always been amongst the avant-garde of British playwrights, first working with David Hare and Tony Bicat in the Portable Theatre Company. He remains deeply critical of traditional proscenium-arch theatre and the attitudes of conventional managements and theatre-goers. He began by writing 'long'-short plays such as *Blowjob* (two skinheads seeking to blow up a factory), *Pignight* (a kind of dark Animal Farm-like story) and *Lay By*.

In a later one-act play, *The Soul of the White Ant* (1976), the life and friends of the South African naturalist Eugene Marais, seen by Wilson as part-visionary and part-charlatan, are intertwined in a bizarre series of events. Wilson might be characterised as a 'political absurdist': performance and appreciation of his material needs insight and courage from both performers and audiences.

Publishers: Methuen

Valerie Windsor (1946–) British dramatist and scriptwriter

Actress and television scriptwriter, Valerie Windsor is best known for her one-act play *Effie's Burning* (1987), a tightly-written play with themes of control, injustice, power and anger. Yet counter-pointing these strong feelings there is also humour; indeed the play has been described as an emotional switchback ride. The play explores the relationship between a sensitive, insecure nurse and an elderly lady with learning difficulties who has been admitted to hospital with severe burns. It is the exploration of both characters and their growing understanding which is at the heart of the play. With two strong roles for women *Effie's Burning* has proved a popular festival script.

Publishers: Samuel French

Charles Wood (1932–) English dramatist and film script-writer

Wood's experience of the army has coloured much of his writing, but he is by no means a simple anti-war propagandist. Rather, his plays are black comedies about army life which betray no obvious political stance, such as *Prisoner and Escort*. Another frequent topic of his writing is the business of film-making, in which he has also been deeply involved (most notably as the scriptwriter of the Beatles' film *Help!*).

Other plays to consider: *Don't Make Me Laugh*; *John Thomas*; *Labour*; *Meals on Wheels*; *Spare*; *Tie up the Ballcock*
Publishers: Samuel French

Margaret Wood (1911–2002) English dramatist

Margaret Wood established herself as a popular playwright specialising in the one-act form in the 1950s and her plays have proved durable. She was born in Great Yarmouth and educated at Royal Holloway College, London University and Cambridge. She taught in schools and wrote scripts for BBC Schools Radio before branching out into work for the theatre. She was five times the winner of the British Drama League's Original Play Award in the years following World War II and she also won an *Amateur Stage* playwriting competition.

She has adapted a number of historical themes (e.g. *Cato's Daughter* (1957) set in ancient Rome; *Martyred Wives*, about the wives of the 19th-century Tolpuddle Martyrs) for all-women casts, but she has also written for mixed casts and youth performers. The themes of her work are varied and have ranged remarkably from village-hall tensions (*Parochial Politics*) to international diplomacy (*Top Table*, 1973). Religion and pacifism were amongst her main interests and these are reflected in some of her best-known pieces (e.g. *Peace hath her Victories*, 1975; *The Road to Damascus* 1956). She has written over a hundred published plays, most of them one-acters and her work is always neatly crafted and recognises the possible limitations of cast size and settings in amateur theatre. The roles she creates are credible and well within the compass of amateur actors.

Other plays to consider: *The Copper Kettle*; *Courting Disaster*; *Covenant with Death*; *Crying in the Wilderness*; *The Day of Atonement*; *A Dog's Life*; *Donatus and the Devil*; *Edward*; *A Fishy Business*; *Fools' Errand*; *The Guilty Generation*; *Home is the Sailor*; *Instruments of Darkness*; *A Kind of Justice*; *Last Scene of All*; *A Moving Story*; *Outpatients*; *Person of no Consequence*; *Pilgrim's Way*; *The Primrose Path*; *Root of all Evil*; *Susannah of the Five Elders*; *The Witches*; *The Withington Warrior*
Publishers: Samuel French

* Victoria Wood (1953–) English comedienne and dramatist

Best known as one of the foremost comediennes of her generation, Victoria Wood has also penned several stage plays. Though not working so far in the one-act stage form, she has been a skilful writer of TV sit-coms. The publication of some of her scripts of *Dinnerladies* (1999) in book form offers the opportunity for enterprising directors to fashion stage pieces from them. The original episodes were 30 minutes in length and confined to a single set in a works canteen: the key question and challenge is whether to replicate or deliberately deviate from the characterisations which brought the scripts to life on television.

Other plays to consider: *Talent*
Publishers: Methuen

Olwyn Wymark (1932–) American dramatist

Although American-born, Olwyn Wymark has spent much of her creative life in Britain. Of the many plays that she has written for radio, television, children and the theatre, many are short, intriguing pieces. Her universal themes cover tension, guilt, isolation and desperation, but these feelings are revealed in a ingenious, theatrical ways.

Comparisons have been made with Pinter's early work, and this can be seen particularly in the claustrophobic *Stay Where You Are* (1969). In the same collection of her scripts *Neither Here nor There* (1971) is a fascinating box of tricks where, as in several of her plays, there is an element of ritual and the playing of mind games. *The Twenty Second Day* (1984) was originally a radio play but has worked effectively on stage, while *Mothering Sunday* is a quirky comedy

Perhaps her best-known play is *Find Me* (1997), based on the true story of a mentally disturbed girl and the effect her disability has on her caring but distraught family. As the structure is episodic, it is sometimes sympathetically abridged to fit the one-act format. Wymark has also made translations of the plays of the Italian playwright, Dario Fo.

Other plays to consider: *And After Nature – Art*; *Coda*; *The Gymnasium*; *The Inhabitants*; *Jack the Giant-Killer*; *Lunchtime Concert*; *The Technicians*; *We Three*
Publishers: Calder and Boyars; Samuel French; Arnold

WB Yeats (1865–1939) Irish dramatist

One of the greatest of Irish literary figures, Yeats was amongst the founders and encouragers of Irish theatre at the turn of the 20th century but his hope for a distinctive Irish style of play which would be a poetic celebration of both legend and history was only fitfully achieved. He both wrote and produced plays for the Abbey Theatre. Many of his one-act plays were lyrical, meditative and expository, but not, in the end-product, particularly dramatic.

Of his one-act work, *The Words Upon the Window Pane* (1930) is best-known. In this play, the vision of Jonathan Swift is created in a spiritualist séance. The part of the medium, Mrs Henderson, makes great demands on an actress, since she also has to play the characters who are brought to life through the séance. Though the play reflects Yeats's pre-occupation with the identity of Ireland, as much can be inferred from the Introduction to the play (33 pages long) as from the play (which is 25 pages long) in the original published edition. It is, in the end, more of literary and biographical rather than dramatic interest.

Other plays to consider: *Cathleen ni Houlihan*; *The Land of Heart's Desire*; *The Pot of Broth*; *Purgatory*; *The Shadowy Waters*
Publishers: Oberon Books

Entries which are starred (*) in the above listings include a comment of general significance beyond the information about the particular writer.

an extra 'lucky dip' of one-act plays

Here is a personal choice of some notable one-act plays (from all periods) by authors who have not been included in the biography section.

Anthony Armstrong – **In the Dentist's Chair**
Dana Bagshaw – **Cell Talk**
Laurence Binyon – **Godstowe Nunnery**
Ian Blair – **Gilhooley Came**
Elda Cadogan – **Rise and Shine**
Richard Cameron – **Can't Stand up for Falling Down**
Gwyn Clark – **When the Bough Breaks**
Beverley Cross – **The Crickets Sing**
Heather Dinsmore – **Blue**
Oliphant Down – **The Maker of Dreams**
Donald East – **Once Upon a Seashore**
Bruce Fisk – **Strawberry Jam**
Terence Frisby – **Seaside Postcard**
Henri Gheon – **The Farce at the Devil's Bridge**
Alan Gosling – **A Dead Liberty**
Sacha Guitry – **Villa for Sale**
Holworthy Hall and Robert Middlemiss – **The Valiant**
Lee Hall – **Spoonface Steinberg**
Cecily Hamilton and Christopher St John – **How the Vote was Won**
Ron Hart – **Lunch Girls**
June Hornby – **The Education of Meg**
Ann Jellicoe – **The Rising Generation**
Elizabeth Johnson – **A Bad Play for an Old Lady**
Jennifer Johnson – **The Nightingale and Not the Lark**
Patricia Joudry – **The Song of Louise in the Morning**
Sarah Kane – **4.48 Psychosis**
Garrison Keillor – **The Mid-life Crisis of Dionysus**
William Kozlenko – **The Earth is Ours**
Barry Kyle – **Sylvia Plath**
Eugene Labiche – **90 Degrees in the Shade**
Eugene Labiche and Martin – **The 37 Sous of M. Montaudoin**
Michael Lambe – **The Treatment of Mungo Tweet**
Benn Levy – **The Truth About the Truth**
Neville Malin – **Let's Be Devils**
Tony Marchant – **Raspberry**
Paul Avila Mayer – **Eternal Triangle**
Stephen McDonald – **Not About Heroes**

John Ford Noonan – **A Coupla White Chicks Standin' Around Talkin'**
Sean O'Casey – **Bedtime Story**
Louise Page – **Tissue**
Ronald Parr – **When Dames Were Bold**
David Perry – **As Good as New**
Tony Powell – **Spitfire Nativity**
Ayshe Raif – **Café Society**
Don Roberts – **The Ragwoman of the Shambles**
Jeannie van Rompaey – **Afternoons on the Keyserlei**
Tony Rushforth – **Seascape**
Ardine L Rushkin – **The Art of Remembering**
David Schutte – **A Bite of the Apple**
Rosemary Anne Sisson – **The Acrobats**
Philip Stagg – **Where the Brass Bands Play**
Philip Stagg – **The Last Time I Saw Paris**
Alfred Sutro – **A Marriage Has been Arranged**
Arthur Swinson – **The Sword is Double-Edged**
Dylan Thomas – **Return Journey**
Sean Vincent – **The Audition**
Dick Vosburg and Frank Lazarus – **A Day in Hollywood, a Night in the Ukraine**
Oscar Wilde – **A Florentine Tragedy**
Heathcote Williams – **The Local Stigmatic**

the history of the **one-act play**

from early history to 1850

the Greeks

The one-act play is no recent phenomenon. It came into existence 25 centuries ago in ancient Greece, when the plays of Aeschylus, Sophocles, Euripides, Aristophanes and others were presented in the Temple of Dionysus, the most sacred spot in Athens, in honour of the god who gave his name to the temple.

These plays were quite long by modern one-act standards (60–80 minutes to judge by copies of the texts that we have) but they were presented without interval to vast audiences who watched them in rapt attention, well aware of their cultural significance.

References in Aristophanes' *The Birds* suggest that they were often played in groups before judges who marked them and placed them in order, as in a modern-day drama festival. The credit for the institution of the first 'drama festival' in 534 is usually given to the Athenian statesman/demagogue Pisistratus (c. 605–527 BC)

The conditions of performance were enviable. The state paid the bills of the production and of the actors, and the directors of the plays were treated with great respect, and seen as akin to ministers of religion. Places of business were closed, the law courts adjourned, and prisoners were released temporarily from gaols so that they might be 'improved' by the plays.

Most of the plays had a religious and moral emphasis and posed dilemmas of cosmic significance, e.g. in Sophocles' *Antigone*, the audience is invited to consider whether the citizen should obey the state or the Gods, when the two are in conflict. Dramatists looked at life from the standpoint of an undoubted eternity.

The one-act play stood at the heart of Greek cultural life and it is estimated that, on average, two-thirds of the population of Athens (some 30,000 people) saw each play. The selection of plays for the festival was the responsibility of a member of the Athenian Assembly called the Archon. The winning dramatist had his name proclaimed by a herald and was crowned in the theatre with a wreath of ivy by the Archon.

The comedies of Menander were still being performed in Antioch (in modern-day Syria) as late as the 5th century and records suggest that short dramatic entertainments were also staged in the cultural life of Rome (for instance, in the intervals between chariot races at the hippodrome).

the middle ages

Undoubtedly there were dramatic elements in the secular story-telling of later ages (from the recounting of the legend of Beowulf to the stories of the Canterbury Tales), but we have no surviving detailed texts to confirm this. We know more about the evolution of one-act drama in the early Christian church.

From the very beginning, the tradition of 're-enacting' the Last Supper of Jesus and his disciples was enshrined in the ritual of the Eucharist; the usually elevated area of the sanctuary of a church was the 'stage' on which this occurred. The chancels of churches were also used at this time as simple dramatic episodes were developed in the liturgy of services: for example, on Good Friday a crucifix was processed through church, to the accompaniment of Misereres sung by the choir; on Easter Sunday, a tomb was represented, and a stone rolled away to the accompaniment of the choir singing Alleluias. Other incidents in the Old and New Testaments (the Garden of Eden, the troubled relationship of Cain and Abel, the building of Noah's Ark, the Birth of Christ, the adventures of St Paul) began to be dramatised and inserted into church services at certain times of the year, sometimes replacing the sermon.

By the 11th and 12th centuries, priests had been replaced by lay-people as actors, and members of craft guilds often took on roles and stories which were akin to their own working occupations. Thus masons might act out a play concerned with the creation of the world, fishmongers the story of Jonah and the whale, and shipwrights the story of Noah and his ark. In time the plays moved from presentation in church (in the chancel or nave) to the porch and eventually to outdoors and they became events in themselves. Then came the desire to play them on movable carts, so that they might be seen by the whole population of a town as they went through the streets.

Thus in Britain, sequences of one-act plays, the elements of the Mystery and Morality plays of York, Lincoln, Coventry, Wakefield and other cities, came into being. These sequences (between 10 and 20 minutes long) dramatised the spiritual history of the human race as seen from a Christian perspective. They included comedy (such as the episode of Mak, the sheep-stealer in the Wakefield plays), as well as drama and melodrama. From the porches of churches these plays progressed to small mobile theatres – carts which processed around the town. On these, makeshift stages were developed, with the performers often changing beneath them or at the side.

Continental equivalents grew up under different names in France, Italy, Spain and Germany. The famous Oberammergau Passion Play – now a full-length theatrical event – owes its origins to a shorter 'mystery' play performed in this remote Bavarian village from 1634 onwards.

Outside the church, *Commedia del arte* was the name given to a form of popular improvised comedy which flourished in Europe from the 16th to the early 18th century, and which originated from the rustic farces performed at Carnival time by amateur groups in southern Italy. Each member of a professional touring *Commedia del arte* company had his own character or 'mask' (the old man, the learned pedant, the swashbucking soldier, etc) and the pieces performed were often quite short in length. It is believed that English pantomime has its origin in this form of theatre.

Elizabethan times

Though Shakespeare left us no specifically short-play texts, we know from the internal evidence of his plays that the one-act form was alive and well in Elizabethan times. The Players come to Elsinore to play the short one-act play *The Tragedy of Gonzago* before Hamlet's parents, unaware of the unfortunate context of their story; Peter Quince and his fellow-players demonstrate that the one-act form could be attempted by the working-classes, as they labour enthusiastically through *The Tale of Pyramus and Thisbe* before an amused audience of courtiers in *A Midsummer Night's Dream*. There are other references to particular 'entertainments' which are presented before court and which are clearly short dramatic episodes rather than full-blown theatrical constructions. Thomas Middleton wrote some one-act plays, among them pageants for the Lord Mayor of London, though these are much less-known and less revived than his full-length plays.

the eighteenth and nineteenth centuries

The public theatre languished somewhat after the Restoration period in England, partly through the restriction of performance to theatres which were licensed by Patent. However, in London, the monopoly of Covent Garden and Drury Lane was circumvented by people like Samuel Foote, who leased the Haymarket Theatre. It is reported that Foote evaded the restrictive terms of the Licensing Act of 1737 by 'inviting his friends to a dish of tea or chocolate', their invitation-card also incidentally giving admittance to short entertainments in which Foote mimicked his fellow-actors and other public characters – an early form of 'cabaret'.

Novelists such as Jane Austen provide us with plenty of evidence that 'amateur theatricals' were also alive and well in the country houses of the land in the early 19th century. The young ladies of *Mansfield Park* work excitedly to present a piece of drama in the drawing room after dinner, but it is clearly not a full-length play, Charles Dickens himself was an enthusiastic amateur actor and spent much of his spare time acting in one-act plays with his friends, as well as giving dramatic recitals of his own work.

the beginnings of the modern one-act play 1850–1918

the purpose-built theatre

The beginnings of the modern one-act play in the English-speaking world can be traced to a period in the middle of the 19th century, when, in Britain, Ireland and the USA, pieces were written for performance in purpose-built theatres – either as adjuncts to vaudeville bills or to longer plays.

These pieces were played by professional performers either as 'curtain-raisers' or as 'after-pieces' and were seen as an additonal attraction to lure in patrons. One early example, popular on both sides of the Atlantic, was JM Morton's farce **Box and Cox** (1847), a light-hearted 30-minute piece in which a landlady lets a room to two lodgers, who keep conveniently complementary working hours. When the two lodgers fall in love with the same girl, complications ensue, and the girl eventually goes off with a third man, Mr Knox, whilst Box and Cox derive a resigned friendship from their earlier rivalry.

in the USA

In the USA, the plays of Brandon Howard, known as the father of American theatre, included some one-act pieces, the most famous of which was **Old Love Letters** (1878). Edward Harrigan wrote 75 short pieces for inclusion in his vaudeville shows in the 1870s, but, by their brevity and low comedy style, these were really more akin to revue sketches than plays. Augustus Thomas had published 12 one-act plays by 1898, alongside his more major work for the theatre.

Perhaps the most significant of the early American one-act dramatists was William D Howells who wrote mostly one-acters and published them in magazines of which he was the editor. He was also the author of the well-known poem *The Night Before Christmas*. American theatre historian Glenn Hughes suggests that, 'His plays possessed a grace of expression and a refined humour which set them apart from the rough and ready pieces written directly for the theatre', in this period. Two of the plays, **The Garroters** and **The Mousetrap** were played professionally in London, and hailed by GB Shaw, amongst others, as a welcome change from the farces which were the staple diet of curtain-raisers.

In the USA, the one-act play was given a further stimulus by the 1911 tour of the Irish Players from the Abbey Theatre, Dublin. This company performed short plays by JM Synge, WB Yeats and Lady Gregory, and, as they toured provincial cities, after their initial New York performances, they fired an interest in the creation of short plays with local contexts.

A second significant event was the season of one-act plays instituted by the Washington Square Players (later to become the nucleus of the Theater Guild) at the Bandbox Theater, New York in 1916. In the first three years of its existence this regular programme gave airings to over 60 one-act plays.

Local professional theatres were founded (such as the Toy Theater in Boston and the Chicago Little Theater) and budding writers were aided by playwriting 'laboratories' run annually by universities, most notably by Professor GP Baker, first at Harvard (1912–25) and then later at Yale. The manageable context of the one-act play was the usual starting place for these writers. Adventurous amateur groups such as the Provincetown Players in New England (the group which nurtured Eugene O'Neill as a playwright) and the Cornish Theater Players in Seattle (prompted by the English director, Maurice Browne, who had also worked in Chicago) grew up, featuring the one-act form in their repertoire.

Margaret Mayorga, an academic and a tireless early crusader for the short play to be regarded as a distinctive art-form, was the editor of the first published anthology of US one-act plays at the end of World War I.

in Britain

There is no doubt that, in Britain, the performance of a short play before the major attraction was a popular feature of evenings at the theatre in late Victorian and Edwardian times. Not all the audience attended such an event (those who were dining at a restaurant or a club knew that they had a certain amount of leeway if they had not finished their meal by the advertised starting-time of the performance) but the curtain-raiser was seen as an attractive (and usually light-hearted) *hors d'oevre* to the main piece of the evening. JA Ferguson suggested that, '[its] function was best-fulfilled when the curtain-raiser was of a quality so poor and trifling that the late-arrivals in the stalls could become objects of interest rather than of irritation to the occupants of the cheaper seats…'

But inevitably some pieces, such as Alfred Sutro's light piece **A Marriage Has Been Arranged**, attracted more attention and had success. In October 1903 Louis N Parker's adaptation of a WW Jacobs' horror short-story **The Monkey's Paw** played so well as a curtain-raiser that some members of the audience came specially early to see it and then left before the main fare of the evening, a matter of considerable concern to the theatre manager who was staging it, as well as to the cast of the later play.

Shaw wrote several such pieces, as did JM Barrie, Harley Granville-Barker, AW Pinero, and other notable British dramatists of the time. The curtain-raiser or after-piece served as a useful showcase for the work of up and coming writers, as well as a place in which established dramatists might offer a light trifle or experiment in theme and style. Harold Brighouse of the Manchester school, for instance (best known for his full-length play *Hobson's Choice*) wrote many more one-act plays (50) than full-length plays (15) in the course of a long writing career, and largely established his reputation with the first of his one-acters, *Lonesome-like*, first performed in 1911.

But, with the coming of World War I and the disappearance of a leisurely attitude to theatre-going, the curtain-raiser dropped out of the theatre bills.

Troops home on leave and their wives and sweethearts did not have the time or inclination for a long evening in the theatre and often sought the immediate (and quick-fire) delights of revue or of musical comedy. Evenings in the theatre became shorter. There was no room for curtain-raisers if a major play was being presented. By 1918, the one-act play had largely disappeared from the repertoire of the professional West End theatre.

the inter-war years

new opportunities for drama

In Britain, interest in and performance of one-act plays passed dramatically from the professional to the amateur theatre in the inter-war years. The end of World War I presaged a change in life-style for many Britons. Working-hours were reduced for many, and new pastimes became available. New settlements were created as the population expanded and in many places, children left the life of extended family groups in the centre of cities to make their own way in fast-growing suburban communities, with the help of a partner, a mortgage and a new semi-detatched house.

In many of these new areas, drama was one of the activities which came to bond people together. The local church or tennis club or community centre was likely to spawn a dramatic section, and in winter months this provided a suitable indoor focal point for socialising as well as performing. RC Sherriff describes one such example in his autobiography; his early writing efforts in the 1920s, before *Journey's End*, were devoted to providing entertainments for the drama section of his local rowing club at Kingston. He wrote his first one-act play as a climax to an evening of variety turns.

> The problem was to invent a story that would meet the requirements. It wasn't to run for more than twenty minutes; it had to have as many characters as possible; and every character must have his fair share of dialogue and things to do.
>
> I finally hit upon an idea that promised everything we needed. The curtain would rise upon a motor coach in the centre of the stage, facing the audience ... the coach is empty at first, with a solitary nondescript person lounging beside it. The passengers enter in twos and threes and enquire of the nondescript person whether this is the coach for the Brighton excursion. He replies that it is, collects the fares, and requests them to be seated. When the coach is full he goes off, informing the passengers that he will tell the driver that all is ready for departure.

The denouement may be anticipated — when the driver eventually turns up, having been delayed, it turns out that the 'nondescript person' was nothing to at all to do with the coach company and has relieved the unsuspecting passengers of their money. A classic small-scale drama that typifies one-act plays of the 1920s and 1930s.

Another writer of the period, Mabel Constanduros, reveals a similar genesis to her one-act play work:

> Soon after I began to work for the BBC, I wrote two one-act plays which were to be performed by amateurs at our local tennis club at Sutton. I approached Samuel French and asked if they would consider publishing them. Arthur Elsbury, who came down from French's, accepted the plays and so began a long and profitable business association. I have written them many plays since...

The widening of both content and pedagogy in the school curriculum provided another outlet for short plays. JW Marriott's introduction in the collection *One-Act Plays of Today*, published in 1924 reports that, 'The need for such a book was suggested by the Board of Education's new attitude towards the teaching of English (i.e. no longer only recitation of poems, or reading aloud of prose)'. Thus it became likely that a new generation of adults who might take part in amateur drama would receive their first introduction to the one-act play by acting a piece out in the classroom.

the British Drama League

The British Drama League was founded in 1919 by Geoffrey Whitworth to cater for the needs of this army of new amateur drama groups, its original aim being 'the encouragement of the art of the theatre, both for its own sake, and as a means of intelligent recreation among all classes of the community'. It published a regular magazine, organised annual summer schools and built up a library of play texts and theatre books. Along the way it incorporated the Village Drama Society, a similar umbrella organisation which had been founded to foster drama in rural communities immediately after the end of World War I. The enlarged BDL set up a National Festival of Community Drama in 1927, a competition based on the one-act play, and this was organised in local and regional rounds all over England. A comparable festival was set up in Scotland at the same time, and Wales and Ireland quickly followed suit.

The first annual competition in England produced over 150 entries from groups in villages, towns and cities; by 1930 the figure had risen to nearly 400. In 1933, the entry figure was 458 plays, and this had grown further to 747 by 1936. The one-act festival of the Scottish Community Drama Association also began in 1927 and grew from an initial entry of 35 to one of 170 in 1930, 207 in 1933 and 386 in 1936.

Coincident with this, local drama festivals (lasting up to a week) grew up to accommodate the early rounds of these competitions. In Welwyn, in 1934, for instance, 26 one-act plays were entered for the week's festival (the sixth to be organised annually at the Welwyn Theatre), and on two nights no fewer than five plays were performed. Fourteen of the plays were unpublished, including the winning play, *Tails Up*, by Cyril Roberts. Among more established authors represented were Harold Brighouse, Thornton Wilder, L du Garde Peach, John Masefield, Eugene O'Neill, Gordon Bottomley and AJ Talbot. Early winners of the Welwyn Festival also made the trip across the Atlantic by sea to compete in the New York Little Theater Festival (see Appendix 2).

Hundreds of short plays were also being performed by Women's Institutes, village drama societies, Girl Guide companies, Boy Scout troops, and youth clubs as the drama bug took strong hold in the social contexts of 'middle-England' in the 1920s and 1930s. Working-class communities also sought to provide their own entertainments and social clubs attached to factories, mines, and large retail stores began to sprout drama sections.

From 1931 onwards Harrap published an annual anthology of nine or ten of the best one-act plays of the year. Other publishers discovered that the one-act play was a market which they could profitably exploit. Robert M Rayner in his history of Britain, *Modern Times*, commented, 'By the close of our period (1939), they [Amateur Dramatic Societies, fostered by the British Drama League] had, in the aggregate, over a million members and were making the drama a more integral part of the national life than ever before'.

drama and politics

There were also moves to enlist the power of drama for political ends. The Independent Labour Party set up an Arts Guild in 1925 to encourage the production of plays with a socialist message. Many of the ILP constituency parties also had related drama groups which presented propagandist plays of varying subtlety, sometimes to their own members and at other times to gathered audiences. A Workers' Theatre Movement was established.

This desire to proselytise led to the development of particular forms of short drama, notably the 'living newspaper' and the symbolic chorus-led play. These carried punch, even when performed in the open-air to a potentially indifferent or hostile audience. Joan Littlewood, later to pioneer many interesting dramatic experiments with her Theatre Workshop company at Stratford East, began her acting career with a group called Red Megaphones which, as its name implied, presented short and pointed political fables at factory-gates as workers came out for their lunch-break. In Scotland the vigorous one-act plays of Joe Corrie 'the miner-playwright' were favoured by some amateur groups.

In America, there were similar political currents, and the development of a workers' theatre movement spearheaded by the writing of Clifford Odets and Paul Eliot Green. Odets' *Waiting for Lefty* (1936) was one of the most notable short politically-oriented plays to capture public imagination. This play also owed something to the rising interest in film as a medium, and its multiple-scenes and minimal props reflected techniques used in the cinema. Green's *Hymn to the Rising Sun* (1935) was a powerful one-act play which eloquently drew attention to conditions in prisons and to the need for civil rights.

The emerging medium of radio also was an influence on the one-act form; its power to capture the imagination was graphically illustrated in Orson Welles's series of 30-minute radio plays for the Mercury Theater in 1938. These included the famous broadcast of an adaptation of HG Wells's *The War of the Worlds*, which had such realism that it scared much of the American Eastern seaboard into believing that the landing of aliens was actually about to take place. Radio provided an alternative outlet for the work of dramatists, and the process was two-way; some pieces were trialled first over local airwaves and then adapted for the stage; others went from initial stage tryouts in a local community to greater audiences when adapted for radio.

Another area of growth for the one-act play was the increasing use of drama in and by churches. The founding of the Religious Drama Society in 1929 signalled a significant return of the church's interest in the use of drama, both within the liturgy and outside it, after some centuries of suspicion about it. Some writers (such as HF Rubinstein, TC Thomas TB Morris, and Wilfrid Grantham) re-cast Biblical episodes in short dramatic form and in modern speech; others such as Clifford Bax and Cedric Mount used symbolism and poetic imagery to pose important challenges and questions about faith and ethics.

increasing adventurousness

Such a blossoming of opportunities for the one-act form led in turn to a greater variety of play and an increasing adventurousness of style on the part of playwrights who sought to meet the needs of this growing market. Experimental plays became more frequent and John Bourne, a knowledgeable chronicler of the national drama scene, wrote of the one-act play in 1934:

> Although its very existence – in concise writing and mainly amateur performance – prevents its development into the realms of the spectacular or mechanical, it has had a definite growth into the spheres of the imaginative, the poetic and the expressionist. The old 'roaring farce', the cottage-drama that provided sordid slices of life, the drawing-room fatuity and the melodramatic thriller are giving place to plays in which character, atmosphere and spiritual purpose are the dominant notes.

Some playwrights (amongst them notably Sydney Box and Philip Johnson in England and Percival Wilde in America) specialised in the one-act form, aiming their work towards the capabilities and interests of amateur companies, and had many of their plays published and anthologised.

Professionally, the one-act play languished, though in London's West End, there was one notable landmark. In 1936, Noël Coward presented a suite of no fewer than ten one-act plays (principally to showcase the versatility of himself and Gertrude Lawrence) and all were played in a three-nightly repertory for a season under the title *Tonight at Eight-Thirty*. Several of these – **Red Peppers**, **Hands Across the Sea, Fumed Oak** among them – became enthusiastically taken up by amateur companies in the years following, and are still seen occasionally on stage in the 21st century. Other than this isolated *tour de force*, however, in the professional theatre, the one-act play was now becoming a rarity.

post-1945 ups and downs
the post-war honeymoon

World War II disrupted the growth of amateur theatre in conventional settings, although the one-act play survived when sporadically presented as part of troop entertainments, or as an entertainment for shelter-dwellers during air-raids. But, life was altogether too hurried and fragmented even to allow the 30 or 40 minute play to command attention and the brief revue sketch or song was a much more likely component of such events.

After the war there was a return of the enthusiasm for artistic and recrea-tional pursuits in local communities. The drama festival movement revived and there was a honeymoon period in the late 1940s and 1950s when the British Drama League's national competitions were deluged with entries and when local festivals burgeoned and were awash with entries. Plays were usually of about 30 minutes in length, with some festivals staging as many as four plays each night.

Festival activity reached a climax in the early 1950s. From then on the theatre had to deal with the growing alternative attraction of television. Though TV itself provided another outlet for writers, the novelty of it as a medium meant that audiences were less disposed to go down to their local hall to see theatrical performances which might be variable in quality. Both the professional theatre (notably the variety circuits) and the amateur suffered from this powerful competitor.

This led to a certain re-trenchment which was of benefit to the amateur theatre – a realisation by many amateur companies that their work had to maintain some credible standard if potential customers were to be tempted away from their firesides. Weaker companies, which had perhaps in the past depended on the indulgence of friends to sustain their audiences, went to the wall.

Some amateur groups had by now been able to consolidate to the extent of finding, equipping and maintaining their own premises. Many who had their own premises had banded together in the Little Theatre Guild of Great Britain and were able to offer a pleasingly varied repertory of plays, which was more challenging than the predominant diet of the inter-war years for many companies – light comedies and farces.

decline and fall of the BDL

In the later years of the 20th century, however, the one-act play had a somewhat chequered existence. In the amateur world in the UK , the British Drama League (later transformed into the British Theatre Association) lost both its dynamism and its pre-eminence, eventually succumbing to dissolution through imprudent financial management during a time of decline. Thus a source of advice, a useful library and a training organisation were removed from the scene in England, leaving amateur companies to survive as best they could. A new organisation, specifically set up with volunteer help, managed to maintain the infrastructure of a national one-act festival in England, but the number of entries nowadays (382 performances at 50 venues in 2004) is not to be compared with the halcyon days of the 1930s and late 1940s. Despite the demise of the overall British organisation, national organisations devoted to amateur theatre have continued to do good work in Scotland, Wales and Ireland.

In the USA, after World War II, the one-act play generally came to assume a minor position in dramatic programmes both professional and amateur. Professional theatre occasionally staged double-bills and some well-known playwrights such as Arthur Miller, Tennessee Williams and Edward Albee produced short plays for this. But in the world of 'community theatre' the one-act piece often became either a vehicle to occupy extra players, a stop-gap in the schedules, or an 'arts-y project' for those with specialist interests. There were some theatre festivals which featured one act plays, but these were less rooted as notable local community events than in Britain.

Leonard Jacobs, a noted historian of the American theatre, reckons, however, that there has been 'a rapturous renaissance' of the one-acter in some places in the last 25 years and cites some notable annual events, such as the New York Ensemble Studio Theater's annual Marathon Series, the Samuel French Off-Off-Broadway Original Short Play Festival and the Actors Theater of Louisville's National Ten-Minute Play Contest as examples of this. On visiting the EST Marathon series, which has been held annually since 1978, a critic from a major New York daily used to reviewing Broadway fare, opined, 'The one-act play is in better health than I had imagined'.

For many amateur companies the general economics of producing shows became increasingly problematic in the later years of the century as the goodwill of community provision evaporated in the face of a harsher economic climate. Thus, the decision to perform a one-act festival play (once comfortably able to be financed from the profits of other box-office successes) became more difficult to justify as costs (notably of transport to other venues and scenery) increased, since it was probably not likely to be a money-spinner in itself.

However, some counter influences to decline can be recognised. In the UK, some one-act festivals (among them those staged in Welwyn, Woking, the Orkney Islands, Manchester, Cambridge, Sedgefield, Southend and Birmingham) have continued to thrive, even though they are beyond their most halcyon days. Writing in 1971, Dora Kolker, the Secretary of the Welwyn Festival could say, 'Our audiences are steadily growing and we are happily within sight of the very high attendances of the immediate post-war years'. There was a down-turn in audiences after that, but not catastrophically so.

The growth of lively 'alternative' theatre companies outside London (often with eager young actors surviving on minimum salaries and working with shoestring budgets) and the creation and maintenance of some small studio theatres in smaller towns has provided some sprigs of growth in theatre in the last 50 years. There is, in these newer venues, often an acceptance of relatively experimental short pieces by well-informed and theatrically-educated audiences, but even so, the performance of one-act plays by professional actors is now comparatively rare.

As dependence on a single major annual production has declined in schools, youth and school companies have become more inclined to experiment with material other than the classics. The move towards more general participation in drama in schools has encouraged the development of more self-generated (and often, improvised) short pieces. In recent years, the National Theatre has sponsored the creation of short plays for young actors by some established writers; these are then performed in regional theatres in the context of a national festival called Connections.

Another recent London initiative to support the short-play form has been the London New Play Festival which began at the tiny Old Red Lion Theatre, Islington, in 1988, and has since operated annually since in a variety of venues on a small budget. This festival, run by a devoted small band of enthusiasts, has usually included a mixture of full-length and one-act plays. Some central London theatre managements have now expressed interest in giving this festival a higher profile.

Radio and TV have provided a fertile ground for shorter pieces of drama (30–60 minutes long) from writers such as Harold Pinter, Tom Stoppard, and Caryl Churchill and there is still a cadre of playwrights (David Campton, Jimmy Chinn, Gillian Plowman, Nick Warburton prominent amongst them) who continue to provide high-quality work written specifically for the theatre in the one-act form. The continuance of widespread performance of one-act plays on the stage, however, is presently more at risk than the provision of suitable material.

Occasional professional touring companies stage double-bills of famous one-act plays by writers of proven box-office appeal (e.g. *The Browning Version* and *Harlequinade* by Terence Rattigan or *The Dumb Waiter* and *A Slight Ache* by Harold Pinter) but at the beginning of the 21st century, the one-act play survives as a viewable art-form mainly through the continuation of drama festivals in local communities, organised by bands of devoted theatre enthusiasts.

Not all these festivals are over-flowing with entries and support, but they continue to provide a valuable outlet for new writing as well as a vehicle for the considerable amount of one-act writing amassed over a century of development. Enough of them offer imaginative presentation and good-quality drama to attract sizeable audiences. Though, on any one night, some of the audience will be supporters of a particular society, others will be season-ticket holders, who come to see all or most of the plays of the week. The continuing strength of these events is sufficient to provide hope for the future and to sustain a focus of interest for theatregoers who value the particular charm and quality of the one-act form.

appendix 1

A classification by nationality (other than English) of the playwrights who appear in the main biographical section.

North American dramatists

Edward Albee

Woody Allen

John Lewis Carlino

Rachel Crothers

Christopher Durang

Charles Dizenzo

Harvey Fienstein

Lucille Fletcher

Horton Foote

Frank Gilroy

Susan Glaspell

Stephen Gregg

Lily Anne Green

Paul Green

John Guare

AR Gurney Jnr

Jack Heifner

Beth Henley

Israel Horovitz

William Inge

Tim Kelly

Arthur Koppit

Neil LaBute

Romulus Linney

David Mamet

George Middleton

James McLure

Terrence McNally

Terrence McNally

Leonard Melfi

George Middleton

Arthur Miller

Jason Milligan

Josephina Niggli

Don Nigro

Clifford Odets

Eugene O'Neill

Dorothy Parker

John Patrick

Robert Patrick

James Prideaux

Jack Richardson

William Saroyan

Murray Schisgal

Sam Shepard

Martin Sherman

Neil Simon

Jules Tasca

Michel Tremblay

Jean-Claude van Itallie

Percival Wilde

Thornton Wilder

Tennessee Williams

Lanford Wilson

Olwyn Wymark

Scottish dramatists

JM Barrie

JJ Bell

James Bridie

Stewart Conn

Joe Corrie

Gordon Daviot

Harry Glass

George MacEwan Green

Ian Hay

Alan Richardson

James Scotland

CP Taylor

Mike Tibbetts

Welsh dramatists

Peter Gill	Gwyneth Jones	Leonard Morley
Rae Shirley	TC Thomas	Frank Vickery

Irish dramatists

Geraldine Aron	Brian Friel	Lady Isabella Gregory
Hugh Leonard	Frank McGuinness	GB Shaw
JM Synge	William Trevor	WB Yeats

European dramatists

Jean Anouilh (France)	Fernando Arrabal (Spain)	Bertold Brecht (Germany)
Anton Chekhov (Russia)	Marguerite Duras (France)	Dario Fo (Italy)
Jean Genet (France)	Jean Giraudoux (France)	Vaclav Havel (Czech Rep)
Eugene Ionesco (France)	F Garcia Lorca (Spain)	Rene de Obaldia (French)
Luigi Pirandello (Italian)	Jean Paul Sartre (France)	August Strindberg (Sweden)
Jean Tardieu (France)	Frank Wedekind (Germany)	

other dramatists...

Michael Gow (Australia)	Alexander Guyan (New Zealand)	Yukio Mishima (Japan)
Michael Olsen (Australia)		

appendix 2

one-act plays which have won or have been runner-up at the Welwyn Drama Festival 1929–2005

The Welwyn Drama Festival in Hertfordshire was possibly the first one-act play festival staged in a particular location in Britain. With the exception of the years of World War II and 1963, it has run annually for a week in June ever since, attracting not only local companies, but teams from further afield. The list below shows winners and runners-up at the festival in each year.

1929	The Autocrat of the Coffee Stall	Harold Chapin
	Trifles	Susan Glaspell
1930	The 300th Performance	Stephen Barnett
	The Long Voyage Home	Eugene O'Neill
1931	Exit	Cyril Roberts
	The Fourth Riddle	Edward Williams
1932	Young and so Fair	Lal Norris
	A Knight Came Riding	Cyril Roberts
	The Cab	John Taylor
1933	The Last Rib	Cyril Roberts
	Symphonie Pathetique	Sydney Box
1934	Tails Up	Cyril Roberts
	Not This Man	Sydney Box
1935	Portrait of the General	Frank Herbert
	Night Episode	WS Plymouth
1936	Salve Festa Dies	PAM Long
	The Perfect Ending	Ryerson and Clements
1937	The Tree	Sydney Box
	Willow, Woe is Me!	Dorothy Carr
1938	After the Tempest	Geoffrey Trease
	The Apostle Play	Max Mell
1939	Plant in the Sun	Ben Bengal
	The Sword is Double-edged	Arthur Swinson
1940	The Rising of the Moon	Lady Gregory
	Beauty Spot	Ivor Brown

Between 1929 and 1940, the one-act plays of Philip Johnson were most numerous among those chosen by teams entering the festival (13) with those of Sydney Box (10) the next most popular. None of the winners or runners-up were excerpts from longer plays

1946	**The Importance of Being Earnest (excerpt)**	Oscar Wilde
	The Song of Rhiannon	David Monger
1947	**The Proposal**	Anton Chekhov
	Children in Uniform	Anon
1948	**And Gathered Flowers are Dead**	Eric Salmon
	First Gleam	Frederick Lidstone
1949	**Spice of Life**	Frederick Lidstone
	Willow, Woe is Me!	Dorothy Carr
1950	**A Sunny Morning**	S and J Quintero
	The Valiant	Hall and Middlemass
1951	**A Phoenix Too Frequent**	Christopher Fry
	The Fish	Yves Cabrol
1952	**The No 'count Boy**	Paul Green
	Overruled	GB Shaw
1953	**A Sleeping Clergyman (excerpt)**	James Bridie
	The Southern Cross	Paul Green
1954	**Davy Jones's Locker**	TC Thomas
	The Laboratory	David Campton
1955	**Hands Across the Sea**	Noël Coward
	Davy Jones's Dinner	TC Thomas
1956	**Dark of the Moon (excerpt)**	Richardson and Berney
	The Wedding Morning	Arthur Schnitzler
1957	**The Sleeping Prince (excerpt)**	Terence Rattigan
	Davy Jones's Clock	TC Thomas
1958	**Captain Carvallo (excerpt)**	Dennis Cannan
	Interlude of Youth	Unknown; 16th century
1959	**Red Peppers**	Noël Coward
	The Magistrate (excerpt)	AW Pinero
1960	**The Crucible (excerpt)**	Arthur Miller
	Rise and Shine	Elda Cadogan

1961	Ile	Eugene O'Neill
	Madame de....	Jean Anouilh
1962	On the High Road	Anton Chekhov
	The Birthday Party (excerpt)	Harold Pinter
1964	Sotoba Komachi	Kwanami Kiyotsugu
	Ton	Graham Cranmer
1965	The Devil Among the Skins	Ernest Goodwin
	A Sunny Morning	S and J Quintero

In the period 1946–65 the plays of GB Shaw were the most numerous of those chosen by teams entering the festival (15), followed by those of Anton Chekhov (7) and Yves Cabrol (7). Eight of the winning or runners-up entries were excerpts from longer plays.

1966	The Private Ear	Peter Shaffer
	Philip Hotz's Fury	Max Frisch
1967	Passion Poison and Petrifaction	GB Shaw
	As Good as New	David Perry
1968	Great Catherine (excerpt)	GB Shaw
	The End of the Beginning	Sean O'Casey
1969	The Audition	Sean Vincent
	Little Doris	David Perry
1970	The Real Inspector Hound	Tom Stoppard
	Oldenberg	Barry Bermange
1971	Red Spy at Night	Robert King
	The Ring Game	Leonard de Franquen
1972	Getting and Spending	David Campton
	Barefoot in the Park (excerpt)	Neil Simon
1973	Marble Arch	John Mortimer
	Albert's Bridge	Tom Stoppard
1974	The Devil in Summer	Michele Faure
	The Tail of Fire	TB Morris
1975	Almost Like Being	JC van Itallie
	The Footsteps of Doves	Robert Anderson
1976	Knock for Knock	Clive Wiseman
	Ritual for Dolls	George MacEwan Green

1977	**Sweeney Todd**	Terry Hawes
	The Wedding Morning	Arthur Schnitzler
1978	**Sequence of Events**	George MacEwan Green
	The Bald Prima Donna	Eugene Ionesco
1979	**The Room**	Harold Pinter
	Willow, Woe is Me!	Dorothy Carr
1980	**Zigger Zagger**	Peter Terson
	The Purification	Tennessee Williams
1981	**The Crucible (excerpt)**	Arthur Miller
	Poppy	Leonard Rogers
1982	**Seaside Postcard**	Terence Frisby
	The Daurk Assize	James Scotland
1983	**The Erpingham Camp**	Joe Orton
	Metamorphosis	Steven Berkoff
1984	**Not about Heroes**	Stephen Macdonald
	27 Wagons Full of Cotton	Tennessee Williams

Between 1965 and 1984 the plays of David Campton were most numerous among those chosen by teams entering the festival (17) with those of Harold Pinter (13), GB Shaw (11) and Noël Coward (11) the next most popular. Three of the winners or runners-up were excerpts from longer plays.

1985	**Abelard and Heloise (excerpt)**	Ronald Millar
	The Bespoke Overcoat	Wolf Mankowitz
1986	**The Perfect Servants**	Donald Ritchie
	Domino Courts	William Hauptman
1987	**The Wooden Pear**	Gillian Plowman
	The Long Goodbye	Tennessee Williams
1988	**Lone Star**	James Maclure
	Home Free	Lanford Wilson
1989	**Me and My Friend (Act 2)**	Gillian Plowman
	Nathan and Tabileth	Barry Bermange
1990	**A Day in Hollywood, A Night in the Ukraine**	Dick Vosburgh and Frank Lazarus
	September in the Rain	John Godber

1991	**Bouncers**	John Godber
	Sylvia Plath	Barry Kyle
1992	**The Fall of the House of Usher**	Steven Berkoff
	Skoolplay	A Brown
1993	**A Coupla White Chicks Sitting Around Talking**	John Ford Noonan
	A Kind of Vesuvius	Gillian Plowman
1994	**Beata Beatrix**	Gillian Plowman
	The Open Couple	Dario Fo and Franca Rame
1995	**Elegy for a Lady**	Arthur Miller
	Fool for Love	Sam Shepard
1996	**The Song of Louise in the Morning**	Patricia Joudry
	Idyll	William Emrys
1997	**The Death Artist**	David Henry Wilson
	Shakers	John Godber and Jane Thornton
1998	**The Indian Wants the Bronx**	Arthur Kopit
	Unprogrammed	Carol K Mack
1999	**Please Mrs Butler!**	Alan Ahlberg, adapted by Coral Walton
	Final Placement	Ara Watson
2000	**Several Slices of Pie**	Ray Newton
	In the Blinking of an Eye	Jeremy Hylton Davies
2001	**Home Free**	Lanford Wilson
	Excerpts from Grimm's Tales	Grimm, adapted by Tiffany While
2002	**The Boundary**	Tom Stoppard and Clive Exton
	Canterbury Tales	Chaucer, adapted by Tiffany While
2003	**Me and My Friend (Act 2)**	Gillian Plowman
	The Lure of the Reichenbach	Lesley Bilton
2004	**Oedipus**	Seneca, adapted by Ted Hughes
	Patio	Jack Heifner

2005 **April in Paris**   John Godber
      Bang! Bang! You're Dead!   William Mastrosimone

Between 1985 and 2005, the one-act plays of Gillian Plowman were most numerous among those chosen by teams entering the festival (16), with those of John Godber (11), David Campton (9), Harold Pinter (8), Tom Stoppard (8) and Nick Warburton(8) the next most popular. Three of the winners or runners-up were excerpts from longer plays.

appendix 3

publishers

Below are the addresses of presently-active publishers who have published or are publishing a significant number of one-act plays. Publishers who go out of existence usually pass on their stock and their rights. Consult the list on p. 185 if the name of a publisher you seek is not listed below. That list indicates which present-day publisher is now responsible for the material of defunct publishers.

Amber Lane Press
Cheorl House, Church Street,
Charlbury, Oxon, OX7 3PR
Tel: 01608 810024
info@amberlanepress.co.uk

Angus and Robertson
1/1 Talavera Road, North Ryde,
NSW, 2113, Australia
Tel: 00 61 29889 3611
www.angusrobertson.com.au

Arno Press
3 Park Avenue, New York, NY
10016, USA

Arnold (now part of the Hodder
Group)
338 Euston Road, London NW1 3BH
Tel: 020 7873 600
arnold@hodder.mhs.compuserve.com
www.arnold.publishers.com

Bakers Plays
100 Chauncy Street, Boston,
Massachusetts, 02011, USA
Tel: 001 617 482 1280

BBC Publications
35 Marylebone High Street,
London W1M 4AA
www.bbcshop.com

Black Apollo Press
PO Box 173, Cambridge, CB5 8YB
Tel: 01223 367201

Editor@blackapollo.com
www.blackapollo.com

Brown, Son & Ferguson Ltd
4–10 Darnley Street,
Glasgow G41 2SD
Tel: 0141 429 1234
sales@scottishplays.co.uk
www.scottishplays.co.uk

Calder Publications Ltd
51 The Cut, London SE1 8LF
Tel: 020 7633 0599
info@calderpublications.com
www.calderpublications.com

Cambridge Publishing Services
PO Box 62, Cambridge, CB3 9NA
Tel: 01223 323519
raw1000@cam.ac.uk

Cambridge University Press
The Edinburgh Building,
Shaftesbury Road,
Cambridge, CB2 2RU
Tel: 01223 312393
www.cambridge.org

David Campton
35 Liberty Road, Glenfield,
Leicester LE3 8JF
davidcampton@aol.com

Chambers Harrap
7 Houpton Crescent,
Edinburgh, EH7 4AY, Scotland

Tel: 0131 556 5929
admin@chambersharrap.co.uk
chambersharrap.co.uk

IE Clark
PO Box 245, Schulenberg,
Texas, USA
Tel: 001 979 743 3232
ieclark@cvtv.net
www.ieclark.com

Constable (now part of Constable
and Robinson)
3 The Lanchesters, 162 Fulham
Palace Road, London W6 9ER
Tel: 020 8741 3663
enquiries@constablerobinson.com

Cornell University Press
Sage House, 512 E State Street,
Ithaca, New York, 14851, USA
Tel: 607 277 2338
www.cornellpress.cornell.edu

Contemporary Drama Service, USA
(see Hanbury Plays)

Cressrelles (for Garnet Miller,
Kenyon-Deane, New Playwrights
Network)
10 Station Road Industrial Estate,
Colwall, Nr Malvern, WR13 6RN
Tel: 01684 540154
simonsmith@cressrelles4drama.fsbusi
ness.co.uk

Currency Plays
PO Box 452, Paddington,
New South Wales 2021, Australia

Drama Association of Wales
The Old Library, Singleton Road,
Splott, Cardiff, CF24 2ET, Wales
Tel: 029 2045 2200
aled.daw@virgin.net
(DAW also houses the most compre-
hensive library of one-act plays in
Britain – see below, Useful addresses.)

Dramatic Publishing Co
311 Washington Street, Woodstock,
Illinois, USA

Dramatists Play Service
440 Park Avenue South, New York,
NY 10016, USA
Tel: 001 212 683 8960
postmaster@dramatists.com
www.dramatists.com

Duckworth
90–93 Cowcross Street,
London EC1M 6BF
Tel: 020 7490 7300
infor@duckworth-publishers.co.uk

Faber and Faber
3 Queen Street, London WC1N 3AU
Tel: 020 7645 0045
www.faber.co.uk

Flying Duck Publications
Oakridge, Weston Road,
Stafford, ST16 3RJ

Gallimard Press
5 Rue Sebastien-Bottin, 75341,
Paris, France
Tel: 00 33 4954 4200

Garnet Miller (see Cressrelles)

**Victor Gollancz (now part of Orion
Publishing Group)**
Orion House, 5 Upper St Martin's
Lane, London WC2H 9EA
Tel: 020 7240 3444

Hamish Hamilton (now part of
Penguin, USA)
375 Hudson Street, New York,
NY, 10014, USA
Tel: 212 366 2000
pmcarthy@penguinputnam.com
www.penguinputnam.com

Hanbury Plays (also Contemporary Drama Service, Pioneer Drama Service) Keeper's Lodge, Broughton Green, Droitwich Spa, Worcs, WR9 7EE
Tel: 01905 23132 and
01527 821 564
hanburyplays@onetel.com
www.hanbury plays.co.uk

Harcourt
525b Street, Suite 1900, San Diego, California, 92101-4495, USA
Tel: 619 231 6616
apbcs@harcourtbrace.com
www.harcourtbooks,com

Harcourt Brace and Co
30–52 Smidmore Street, Marrickville, NSW, Australia

HarperCollins
77–85 Fulham Palace Road, London W6 8JB
Tel: 020 8741 7070
www.harpercollins.co.uk

Henry Holt and Co
115 West 18th Street, 5th Floor, New York, NY, 10011, USA
Tel: 001 212 886 9200
infor@hholt.com
www.henryholt.com

Hodder Wayland
338 Euston Road, London NW1 3BH
Tel: 020 7873 6000
www.hodderwayland.co.uk

Joint Board of Christian Education of Australia and New Zealand
(now Uniting Education)
PO Box 1245, Collingwood. Victoria, 3066, Australia
Tel: 00 63 9416 4262

Kenyon-Deane (see Cressrelles)

A A Knopf
299 Park Avenue, New York, NY 10171, USA
Tel: 001 212 751 2600
customerservice@randomhouse.com
www.radomhouse.com/knopf

Macmillan
Brunel Road, Houndmills, Basingstoke, Hants, RG21 6XS
Tel: 01256 393859
www.macmillan.com

Maverick Musicals Pty Ltd
89 Bergann Road, Maleny, 4552 Queensland, Australia
Tel: 0067 5494 4007
Helen@mavmuse.com
www.mavmuse.com

Methuen Publishing,
11–12 Buckingham Gate, London SW1E 6LB
Tel: 020 77981 1609
www.methuen.co.uk

Nelson (see Nelson Thornes)

Nelson Thornes
Delta Place, 27 Bath Road, Cheltenham, Gloucs, GL53 7TH
Tel: 01242 267 284
nelsonthornes.com

New Playwrights Network (see Cressrelles)

New Directions Publishing Corporation
80 Eighth Avenue, New York, NY, USA
ndpublishing.com

New Theatre Publications
13 Mossgrove Road, Timperley, Altrincham, Cheshire, WA15 6LF
Tel: 08700 275 297

ian.hornby@btinternet.com
www.plays4theatre.com

Nick Hern Books
The Glasshouse, 49a Goldhawk
Road, London W12 8QP
Tel: 020 8749 4953
orders@nickhernbooks.demon.co.uk
www.nickhernbooks.co.uk

Oberon Books Ltd
521 Caledonian Road,
London N7 9RH
Tel: 020 7607 3637
oberon.books@btinternet.com
www.oberonbooks.com

Oneactplays
50 Marlborough Way,
Ashby-de-la-Zouch, LE65 2QR
Tel: 01530 416251
brian@langtry.fslife.co.uk
www.oneactplays.org.uk

Oxford University Press
Great Clarendon Street,
Oxford, OX2 6DP
Tel: 01865 556767
UK@oup.com
www.oup.co.uk

Parthian Books
The Old Surgery, Napier Street,
Cardigan, SA43 1ED
Tel: 01239 612059
parthianbooks@yachoo.co.uk
www.parthianbooks.co.uk

Pederson Press
44 Redburn Road, Cumbernauld
Glasgow, G67 3NR
Tel: 01236 729228
harryglass1@activemail.co.uk

Penguin UK
27 Wrights Lane,
London W8 5TZ

Tel: 020 7416 3000
www.penguin.co.uk

Pioneer Drama Service, USA
(see Hanbury Plays)

The Playwrights Publishing Co
70 Nottingham Road, Burton Joyce,
Notts, NG14 5AL
Tel: 0115 931 3356
platwrightspublishingco@yahoo.co.uk
www.geocites.com/playwrights
publishingco

**Radius (The Religious Drama
Society of Great Britain)**
58–60 Lincoln Road,
Peterborough PE1 2RZ
Tel: 01733 565613
info@radius.org.uk
www.radius.org.uk

Random House
20 Vauxhall Bridge Road,
London SW1V 2SA
Tel: 020 7640 8400   And
1540 Broadway, New York, NY,
10036, USA
Tel: 212 782 9000
customerservice@randomhouse.com

Rigby
18 Dequetteville Terrace, Kent Town,
South Australia 8000, Australia
Tel: 0068 8363 2055

Samuel French (UK)
52 Fitzroy Square, London W1T 5JR
Tel: 020 7387 9373
theatre@samuelfrench-london.co.uk
www.samuelfrench-london.co.uk

Samuel French (USA)
45 West 25th Street, New York,
NY 10010, USA
Tel: 001 212 206 8990
www.samuelfrench.com

The two Samuel French companies are in the same ownership and have constant business dealings with each other. They carry stock of each other's plays in their bookshops. Prospective customers, whether British or American, are advised to contact the address in their own country, in the first instance, in matters relating to play-copy purchase and performing rights.

Schoolplay Productions Ltd
15 Inglis Road, Colchester,
Essex, C03 3HU
Tel: 01206 540111
schoolplay@inglis-house.demon.co.uk
www.schoolplayproductions.co.uk

Sheffield Academic Press Ltd
The University of Sheffield,
343 Fulwood Road, Sheffield, S10 3BP

Simon and Schuster
1230 Avenue of the Americas,
New York, NY, 10020
Tel: 001 212 698 7000
ssonline.feedback@simonsays.com

Smith and Kraus
PO Box 127, Lyme, New Hampshire,
03768, USA
office@smithkraus.com
www.smithandkraus.com

Southern Methodist University Press
PO Box 750415, Dallas, Texas, USA

SPCK
7 Tufton St, Faith House,
London SW1P 2QN
Tel: 020 7799 5083
London@speck.org.uk
spck.org.uk

Spotlight Productions
Penklin Garden Flat,
Cumloden Road, Newton Stewart,
Scotland, DG8 6AA
Tel: 01671 403724
enquiries@spotlightpublications.com
www.spotlightpublications.com

Theatre Centre – Aurora Metro Press
3 Gunthorpe Road, London E1 7RQ
Tel: 020 7377 0379
admin@theatre-centre.co.uk
www.aurorametro.com

University of Queensland Press
Staff House Road, PO Box 6042,
St Lucia, Queensland, 4067, Australia
Tel: 0061 73365 2127
uqp@uqp.uq.edu.au

Viking Press (now part of Viking
Penguin)
375 Hudson Street, New York, NY,
10014-3657, USA
Tel: 001 212 366 20000
publicity@warnerbooks.com

Josef Weinberger Plays
12–14 Mortimer Street,
London W1T 3JJ
Tel: 020 7580 2827
general.info@jwmail.co.uk
www.josef-weinberger.com

Weinberger's hold the performance rights in the UK to most scripts published by Dramatists Play Service

Yennadon Plays
Heatherdene, Dousland,
Devon PL20 6LU

publishers no longer active (and the holder of their rights and archive, where known)

G Bell	now Harper Collins
Calder and Boyars	now Calder
Collins	now Harper Collins
Deane	now Cressrelles
English Theatre Guild	now Weinberger
Evans Plays	now Samuel French
Gowans and Gray	now Samuel French
Garnet Miller	now Cressrelles
Grant Richards	now Methuen
Harrap	now Chambers Harrap
Heinemann	now Random House
Hutchinson	now Random House
Kenyon-Deane	now Cressrelles
Lovat Dickson	
Maynard	later Small, Maynard and Co
Hugh Quekett Publications	now Samuel French
Sidgwick and Jackson	now Macmillan
The Bodley Head	now Random House

appendix 4

other useful addresses

National Drama Festivals Association (NDFA)
c/o The Hon Secretary, Tony Broscomb,
Bramleys, Main Street, Shudy Camps, Cambridge, CB1 6RA
Tel: 01799 584920
tonybroscomb@compuserve.com

All-England Theatre Festival (AETF)
c/o The Hon Secretary, Joan Pickthall,
6 Fallodon Court, Fallodon Way,
Henleaze, Bristol, BS9 4HQ
Tel: 01179 622947
www.aetf.org.uk

Scottish Community Drama Association (SCDA)
5 York Place, Edinburgh, EH1 3EB
Tel; 0131 557 5552
e-mail; headquarters@scda.org.uk
web-site: www.scda.org.uk

Drama Association of Wales (DAW)
The Old Library, Singleton Road,
Splott, Cardiff,
CF 24 2 ET, Wales, UK
Tel: 029 2045 2200
aled.daw@virgin.net

The Drama Association of Wales houses the largest English language theatre lending library in the world, with over 350,000 play scripts. In recent years it has absorbed into its collections the libraries of the British Theatre Association (formerly the British Drama League), the Inner London Education Authority, large sections of the Research Library of the British Broadcasting Corporation, duplicate materials from the London Theatre Museum, the theatre sections of several county libraries and many smaller libraries and private collections.

Where a play is out of print, the DAW Library is happy to investigate who are the rights holders and get permission to photocopy. If a play is out of print and the Library does not have a copy, they work with the Theatre Museum to acquire and place a reference photocopy in the Library. They are willing to then negotiate access and produce copies, subject to agreement with the rights holders.

Though not one of the official Deposit Libraries of the UK, DAW recieve review copies from most play publishers in the UK and Ireland, and also from some publishers in Canada, the USA and Australia.

Association of Ulster Drama Festivals
c/o The Hon Secretary, Alan Marshall,
31 Shorelands, Greenisland,
Carrickfergus, BT38 8FG
Tel: 02890 861234
www.audf.org.uk

The Drama League of Ireland
Carmichael House,
North Brunswick Street,
Dublin 7, Ireland
Tel: 00 3531 874 9084
dli@eircom.net
www.dli.ie

Central Council for Amateur Theatre (CCAT)

c/o Hon Chair, Tom Williams,
39 Harestock Road, Winchester,
Hants, SO22 6NT
Tel: 01963 669 356
ccatchair@aol.com

International Theatre Exchange (the UK centre for the International Amateur Theatre Association)

c/o Marjorie Havard
19 Lease Road, Leeming Bar,
North Yorks, D17 9DB
Tel: 01677 423 047

Little Theatre Guild of Great Britain

c/o 181 Brampton Road,
Carlisle, CA3 9AX
Tel: 01228 522649
webmaster@little theatreguild.org
www.littletheatreguild.org

National Association of Youth Theatres

Arts Centre, Vane Terrace,
Darlington, DL3 7AX
Tel: 01325 363 330
nayt@btconnect.com
www.nayt.org.uk

National Operatic and Drama Association (NODA)

c/o Chief Executive,
58–60 Lincoln Road,
Peterborough, PE1 2RZ
Tel: 0870 770 2480
everyone@noda.org.uk
www.noda.org.uk/

Religious Drama Society of Great Britain (RADIUS)

c/o General Secretary,
58–60 Lincoln Road, Peterborough,
PE1 2RZ
info@radius.org.uk
www.radius.org.uk

Shell Connections

Education Dept, National Theatre,
Upper Ground, Southbank,
London SE1 9PX
Tel: 020 7452 3313/4
hprosser@nationaltheatre.org.uk
www.nationaltheatre,org,uk

Young Farmers

www.yfc-web.org.uk

Many branches and regions of Young Farmers run one-act play competitions for their members.

adjudicating bodies

Guild of Drama Adjudicators (GODA)
c/o Hon Secretary, Joan Crossley,
25 The Drive, Bengeo, Hertford,
Herts, SG1 3DE
Tel: 01882 581 993
crossley@bengeo25.freeserve.co.uk

Scottish Association of Speech and Drama Adjudicators
c/o Jim Gibson,
104 Argyle Road, Saltcoats,
Scotland KA21 5NE
Tel: 012 94559 274
jagibsonht@yahoo.com

Association of Drama Adjudicators (Ireland)
Edenmore, Courtown Harbour, Mill
Grove, Gorey, Co. Wexford, Ireland
Tel: 00 353 55 25124

print media

Amateur Stage (a monthly magazine)
Hampden House, 2 Weymouth Street,
London, WIW 5BT
Tel: 020 7636 4343
cvtheatre@aol.com

The Stage (a weekly newspaper)
47 Bermondsey Street,
London, SE1 3XT
Tel: 020 7403 1818
www.thestage.co.uk

websites

Amdram
PO Box 536, Norwich MLO,
Norfolk, NR6 7JZ
editor@amdram.co.uk
www.amdram.co.uk

UK Theatre Web
info@uktw.co.uk
www.uktw.co.uk

The Irish Playography is a comprehensive, on-line searchable catalogue of all new plays produced professionally throughout Ireland since 1975. For each play it lists all credits including details of copyright-holders and publishers.
www.irishplayography.com

general index

(see also index of play titles and index of playwrights)

play titles

Note: only one-act and short plays are included in this index. Full-length plays mentioned in the text are not listed. *Some collections and notable double-bill titles are included and are italicised in this index.*

playwrights

Note: entries in **bold type** refer to main entries in the biographies.